CHILDREN OF THE REVOLUTION

The lives of sons and daughters of activists in Northern Ireland

Bill Rolston

GUILDHALL PRESS

ISBN: 978 1 906271 38 1

First published July 2011 by

Guildhall Press
Ráth Mór Business Park
Bligh's Lane, Derry
BT48 0LZ
T: 00 44 28 7136 4413
F: 00 44 28 7137 2949
E: info@ghpress.com
W: www.ghpress.com

Designed by Guildhall Press

This book has received financial support from the Northern Ireland Community Relations Council which aims to promote a pluralist society characterized by equity, respect for diversity and recognition of interdependence

Views expressed in this book do not necessarily reflect those of the Community Relations Council.

A catalogue record for this title is available from the British Library.

For Anna.

Let us be lovers,
We'll marry our fortunes together.

Let's hope we never have to choose
Between our children and the land we love so well,
'Cause either way we're bound to lose …

Gerry Creen, *A Rose By Any Other Name*

Acknowledgements

My thanks to those who provided ideas and assistance or who helped me in my search for people to interview, even if in some cases the quest reached a dead-end. These include: Gerry Adams, Joe Austin, Pam Brighton, John Bunting, Suzanne Bunting, Ann Carr, Cath Collins, Sammy Douglas, Geoff Dudgeon, Anna Eggert, Maria Eggert-Stumpenhorst, Frankie Gallagher, Lisa Gormley, Claire Hackett, Deena Haydon, Paddy Hillyard, Ann Hope, John Howcroft, Colin Halliday, Marion Jamison, Mary Kennedy Snr, Paddy Kelly, Alistair Little, Patricia Lundy, Deirdre McAliskey, Alan McBride, Margaret McCann, Jackie McDonald, Laurence McKeown, David McKittrick, Rose McLarnon, Robbie McVeigh, William Mitchell, Cyril Moorhead, Brenda Murphy, Danny Murphy, Féilim Ó hÁdhmaill, Dawn Purvis, Winkie Rea, Phil Scraton, Louise Spence, Gerry Spence, Séanna Walsh, Mina Wardle, Debbie Waters, Marion Weir and Sam White.

Thanks also to the Community Relations Council for their support with this project and to Paul, Declan, Joe, Kevin and Jenni from my publishers, Guildhall Press, for their professional advice and input.

Contents

Introduction

There has been an uneven set of narratives coming out of the Northern Ireland conflict. While everyone in the society was affected in some way or other over the three decades-plus of violence, some were more touched than others. Yet not all of those who suffered have had equal space to tell their stories. There are social, psychological and cultural reasons for this disparity, but the results are clear to see. For example, ex-prisoners have publicly told their stories more, and more successfully, than British Army personnel (officers excluded) and police personnel. Republican ex-prisoners have been more vocal than loyalist ex-prisoners. And the story of male republican ex-prisoners has received more publicity than that of female republican ex-prisoners.

Towards the bottom of the narrative ladder is the story of children and the conflict, and within that, the direct voice of children of combatants has barely been heard at all. To tell at least part of that story is the reason for this book.

By combatants, I mean members of the non-state militarised groups in the North throughout the conflict. This includes the Irish Republican Army (IRA) and Irish National Liberation Army (INLA) on the republican side, and the Ulster Volunteer Force (UVF) and Ulster Defence Association (UDA) on the loyalist side, as well as a number of smaller groups such as the Irish People's Liberation Organisation (IPLO), the Red Hand Commando (RHC) and Loyalist Volunteer Force (LVF). All but one of these groups was illegal during the entire conflict. The UDA was not outlawed until August 1992, even though by that point it had killed approximately 350 people under the label of the Ulster Freedom Fighters (UFF). Most of the people interviewed in this book have had a mother or father who is acknowledged as a combatant in one of these groups. There are two main exceptions: the son and daughter of two separate prominent republican activists – Gearóid Adams and Cathy Nelis.

The Problem of Access

Locating the focus for the book intellectually was relatively straightforward, but finding people who were eligible and willing to talk proved more difficult. I had some advantages, however. As a person born and raised in this society, who has lived in it for all but seven years of his life, who has been active in community politics over more than three decades and who has researched issues related to prisoners and activists, I had a level of access that was greater than that of someone coming in fresh from the outside. Thus, one woman I interviewed, Mary Kennedy, was the daughter of someone I had got to know fairly well when I worked in the early 1970s as a youth worker in Divis Flats, an area in West Belfast with high levels of deprivation and of political and military involvement in republican activity. Mary Kennedy senior and her husband Billy were both interned, the first married couple to be treated that way, while I was working there. I visited Mary on a number of occasions in Armagh Jail. And although I was moved shortly afterwards to another youth centre in North Belfast, I was well aware of the successful efforts of youth workers, relatives and neighbours in Divis to keep Mary junior and her sister and brothers in their own home and out of the clutches of the care system until Mary senior was released. So when I approached Mary junior, now a grandmother, for an interview about her experiences in relation to her own mother, she replied that she would not have agreed to an interview with anyone else but me.

Sometimes this personal advantage appeared without planning. Through a family friend, I approached the daughter of Dan McCann, killed by undercover British agents in Gibraltar in 1988. The friend spoke to Dan's widow, Margaret, but neither she nor her daughter was enthused about the idea of the daughter being interviewed. I asked the friend to approach Margaret again, and when he did, he happened to mention my name. Dan's widow's reply was: 'Why didn't you tell me who it was?' The interview took place within a few days. Here is the reason. After I had worked in Divis Flats, I was moved to a youth centre in the New Lodge area of North Belfast. Around the corner was the home of Mrs Doherty; most of her children came to the youth centre, while we, the youth workers, often used to escape temporarily to her house for a cup of tea and lively political conversations. Her oldest daughter, Margaret, flitted in and out, but I didn't know her well; she did not come to the youth centre. Unbeknown to me, Margaret later met and married Dan McCann. So when I came looking for an interview, I was not an academic or an interloper, but a former friend of her mother.

Of course, reputation is two-edged. I am not a loyalist; moreover, most of my community activity has been in relation to nationalist and republican West Belfast where I was born. During the Troubles, that mere accident of birth, never mind my community activity, was more than enough reason to label me a legitimate target in the eyes of loyalist military groups. Contacting or interviewing loyalists at the height of the conflict would thus have been impossible for me. That has changed since the peace process, as more academics have sought to understand loyalism, and as loyalism has become more open to debate and scrutiny. That said, given my background, I have no history in that community and so less likelihood of identifying or even stumbling across long-lost or inadvertent contacts. Perhaps surprisingly, it has happened on one occasion; in the late 1990s, I was interviewing UVF men in their wing at Long Kesh Prison. I knew that they would not have allowed me in to photograph and talk about their prison murals without having checked me out, but I did not expect the effusive welcome I received from the officer commanding the wing. Only at the end did he reveal that I had taught his sister. But perhaps more telling in relation to the road I had to travel in penetrating loyalism was the comment of one ex-prisoner I approached when researching an article in 2005: 'You're not exactly known as a friend of loyalism, are you?' Despite the changes in loyalism and in my relationship to it in the last decade, there may have been some vestiges of a similar sentiment which stood in the way of my access to some people I might otherwise have been able to interview.

Loyalism posed a difficulty in another way as well. More often than with republicans, the path to an interview with the son or daughter of a loyalist ex-combatant petered out because of refusal on the part of the parent or offspring or both. There were a number of reasons given:

'No-one knows my father was involved, so I don't want to change that.'

'My kids don't know I was involved, and I don't want them to.'

'I can only talk if you don't name me or my parent, and if you cut out anything that could identify either of us.' This is virtually an impossible request in cases where the parent was a high-profile loyalist.

'The past is over and done with; there's no point raking over old coals.' This last reason, incidentally, I found during research in 2005 to be part of the articulation of loyalists in rejecting the possibility of a truth-recovery process for Northern Ireland. A stepdaughter of a UVF ex-prisoner whose story appears here has disguised both her name and that of her stepfather, while the UVF son of a UVF father has provided only the first names of himself and his father.

Republican ex-prisoners have been traditionally more rooted in their community and less likely to be wary of breaking cover. And, unlike loyalism, republicanism has made attempts to embrace the notion of formally coming to terms with the past. I am not claiming that there are no cases where republican ex-combatants have faded back into anonymity in the community and want to remain there, or where their children, especially if born after imprisonment, know nothing of their previous life and activities. On the other hand, only on one occasion did the issue of anonymity arise in relation to republicans; the daughter of Dan McCann did not want her first name used. Sons and daughters of republicans who refused tended to give reasons such as: 'I have no problem being interviewed, but my mother would be very upset if I said exactly what I think.'

In the end, you could say that the people whose stories appear here self-selected themselves. But getting to them to give them the chance to self-select was not always straightforward. Some people were more likely to agree to interviews than others. For example, not all combatants ended up in prison, but it was inevitable that the sons and daughters I interviewed were of ex-prisoners; no-one was likely to 'out' their parent if they had not already been caught. Likewise, there were certain 'categories' of sons and daughters whom I could not pin down for an interview. For example, the ten republican hunger strikers in 1981 were mostly single men without children. An indirect attempt to persuade one of the few children of hunger strikers to be interviewed failed. Similarly, some sons and daughters of republicans became deeply engaged in anti-social behaviour, such as joy riding and petty crime. I collected one powerful story from one such person, but in the end, she withdrew the interview because it would cause hurt to her mother who had been a member of the IRA.

One major structural problem I faced was that often my only access to a person I had identified and sought to interview was through an organisation, military or political. Despite the fact that the peace process has allowed for a relaxation in this regard, some organisations are more controlling than others and police robustly the public profile of their members. When I started out, I expected the least difficulty in accessing republicans, with more difficulty in relation to loyalists, for the reasons I have given above. And within loyalism, I expected to have more luck with the UVF than the UDA, not least because the former views itself as a more sophisticated and ideologically based organisation than its rival, and the latter has been more ambivalent about the peace process. But sons and daughters of UDA people proved to be more amenable to interview than I had expected, and those of UVF people less so.

On the republican side, Sinn Féin proved particularly fortress-like. In trying to contact people I actually knew, I was sometimes directed to the Stormont office of that same person, now an elected politician. After interrogation as to my reasons for interviewing the person, I was promised a call-back which never came. On one other occasion, I approached someone working in a republican ex-prisoners' organisation for some contacts. That person, whom I had not previously known, said his ability to help depended on what capacity I was asking him – as an individual or as a representative of the organisation. I hastily said I was asking him personally, and he was more than generous in helping me. 'If you had asked me as a representative of the organisation, I would have to have sought permission,' he said. And despite the negative thrust of this paragraph, I have to acknowledge that Gerry Adams had no difficulty speaking to his son Gearóid, who quickly agreed to be interviewed for this book.

One way I identified and sought out people to interview was by contacting ex-prisoners, either directly or through an intermediary. Some intermediaries were more enthusiastic and persistent than others, and some had more clout than others. But beyond this is the fact that, given my age, I was dealing with people, parents or intermediaries, of my generation and asking them to persuade people of the next generation to bare their souls in an interview. In effect, it was as if I was approaching a parent with the following request: 'I want you to ask your son if he would like to be interviewed by me as to how your political involvement impacted on him as a child. I know he hardly knew you growing up, that he became a tearaway as a teenager, that your relationship with him since you were released has been at best tense, and that he doesn't share your political world view at all, but I would like you to ask him anyway.' You can guess the answer.

Methodology

The interviews were relatively unstructured. There were three main areas I wanted each person to talk about: how the parent's involvement impacted on their lives as children, what they thought of the parents' politics then, what they think now, and whether there has been a change in their views as they have become adults. Each interview was taped and transcribed, after which I edited the transcript to produce a free-flowing narrative. Sometimes this took extensive editing before a satisfactory account was produced. In this editing process, sections were deleted or moved around. However, no words were added; the final edited account contained only words spoken by the person interviewed, even if not precisely in that order. The edited interview was then given back to the interviewee for approval. They had the freedom to change as much of the account as they wished. Thus, every word in each of these stories has been approved by the person telling the story.

In this way, the book differs significantly from most research involving interviews which is carried out by academics (and indeed journalists). There are other divergences from more traditional social research. For example, there is no 'control group'. In standard research, this would mean having another group of people to interview who differed from this group in at least one major way. One could, for example, when researching the educational achievements of children from one-parent families compare the results with children from two-parent families to see if there were significant differences in educational outcomes. The question which arises is: what would be an appropriate control group for the sons and daughters of combatants in Northern Ireland?

One possibility would be to look at a group of people who did not have parents who were combatants to see how their experiences of the conflict differed and to judge whether the involvement of the parent had made for a substantially different situation. The problem here is that the experience of conflict differed dramatically across class, sectarian, regional and other lines, making it difficult to figure out what exactly was being compared with what.

Another approach would be to consider the sons and daughters of regular prisoners; as we shall see in the next chapter when we consider research carried out by others, there are many resonances in the experiences of both groups; these differences could throw some light on the effects of the parent's involvement in political violence in one case but not the other. Similarly, one could compare the experiences of the sons and daughters of combatants with those of the sons and daughters of regular security personnel; this could allow a focus on whether the illegality of the violence in one case made a difference to the experience. Finally, one could examine the experience of the sons and daughters of combatants elsewhere to see if the Northern Ireland experience was in some way unique.

There are a number of reasons for not pursuing any of these options, time, cost and accessibility among them. But the most significant reason is this: this is not intended to be a traditional social-science report. Rather, it has been planned as a platform on which some stories from a category of people in the Northern Ireland conflict whose stories have not yet been adequately told can be told. Moreover, the stories are in the words of the people themselves, as uninterrupted as possible by me, the researcher.

I would hasten to add that I do not believe that this book reproduces a set of misery memoirs. This genre has recently reached a peak, accounting for around 9% of book sales in the UK alone. While there is some good writing and riveting narrative in books such as Frank McCourt's *Angela's Ashes* and Dave Pelzer's *A Child Called It*, such is the popularity of the genre that it has forced an escalation of horror. Although the books have broken taboos and revealed hidden truths, the popularity has also led to an inevitable lenience as regards truth. In the rush to be Oprah's or Richard and Judy's next choice for stardom, authors have been tempted to exaggerate, even lie. James Frey's blockbuster *A Million Little Pieces* was revealed as partially fictional, while Margaret B Jones' *Love and Consequences* was unmasked as being totally imaginary. Overall, the genre is plagued by a kind of pornographic intent on the part of some authors and publishers, and in that the revelation of truth, concerns about justice, and indeed the whole concept of human decency, have often been diluted.

Ethics

There has been a recent upsurge in concern about ethics in academic research. Given some cavalier practices in the past, such a concern is timely and valuable. On the other hand, there has been a counter-swing towards intense caution, particularly in social research. One measure of this is the focus on vulnerable subjects. The directive is that such people should not be approached, for example, to participate in interviews without a carefully thought-out range of protections. Valuable as that is as a policy, it does not of itself define a 'vulnerable subject'. Some such people are obvious – children, or adults with mental illness, for example. But it is my belief that the definition of vulnerability should be located in the person, not in the topic of research. This is not the current consensus in social research, where it is believed by some that some topics are of their very nature so potentially disturbing that interviewing anyone in relation to them is ethically dubious. That could be said of the people whose stories are in this book; they tell of absent parents, police and army dawn raids, first-hand experience of death and injury, the humiliation of prison visits, the tension in the home when the parent returns from prison. Yet I have neither ruled interviews with these people out of bounds nor indeed sought ethical approval for the research. There are a number of reasons for this.

First, these people are adults, going about their lives successfully, and capable of reaching informed decisions on their own part, either alone or in consultation with those to whom they are close; one such decision is the choice to accept my invitation to be interviewed. Secondly, many of them had come to terms many years ago with the circumstances of their childhood and talking about this period now in adulthood is no longer traumatic for them. Thirdly, even those for whom the experience of telling their life story was difficult benefited from the experience. Let me give one example: one of the women interviewed for this book cried on a number of occasions during the interview. I offered on each occasion to stop the interview, temporarily or permanently, but she asked me to continue. Even then, her account was often disjointed, with jumps in the story, incomplete sentences and faltering narrative. The transcribing and editing of this interview proved the most difficult and time-consuming of all. I gave the completed account back to the person, unsure what her reaction would be. Within an hour, she was on the phone, thanking me profusely and telling me how positive she was about the finished product. It was, she said, the first time since the incidents she spoke about, which happened decades before, that she was able to see her story as a coherent and reasoned narrative. She had never before been able to construct that narrative by herself.

I am neither a counsellor nor a conflict-resolution technician. Nor am I so arrogant as to believe that the people I interviewed were incapable of telling their own stories until I came along. All I can claim as an academic is to have persuaded the twenty people in this book, some of whom took more coaxing than others, to tell their stories for public consumption. Some had told these stories on other occasions, while some had never told them publicly before. Why did they all do so? To get something off their chest? For recognition and acknowledgement for themselves, the parent or the ideals for which the parent struggled? To provide some lessons for a society seeking to transform from violence to peace? As an example to others? I suspect that all of these reasons and others figured at some point in the rationale. But I am not the one to answer the question of motivation. You would have to ask them.

Children and War: Trauma and Resilience

Introduction

The stories which you are about to encounter are those of some people, adults now, who as children had a parent caught up in the violent political conflict that racked Northern Ireland for three decades. Most had a parent who was a militant activist and who paid for that activism through imprisonment or death. The people whose stories are here constitute only a small proportion of all such children. There is no way to tell accurately how representative they are or how typical their experiences were in relation to all the other people who have not been interviewed. One reason for this is that there has been so little research done on this topic. So to put the stories into context, it is worth looking at three distinct areas: the general issue of children and the Northern Ireland conflict; what we know about children of prisoners in particular; and what insights we might get from other conflict zones in the world.

Children and the Troubles

Article 1 of the United Nations Convention on the Rights of the Child defines 'children' as persons up to the age of eighteen. Using this definition, we can begin to explore the extent to which children have been caught up in the Northern Ireland conflict.

There have been child soldiers in both legal and illegal armies. The IRA seems to have been the most likely to recruit child soldiers. But the loyalists were likewise active; Alistair Little (2009) has written of his involvement in murder as a member of the UVF when he was seventeen years of age. The British Army deployed troops under the age of eighteen in Northern Ireland, but after the deaths of two such soldiers in 1974 made eighteen the minimum age to serve in Northern Ireland (seventeen and a half if confined to barracks).

Children in all these armed groups died in the conflict: 223 of the 3,285 victims who were killed between August 1969 and December 1993 were children, that is, 6.78%. (Sutton, 1994) These deaths were not evenly spread among the different sections of society. Catholics bore the brunt of the killing: 150 of the children killed, 67.6%. And working-class children suffered disproportionately; the six postal districts in Northern Ireland where poverty and inequality were greatest saw 33.5% of deaths of people under the age of twenty-five, but 58% of deaths of children. (Smyth, 1998: 55)

The year 1972 was the worst for deaths of children (as indeed it was for casualties overall), with fifty-six such deaths, 25% of the total for the whole period.

All of the armed groups active in the North killed children. To take some examples: eight of the seventeen people killed by rubber and plastic bullets fired by the police and British Army and six of the fourteen Bloody Sunday victims in 1972 were children. An IRA bomb on the Shankill killed a one-year-old boy and a two-year-old girl on 11 December 1971. Unborn twins were victims of the Real IRA bomb in Omagh on 15 August 1998; their mother was one of twenty-nine people killed. A UVF bomb in Dublin on 17 May 1974 killed two sisters, aged five years and seventeen months respectively.

In those areas where the conflict was most intense, children, no less than adults, were witnesses to police and army raids and roadblocks, street rioting, bombings and shootings, and the disruption of everyday life. How did children survive such experiences?

At first, psychologists writing on the subject, such as Fraser (1973), concluded that there was little to worry about; only a minority of children were affected negatively, and the effects were short-term. Fields (1973) raised the stakes by arguing that not only were the effects of the conflict deep and long-lasting, but the Northern Ireland population, adult and child, was at the receiving end of a psychological onslaught by the British state to 'de-individualise' people, leaving them incapable of independent political action. The reaction to this argument from mainstream psychologists was to throw the baby out with the bath water; in rejecting Fields' extreme position, they concluded that the psychological effects of the conflict were being exaggerated and that most people were managing to get on with normal and ordinary everyday lives. 'Contrary to expectations, however, the vast majority of children in Northern Ireland have not become psychological casualties of the Troubles.' (Cairns, 1987: 70)

Underpinning this debate was a traditional psychological focus on individual effects. Later, psychologists attempted to inject a social element into the debate. Connolly (2002) was at the forefront of this approach with his finding that children as young as three were capable of recognising ethnic cultural clues such as colours, emblems and flags. In addition, children as young as six were shown to have already begun to identify themselves as belonging to one of two main communities. (Connolly et al, 2004)

With this focus, the pendulum tended to swing the other direction, ignoring the question of effects of the conflict on children as individuals. There is some strong evidence now that these were greater than was realised while the conflict raged; for example, the dramatic rise in the suicide rate, including among children, post-conflict is seen as having part of its origin in the conflict itself. (Tomlinson, 2007)

Children of Combatants

Children of combatants were likewise caught up in that conflict, perhaps more intensely than most children. So whatever conclusions there are about the ability to cope or the long-lasting effects of the conflict will be at least as relevant for them as for other kids. One way to find out the details of that experience is to look at research which has been carried out on prisoners and their families in Northern Ireland. (McEvoy et al, 1999; Jamieson and Grounds, 2002; Shirlow, 2001)

The partners of prisoners clearly point to the detrimental effects of imprisonment on the whole family. Financial difficulties, psychological effects – from nightmares to temper tantrums – loom large in the literature. Children who witnessed the arrest of their parents were particularly hard hit; 71% of those partners in one study whose children were present at the arrest felt that the children were not coping well, compared to 58% of those whose children were not present at the arrest. (McEvoy et al, 1999: 189)

The research shows that children were frequently told protective lies about the parent's absence. The younger the child the less likely they were to have been told the truth. The parent was 'working away from home' or was 'in hospital'. (McEvoy et al, 1999: 190)

Keeping relationships going despite imprisonment was a major task, yet partners of politically motivated prisoners seem to have done well in this respect. One study revealed that 88% of partners interviewed visited at least once a week and 57% said they brought their children on the visit at least fortnightly. (McEvoy et al, 1999: 185) That is not to say that prison visits were easy. Sustaining open and honest conversation was difficult with young children present and when everyone was intent on not causing additional stress. As one prisoner's wife put it:

> You would always look your best when you went to visit. You would spend all morning getting the children all clean and ready, blow-drying your hair and whatever. Then you would go up and sit and smile and inside you would be saying to yourself, 'Don't let him know how bad you feel. If he knew, he would crack up.' (Shirlow, 2001: 15)

Finally, the release of the prisoner back to the family home was not without problems. One woman told an interviewer: 'When he first came home, I thought that's it, I can't have this big child in the house.' (Shirlow, 2001: 11)

Another woman recounted: 'You are so glad he is back and then all hell breaks loose.' (Shirlow, 2001: 11)

Part of the problem was the new-found independence of the woman and the male ex-prisoner's difficulty in coming to terms with that. Another huge part of the problem was rebuilding relationships with children. One ex-prisoner said of his teenage son: 'He couldn't accept me coming out and being the dominant figure in the house.' (Jamieson and Grounds, 2002: 40)

In Their Own Words

The voices of the children themselves are often absent from these studies. There are a few exceptions: the reports on two focus groups with children of republican prisoners carried out by Tar Anall (2000 and 2005); the report of a focus group with children of republican prisoners in Derry carried out by Cúnamh (2000); and a report on interviews with children of UVF prisoners conducted by Spence (2002).

The children confirmed the findings of the reports on prisoners considered above but added a level of immediacy when they talked of coping with the parent's imprisonment.

They spoke of house raids and of the often frightening experience of prison visits. Some realised that parents had kept secrets from them, especially in relation to why their father was missing: 'I had it in my head it was something ten times worse than what it was.' (Cúnamh, 2000: 13)

And some noted how they, too, had taken part in this culture of secrecy: '... you didn't wanna go and tell your mummy because you didn't want to give her any more hassle, so you kept it to yourself'. (Tar Anall, 2000: 10)

The parent's release figured prominently in the accounts of tension and stress.

> My da used to have loads of rules whenever he got out. You weren't allowed to leave our garden at all, and I was six or older, and my wee mates across the street used to have to come over to me. And I used to cry and all, I used to say: 'I hope ... the peelers shoot you. I hope the English bastards get you!' (Tar Anall, 2005: 18)

Finally, many of those interviewed were clearly resentful of the parent's political activism which led to separation and imprisonment. 'I grew up hating the 'RA, so I did. I didn't like them one bit. Because I felt that *both* sides took my parents away, not just the Brits, for I blamed the 'RA as well.' (Tar Anall, 2005: 20)

As many of them express it, the hardest thing to take is that their fathers' priorities did not include them. One young girl stated: 'I get mad at him an' think, "You didn't raise us." 'Cause I don't understand why he chose to do what he did for his country over us.'

And a young man: 'No offence, but he's more concerned about helpin' other people than his family.' (Spence, 2002: 42)

Children and Conflict Elsewhere

Such information as exists about children of political activists elsewhere in the world reveals that they express sentiments practically identical to those of these children from Northern Ireland. For example, in South Africa, Gillian Slovo grew up one of three daughters of Joe Slovo, head of the ANC's military wing, MK, Umkhonto we Sizwe, and Ruth First, anti-apartheid activist, who was killed when she opened a parcel bomb sent to her in Mozambique by the South African military. She writes of her father:

> All my life I had wanted him to value me as much as he valued South Africa. In moments of past clarity, I would face the possibility that my father was just not capable of giving me what I desired. (Slovo, 1997: 210)

Nelson Mandela recognised this dilemma of the political activist.

> It seems to be the destiny of freedom fighters to have unstable personal lives. When your life is the struggle, as mine was, there is little room left for family. That has always been my greatest regret, and the most painful aspect of the choice I made. (Wiwa, 2001: 235)

From prison, Mandela wrote to his daughter Maki to explain this point: 'Don't make me regret I am here. What I need to do is worthwhile, not only for you and for the family, but for all black people.'

But Maki was having none of it. When he was released, he tried to hug her, but she pulled away: 'You are the father to all our people, but you have never had the time to be a father to me,' she told him. (Slovo, 1997: 214)

Some children of such activists seem to have seen the parent's abandonment of them as the ultimate sign of virtue. Aleida Guevara writes of her father Che:

> ... how wonderful my father really was. He renounced the most beautiful thing a human being can have, which was his love for his children

> and wife, to dedicate himself to a much greater and more important task. (Guevara, 2006)

But the evidence seems to point to most of the children of these parents being ambivalent about the parent's political involvement. Take Slovo (1997: 100):

> We were not asking them to stay silent ... or to put our needs before the needs of the oppressed. All we wanted was a simple acknowledgement that no political movement can ever fight for justice without there being casualties.

Perhaps one of the clearest examples of this is the account of one Chilean woman. Her parents were members of the MIR (Movimiento de Izquierda Revolucionaria, Revolutionary Left Movement), formed in 1965 and militarily active against the Pinochet dictatorship from the mid-1970s. They abandoned their kids to collective childcare arrangements while they pursued the struggle.

> It was as if Chile, what was happening in Chile, was always more important than us children, although I've always been very proud that my parents were MIRistas. I believed in the revolution. I think she did what she had to do and never, never thought any more about it; never thought that it was doing us any harm, never thought that we would feel abandoned until the end of our days. (Castillo, 2007)

Coping and Resilience

If that was all there was to say about the experience of being the child of a combatant, then what you are about to read would be an unmitigated negative tale. Yet, one of the things which comes through from these interviews is the resilience of many of the people concerned; they are survivors, not just victims.

There is an expectation in society that the experiences they had were so unnatural and abnormal for children that they were inevitably severely traumatised as a result. This would be the conclusion of many psychologists. Mainstream psychology as a discipline focuses on the individual person and looks for clear, measurable consequences of experience in the individual, including psychopathology and post-traumatic stress disorder. But it is necessary to see how such expectations and indeed our Western view of childhood as a time of innocence are social constructs. From this point of view, one important element in the experience of trauma is the expectation that trauma is a consequence of experience. If the society or community in which the child lives does not define an experience as traumatic, then people in that society or community, including children, do not necessarily view the experience as traumatic. This is not to presume that these children are invulnerable or immune from the negative effects of violent conflict, but it opens up the possibility of seeing how children can cope with those effects, drawing on not only personal but also communal strengths.

Thus, adolescent Iraqi and Somali refugees have been found to be more resilient than might have been expected because of their strong ties to their culture and community. (Maegusuku-Hewitt et al, 2007) And researchers who have studied Palestinian children during the first Intifada of 1987–93 found that '… the children who glorified war, expressed unfailing support for their national cause, and were ready to join the fight suffered less from anxiety and insecurity, depression, and feelings of failure … than did the children with weak ideological commitment'. (Punamäki, 1996: 66) Children 'viewed themselves as freedom fighters and this ideological commitment functioned as a protective factor and source of resilience'. (Qouta, S, Punamäki, R and El Sarraj, E, 1995: 1205) Most astoundingly of all, the Intifada became 'a therapeutic process that turned Palestinians from victims to masters of their destiny', children included. (Qouta, S, Punamäki, R and El Sarraj, E, 1995: 1198) The conclusion that war and political violence can have therapeutic rather than traumatic effects on children is not merely controversial; it is also a long way from standard wisdom.

Similarly, looking at the South African situation, Feldman concludes that the involvement of children in active resistance to apartheid was not a sign of 'profound disorder' – the collapse of the preciousness and innocence of childhood – but 'the emergence and rediscovery of childhood as a distinctive and separate moral and ethical category in modern South Africa …' (2002: 298)

This is an argument which is open to misunderstanding. Children *should* have the fundamental human rights of safety, equality, economic parity and a meaningful life. (Garbarino, 2008) They *should not* have to cope with the experience of political violence. But in as far as some of them manage to cope, our notions of normality and abnormality are called into question.

If we start with the Western construct, that childhood is precious, vulnerable, in need of constant protection and cosseting, then the answer is clear:

children involved in freedom struggle or resistance represent the collapse of our notion of the innocence of childhood. In as far as such cultural definitions prevail in a society, then they are accepted not just by adults but also by children. Where this is the dominant cultural conclusion in a society, children in that society also accept that they should not have to suffer such distortions, and the experience of doing so is a potential source of stress to them. In other words, even expectations of stress are in many ways socially determined. And the converse is true; in a situation where an opposite social construction exists, then resistance and its consequences are not necessarily regarded as abnormal, not even by children. In short, coping depends on the social/political context which makes it possible for people – including children – to believe that it is possible to cope.

To take one example: to outside eyes, the children of South African liberation were deprived of the things that are regarded as essential to a happy childhood, but this is not necessarily how it appeared from the inside. Listen to Annie Neo Parsons; she grew up in Botswana, where her parents were politically active against apartheid. Their home was firebombed by the South African Defence Forces and the children went into exile in England with their father.

> Living the struggle as a child meant taking on roles and responsibilities as many children all over the world do for different reasons. We are taught to think about childhood as a time of innocence and freedom, but really it was about growing up. In some ways I felt more of a child at fourteen than I did when I was seven years old. The struggle gave me a sense of purpose. It taught me that every second of our lives matters and has meaning. That's as valuable as my memories of climbing trees. (Gunn and Krwala, 2008: 13)

As was said earlier, the people whose stories appear in this book represent only a small proportion of all those whose stories could be told. As such, they may not be representative of all the missing stories. It may be that those who were most traumatised by the experience of being a child of a combatant are unable or unwilling to tell their stories. That said, those who have been able and willing to speak here manage to reveal the ways in which they have survived the experience. What they went through was in many cases horrific, and as such left scars. But that is not the whole story. There is also a story of survival and indeed of resilience in the face of terror.

In the Shadow of Famous Men

I'm not sure that I'll ever be able to get out of his shadow.

Mark Ervine

John Lyttle

Son of Tommy 'Tucker' Lyttle

Tommy Lyttle, nicknamed 'Tucker', was Brigadier of the West Belfast Brigade of the UDA during the period when the UDA was widely involved in killing nationalists. After his demotion from that post, it was claimed that for many years he had acted as a Special Branch agent, and as such had been involved in collusion between state forces and loyalists to carry out operations such as the murder of prominent lawyer Pat Finucane. Tommy Lyttle died in 1995. John Lyttle was born in 1959. He is currently writing a book about his life.

My name is John Lyttle. I'm a journalist. I've been living here in London – in exile, in a way – since I was about eighteen. I'm fifty now, so that's a long time … thirty-two years.

I'm officially an orphan. Both my mother and father are now dead. Painful though that was, I'd be a liar if I didn't admit it has also been kind of liberating.

When my mother died a few years ago, from a massive stroke, I noticed that I was in this better, lighter place, even though the entire family had to endure days of coma and dashed hopes. I felt seedy and guilty for feeling … freed … who wouldn't? But I've made my peace with it. I've finally – finally – been able to leave something behind, not drag it about behind me like a dinosaur's tail, and look at my parents, my mother as well as my father, and see what they'd done between them.

It was a tug of war: between one who was cynical and dark and black and strong and smart – and one who believed in the essential goodness of people and was bound to authority and kindness and good manners: to niceness. I realised when my mother passed how I'd been suspended in the middle between these two conflicting forces and it was, in a very matter-of-fact way, tearing me apart, and had been doing so for decades. And with my mother gone, I went over to my father's side. I thought I saw the world as it was, not as my mother hoped and pretended it was. Having spent a lifetime rejecting him, and at the same time loving him because he was lovable and nurturing and all the private things a public persona doesn't and can't encompass.

He was dedicated to us, his five children, unlike most males loitering on the Shankill Road. Tucker was deeply involved with our upbringing. He believed in education, thought it was absolutely right that we should sit indoors on a blazing hot day with a book. You can imagine what book readers on the Shankill had to go through; it's like an eccentricity. He'd say, 'They don't need to be out in the sunshine, Lily. If they're reading, they're learning. For God's sake, woman, let them alone.'

He was hands-on as a parent. In the time before the Troubles, he'd come back from the night shift at Mackies,[1] the factory where he was a machinist and a foreman, and my mother would still be in bed and, exhausted, he would make breakfast of hot milk and cornflakes and toast and tea. He would dress us. He would clean us. He was tactile. He wasn't afraid of hugging and kissing. I look back on that from here and I think, 'You were blessed.'

There's something peculiarly comforting about knowing you have a father who will quite literally kill for you. In this case, it wasn't just a form of words. We knew that when my father said that, he meant it. We had the proof of it all around us, after all.

So yes; I'm John Lyttle, I'm a journalist, I'm fifty, and I can turn round and look at my childhood and not be swamped by the old, roaring tidal waves of blackness. I've reached an ... let's call it an accommodation.

I have a theory that for a lot of smart working-class men in Northern Ireland, the Troubles were a golden, Gothic opportunity. Routes that were otherwise shut to them in terms of using their skills or their talents opened up to them on both republican and loyalist sides. The Troubles freed these men, allowed them means to use their smarts.

My father was bright, I mean extraordinarily bright. And trapped. He fell into the traps most working-class men in Belfast did and still do: married too young, had children too young, had to work in a job that he didn't particularly want; no life of the mind, no purpose of imagination. Political agitation and explosion liberated Tucker. It came at a time when he was searching for something, even though he may not have known it.

I imagine it began being purely political and very quickly evolved, or devolved. In the land of the blind, the one-eyed man is king. He was immediately involved in the upper echelons of the embryonic UDA and revived UVF.

---

1 Mackies, an engineering company based in West Belfast, at its height one of Northern Ireland's largest employers. Like most Belfast engineering firms, as well as Harland and Wolff shipyard, its workforce was overwhelmingly from the unionist community.

He was smarter than those people – no vast achievement – so he was at the eye of the storm from the very beginning. And it carried him away.

The terrible thing for him, which I now realise, is that he knew what was happening, not just in Northern Ireland but to himself. He saw what he was becoming as the years passed. He was very conscious of himself and he knew he was committing sins God wouldn't forgive him for.

When I was twelve or so and wising up, I remember asking my mother once, 'Why is my da on his knees at the end of the bed every night for hours?'

And she said, 'What do you think he's doing? He's praying.'

And I remember saying to my mother, 'No, he's not; he's negotiating.'

He was becoming monstrous. He did things he thought were necessary, in the sense that they were expedient and because everybody else was doing them: do or be done unto. If he didn't, he would be the next head on the chopping block. It tormented him because he was bright, but at the same time, I don't think he ever thought there were other options, avenues. I thought there were, hence my rage and disgust and disappointment. I realise now that there weren't. Kill or be killed.

My father always thought Catholics had a good case and a true cause. He'd say to us, 'You can't keep anyone second class and expect them to put up with it.' Harland and Wolff, the shipyard, used to drive him crazy. He'd say, 'If they can do the job, they should be doing the job. Refusing people work is practising apartheid.' He knew, understood, words like 'apartheid'.

This isn't to say there weren't figures in the nationalist community he loathed, but that had nothing to do with the fact that they were Catholics. He never saw the Troubles in strictly religious terms. He used to say, 'That's a lazy label.' He wanted to negotiate a peace. He'd say, 'In the end, we'll lose. It's their country. They're going to want it back. We've got to bargain.' He was very involved in those early peace initiatives that were pissed on. They came up with that document *Towards a Negotiated Peace* early on. Odd, isn't it, how a lot of his beliefs, twenty-five years later, were part of the actual peace process?

I had a secret life. I knew I was gay from a very early age. When Diane B, a girl I knew at school, dropped her knickers underneath my grandmother's piano and invited me to have a look, I thought, 'What the hell is that? Are you kidding?' I was about six and remember thinking, 'I'm different from other little boys. I'm not going there. And I had better keep quiet about it.' Which wasn't unique to me; it's every gay child.

Thank God I was gay. I was able to stand outside, live in parallel, and look in. I never bought it. When I heard garbage about Catholics, I thought, 'Well, you're saying it because they're different, and I'm different, and you're wrong about me so I'm guessing you're wrong about Catholics.'

My brothers, to greater or lesser degrees, were involved in my father's life; I never got on board. We had this running joke from the *Godfather* movies that I was Michael Corleone, the one from the outside. I used to say, 'Well, don't think I'm coming back to take over.' We had bitter arguments, terrible arguments, about how he was trying to achieve his aims, or the aims of 'the Organisation'. It was always referred to as 'the Organisation'.

I was critical of my father from an extremely early age – admiring of him, but at the same time wondering, 'You're getting this wrong, and you're hurting us all. Don't you see what you're doing to the girls?' He ruled our lives because of his presence and then he ruled our lives because of his absence. Catholic and Protestant, they jointly sacrificed their children. They were political activists, and then they were terrorists, or whatever word you want to use, freedom fighters, and we were offered up.

Every day of my childhood, and I do mean every day, from the age of about nine until I left at eighteen, I expected to die. I thought about death every day. Getting on the bus, *it's going to blow up*. Walking past Unity Flats,[2] *is a sniper going to take me out?*

The first thing my father did when he left the house every morning was drop to his knees with a mirror on a stick and put it under his car to see if a bomb had been placed. In the house, I couldn't sit with my back to the front window, because every time a car would pass, the blood would drain from me. Even after I left Belfast and came back, my mother said to me, 'Don't sit there. Don't think you're testing yourself. That's stupid. If you don't want to sit there, don't sit there.'

We had people trying to break into the house. We had a security camera. We had CCTV years before anybody else, multiple locks on the door. My mother broke someone's arm who tried to get into the house by slamming the door. Leaving school when I was about sixteen up at Somerdale, three men tried to drag me into a car. I realise today I spent my childhood as an undiagnosed depressive.

My mother was bipolar, got into prescription meds. Who didn't? Much of that had to do with choices my father made. He self-medicated with alcohol. He would be withdrawn. This rumbling thundercloud would come into the

2 Unity Flats, a nationalist estate at the bottom of the unionist Shankill Road and a frequent point of confrontation during the 1970s.

house and we never knew what time it would arrive. And this used to be the person we ran to.

I mean, we fucking adored our dad. He was fun; we would rush him when he came into the hallway. We would throw ourselves around him. He would pick us up. And over the course of years this … this depressed gangster would thump home disguised as him. My siblings might see this differently, because everybody's story's different, but I finally couldn't bear to be in the same room. He could see it. He could see it happening. Awful. Even worse was that towards the end, he grasped what he had done.

My father got involved when we were in Wigton Street, when you had the agitation for civil rights. Wigton Street was literally a stone's throw from the Falls Road. The men started with patrols. I remember my father taking me with him – how insane is that? – and the men talking and I'd be standing there, holding my father's hand and feeling protected and thrilled.

It ramped up pretty quickly. I remember at eleven seeing my father on television for the first time on the evening news. We had our first barney because everyone else lied to him about how he came across and I wasn't willing to. He was angry at me – angry at me like I was an adult. A kid doesn't realise certain repercussions of things, so I was going, 'What were you doing? You didn't answer the questions. Why were you wearing that coat, that fake leather?' There's the gay child for you, criticising your father's fashion sense.

And he shouted at me, and that was the new Tucker. We didn't have screaming and shouting before. My father never lifted his hands to us. I can count two or three occasions when my father ever laid hands on his kids. It was an admission of defeat. He felt that way about violence generally, believe it or not, that if you had to resort to it, then you weren't arguing your case well. Violence won't fix it. It's idiot energy.

There was something he said to me a few months before he died: 'Things will improve now, because everybody is mutually exhausted.' That was shrewd. And he added, 'Don't forget, we've all reached a certain age and we're seeing what we've done, and looking at the people around us and seeing what we've done to them. Now,' he says, 'comes change.'

He didn't live to see it.

The marriage went on and on because when you married in Belfast, you married for life. But the happy period of it ended damn quickly, when I was about ten or eleven. My mother wanted a commitment to some kind of home life and that was impossible. Do you know the feminist adage, 'the personal is political'? Well, the political would often turn very personal in our house.

It was King Kong versus Godzilla. They beat the crap out of one another on occasion. And I can remember the Christmases where my father was out playing football with his UDA cronies and wasn't even there for our Christmas gifts being opened or dinner, and then couldn't understand why my mother was enraged. He would come home loaded. I remember my sisters sitting on the stairs, bawling their eyes out and me sitting with my arms round them, thinking, 'Do you have any idea of what you're doing?'

My mother would needle, 'This isn't a Frank Sinatra movie. This isn't *Robin and the Seven Hoods*.' She could get that. 'You're a husband and a father.' They were emotionally estranged for years. My mother had chronic breakdowns. I remember visiting her in the Mater[3] and she was a zombie. And my father stood at the bed and I knew that he knew that it was his handiwork. We all were. Three boys and then two girls. I was the second child: 'Saturday night's mistake,' my mother would joke.

He was doing it because it was giving him identity, outlet, esteem, history, even power and control. A real life and a fantasy life of a sort combined. Pop culture corrupts absolutely, you know. It's one of the great, unacknowledged influences on the last thirty to forty years in Northern Ireland: the *Boys' Own* adventure side of terrorism. He would take us to see *Tora, Tora, Tora*, all the Bond movies. One of the reasons I don't drive – I know this is the worst kind of Freudianism! – is my father with his eight-track blaring the James Bond theme, almost going up on two wheels, like it's *Diamonds Are Forever*, driving like a maniac. They were spies, him and his friends. Or cowboys: constant references to *The Magnificent Seven* and what have you. Or Mafia: the aforementioned *Godfather* movies. Performance art with real bullets. They had no other frame of reference for what they were doing. The nationalist community had rich Celtic romance and rebellion; we didn't have that. We had WWII flicks and King Billy.

I do remember sitting underneath the stairs on the Shankill Road estate after we moved out of Wigton Street, which was the end of happiness in my life. I remember sitting in the new house under the stairs with a sketchpad, drawing, because I used to compulsively draw. I was like every other kid in Northern Ireland: blood and guts and helicopters and bombs. And my father and his friends would be at the Formica breakfast table in the kitchen, chatting about who needed to be killed. And I'd listen to that. Adults believe children aren't there.

3 Mater Infirmorum Hospital, North Belfast, near the Shankill Road.

I can't believe my father kept guns in the house. Astonishing. Remember those little bags that you got chocolate gold coins in? My father kept his gun in one of those under 'Daddy's chair' in the front room. If anyone came to the door, he could reach down and pull it out. I found another gun in his bedroom. I went looking for his porn, because I knew he had porn. I found a gun. It wasn't loaded, thank God, because I did things with it I shouldn't have. Pressed it to my head. Pointed it out the bedroom window.

I remember once when I was small, stumbling downstairs at Wigton Street in the dead of night for a glass of water and finding some poor bastard roped to a chair. I can close my eyes and recall the smell of cheap beer and cigarette smoke and the gang sprawled around on the plastic sofa and the bare light from the kitchen and the blood soaking this guy's white vest. It was the middle of summer. It was hot. The house was a basic two-up, two-down; you roasted in the summer and froze in the winter. I felt skinny and vulnerable and weak standing there in my Y-fronts. My father stopped belting him to tell one of his 'men' to go and fetch me a glass of water. And this guy looking at me with absolute despair, despair. For years, I tried to convince myself that it was a dream. Around the same time period – events concertina when you're a kid, so I'm not sure of the time frame – but I went to the Stadium Cinema on the Shankill Road and saw a war movie called *633 Squadron* and there's a sequence at the end where the Nazis are torturing the hero and he's tied and they're pulling out his finger nails. And I had what I guess was a panic attack. I didn't make it to the toilets before throwing up.

I think that if my mother knew what was going on she would have stopped it. My mother was pseudo-corrupted; she was aware of what was going on and pretended not to be. But, when your father's saying things like, 'So-and-so is giving me a hard time,' and six weeks later so-and-so just isn't around to give him a hard time, you hardly need to be Einstein to join up the dots.

One of the most troubling things my father did when I left Belfast, I must have been in my late twenties, and I came back for a visit and he was driving back from the airport to return home. He always came to the airport to collect me and he would drive me back, and we had awkward, stilted conversations I realised couldn't be conducted within earshot of anyone else. This day, he talked about an individual who will have to remain nameless … Look, I spent years hating my father for this because basically, he implicated me in his decision making. It was basically 'it's him or me'. What can you say? It's one of those things you cannot *not* reply to. In the end it was, well, if it's my father or somebody else's father, it's going to be somebody else's father. I don't know what it was about that particular thing … well, I do now, but I can't go into it. I think his conscience was raw because it would cause great hurt to another family member. All my posturing on the moral high ground was abandoned. He used to tell me I was naive and I realise in retrospect he was discussing blunt realpolitik, that he would do it anyhow without anyone's permission. Still, it infuriated me. 'Why are you asking me to endorse this?'

Once, I went to UDA headquarters on the Shankill Road to wait for him in his office. He walked in and was surprised. 'How did you get in here?'

And I said, 'Da, I walked in.'

He went to the door and looked out and said, 'Past my praetorian guard?' in his sarcastic voice. I just burst out laughing. That's where he got me. My father could always make me laugh. There were moments that were private jokes. 'You'll get this, John. Not sure if others will.' It was well meant and flattering, but as I grew older and more conscious, it made me feel almost dirty. You're never quite sure of anyone's intentions: was that done out of love for me? Was that done to please yourself?

Surreal hardly covers it. During research for my book, I interviewed men and had to listen to their rationale, like, 'Your father had to have me kneecapped, but he was good about it. The shipment of guns did go missing. Everybody thought I had sold them on to the Provos, though I hadn't. He made sure the boys dropped me outside the A and E.'

I found myself blurting out, 'Do you know how fucking crazy that sounds? You're making excuses for my father putting bullets into your fucking kneecaps? Human beings don't do that to one another.' Except, of course, they do.

My problems didn't start until I got outside the environment. Once I wasn't immediately present in that environment, I awoke to what was not normal, because when we were kids, even though I realised on an abstract level that this was not right, at the same time I was accepting, because I had nothing to compare it to.

In *Godfather 3*, Michael says, 'Every time I try to get out, they keep trying to drag me back.' For years, things would happen where I would feel my father's hand dropping onto my shoulder from hundreds of miles away. When I went to therapy, the suits would say, 'What do you want to talk about?'

And I'd answer, 'I don't want to talk about my father because I'm cool with that now; I've figured it out.'

The fact that I brought up my father first, a good therapist would go, 'Well, he wants to talk about his father and he's not cool with it.'

Part of my secret life was the Shankill Road library and the library down the town. I'd be there for hours, educating myself about myself. When I came out – I was fifteen when I told my parents I was gay – I went off and I read about how to break the news before I did it.

Naturally, one of the reasons I told him was to wound him. I was very aware of it. He sat on my sister-in-law's bed and I told him in a way that sounded adult and mature, or at least as adult and mature as you can be at fifteen, but I waited for the moment when he'd break and I felt triumphant, justified when he did. He said, 'I'm trying to understand, John,' before making the fatal mistake of continuing, 'but what are my friends going to think?'

He was sobbing. Joy rushed through me, God forgive me. I said, 'I don't give a fuck what your friends think.'

I was sleeping with two of his friends. I remember once his car drawing up outside the house. I had pinned this guy to the bed. He said, 'That sounds like your father's car.'

And I said, 'That's because it is.'

We're naked in my parents' bed and this man freaks. How angry must I have been with my da to gamble not just with my life but with this bloke's? He was on the council[4] with him. My father would say to me, 'John, would you take this message round to —?' I was always happy to do that because I would end up in bed with —. That gave me such a huge adrenaline rush. Twisted.

My father turned up in gay bars searching for me once when I was arrested during one of the RUC's anti-gay spasms. I coped better than anyone else because my father trained me. Everybody else ended up signing statements. I was reminding the police, 'You know how old I am? Don't you realise one of my parents has to be here?' It was drummed into us.

Then they did good cop, bad cop: 'Oh dear, my da's right about these people; they're in the police because they're not bright enough to be criminals.' I refused to sign a statement. They let me go.

I didn't get any grief on the Shankill for being gay. People might occasionally pass a drunken remark and I would whisper, 'Black and Decker, Black and Decker,'[5] and it would stop. Later, I found out there had been times when so-and-so was going to do this or that, and so-and-so was told: 'His father's Tucker Lyttle.'

There were guys on the gay scene who were nationalists, hard-line nationalists. It didn't stop them from sleeping with you. The gay scene saved me, because people in the bar – whatever bar it might be, the Whip and Saddle

4 The governing body of the UDA.

5 Sometimes drills rather than guns were used to inflict kneecappings.

at the Europa or the Three Crowns or wherever – would say, 'He's not responsible for what his father does.' Looking back, the idea that it was fine to kill your fellow man but not have sex with him strikes me as brutally comical: Joe Orton stuff. The gay scene was the single safe area for Catholics and Protestants to come together … quite literally. God knows, I got a kick out of sleeping with Catholic guys and with British soldiers. My first serious boyfriend was Catholic and I made sure he was. Even though I knew my father would never know, *I* knew.

After I left Somerdale, I wanted to move into higher education. I was at the College of Business Studies for about three months and soon enough my classmates discovered who my father was. I was in the men's loos and cornered by a crowd and they said, 'We know who you are.'

There was no point in replying, 'Just because you know who I am, don't make any assumptions about what I might believe, or indeed about what my father might believe,' because he always predicted there would eventually be a united Ireland.

They looked at me and said, 'You're dead if you stay in Belfast.'

I thought, 'Hell, I do need to escape.' It was time to leave, because I would never be John Lyttle otherwise. I would be Tucker Lyttle's son forever. Worse than that, Tucker Lyttle's *gay* son.

One of the real reasons he was eventually jettisoned from the UDA was because he refused to allow drugs onto the Shankill. He was old-fashioned about drugs. All that stuff about him working for MI5 – yes and no. No-one who's writing about it is apparently sophisticated enough to realise that it's a two-way street. 'I'll give you information if you give me information.' He wasn't under their control; he wasn't being paid by them. If he was, I'd dearly love to know where the money went. I used to look at all the others on his level in the UDA and their big cars and their holidays in the Caribbean and their vulgar sound systems, knuckleduster gold jewellery and their front rooms being redone every three months; we never had any of that. We never had extra pocket money. Mind you, there were butchers on the Shankill Road who gave him steaks and joints, but as my father said, 'Your mother's just going to burn it.' There was a kind of weird purity. He also had this open-door policy, so when he was home, we never had a moment's peace. There was a flood of people coming in and out. It was like *The Godfather*: 'On the day of your daughter's wedding, will you grant me this request?'

My father died thirteen years ago. My mother died three years after him. No-one thought that he would die a natural death, though, of course, the fact that he had that massive heart attack and the three before that had all to do with the life he had led. My mother pulled something which infuriated me at the time but I realised is the Tennessee Williams' heroine's option; she rewrote the relationship in her head. It was Romeo and Juliet, star-crossed lovers. She transformed it into a pairing she could live with, even though when he died, they were separated.

What I didn't discover until afterwards was my father knew that he was dying. I feel guilty, because he kept making overtures and he wanted to have one heart-to-heart conversation. I couldn't do it. He wanted to talk and I was in the driver's seat now. I refused, and I did it deliberately. It was about being my own man. I regret it to this day.

Towards the end, he was repentant, whatever that word means. He did tell members of the family – because I never had that last conversation with him – that prison had stopped the merry-go-round. All that negotiating on his knees kind of worked out, which infuriated me at the time. When my father decided to forgive himself … you can't imagine my anger. That was one reason I couldn't have that conversation: 'Oh, what about the hundreds of dead you've left behind you?' After he died I wrote a piece for *The Independent* magazine.[6] It was a 5,000-word piece and it's called 'In the Name of My Father'. My sister newspaper *The Mirror*, which was owned by *The Independent*, the Irish edition, said the shame of having an out gay son had killed him, even though I had come out twenty or more years before.

After the piece appeared, his English teacher in prison sent me his writing. She said, 'He was so proud of you. He used to cite things that you had written, even something that had infuriated him, because it had made him laugh.' I read his writing, the essays, and … I wish I could write like that. There was a story about a man who lies about winnings on his greyhound, on a bet, and how he lies to his wife and the banal consequences. It's about penance, and about not treating your family with respect. I read it with my jaw slack. His writing is terrific.

Perhaps my facility with words isn't just environmental because my father said 'let the boy read his books' or because on Sunday mornings he'd have all the newspapers and hand the pile to me. Maybe he passed a skill on.

Perhaps there's a lot more of him in me than I acknowledge. I'll bet there are many sons and daughters of Provos and Sinn Féin who are having variations of this conversation even as we speak. What can you do? The forces

6 30 March 1996.

of history are immense and are tortured, and there's individual circumstance and then there's personality and character and the politics of the moment and it flies together and creates an extraordinarily combustible mix. Fathers and mothers do what they think they have to do. If you must judge, you've got to judge in context. For years, I dragged all this behind me like a dinosaur's tail. It was impossible to move at the speed I wanted to. I couldn't even run from the past. I could barely stagger. It gets better when you drop the baggage: if you want to survive, God, you have to let go.

Mark Ervine

Son of David Ervine

David Ervine joined the UVF at the age of nineteen and two years later, in November 1974, was arrested for possession of explosives with intent to endanger life. In prison, he came under the influence of the charismatic founder of the UVF, Gusty Spence, who influenced his political development. In the mid-'80s, Ervine stood for election for the Progressive Unionist Party, a left-of-centre party with connections to the UVF. In 1998, he was elected to the Northern Ireland Assembly, a position he retained until his death. He played a key role in the loyalist ceasefire of 1994 and was a central figure in the developing peace process. He died of a heart attack in January 2007. Mark Ervine was born in 1971.

My father politically would have been heavily influenced by his father, who was in the Merchant Navy and the Royal Navy and was a member of the Labour Party. That's where a lot of my father's political influence came from. He would have been left-of-centre; he was a socialist, which, coming from a loyalist community, was pretty rare – given the politics of the late 1960s and early '70s and when you had 'big-house' unionism and right-wing conservatism.

I'm not sure that at that age my da would have had his politics formulated. He maybe had an idea of right and wrong politically, but I don't think he had formalised his own politics. I don't think he knew he was a socialist at that point. His father died six months before he got arrested and that was one thing that my da was very thankful for, that my grandfather wasn't there, because he would have been devastated. He'd be deeply, deeply disappointed because he didn't agree with the Paisleys of this world. I don't think my grandfather would have been very enamoured by unionism. Although he wouldn't have been into an all-Ireland, he would have been more left-wing whereas unionism then was more right-wing.

My father never got politically motivated until he went to prison and met Gusty Spence.[7] Gusty Spence asked him why he was there. And my da, not fully understanding the ramifications of the question, said to him, 'Well, what the hell do you think I'm here for?' He was in the process of committing a terrorist act.

Later it dawned on him what he meant. '*Why* are you here? What created the situation that you find yourself incarcerated?'

When you're in prison, you have a lot of time for reflection, so through reflection and engagement with other political prisoners, who were probably going through the same sort of thing, he started to become more politically motivated; he started to analyse things more. And that was the birth of what later was to become the Progressive Unionist Party. They stood for their first election about '85, '86, and I knew nothing about it. I was fourteen, heading home from school and I saw a poster of my da on a lamppost and it's, like, *what the hell is going on?* I had no notion. My mother knew, but I didn't know. And then, of course, you got ribbed about it in school by your mates. And I'm thinking, *why is he doing this?* I thought it was just to get me a hard time! They were pretty small and would have been marginalised by the already established unionist parties, probably because of their more leftist politics and also because maybe a fear within unionism of, 'Hold on a wee minute. What's going on here? This is coming from the bottom up. Is this a revolution?' It's still to get to that point, but I think that it's in the process of happening within the unionist community.

I was one and a half when he got arrested in 1973. I can't really remember much about it until I was in school and I started to get every Thursday off. That was something to remember. All the other kids are sitting doing their school work and I don't have to go in that day because I'm going to the Maze! At that point, I didn't know that it was a prison; I thought this was where my da worked because that was what my mother had told me because she was afraid of me thinking, as you probably would do whenever you're a child, that only bad people go to prison. They're all bad people; and she didn't want me thinking of my da that way. So she told me that he was there working and whenever I inquired what his work entailed, she said, 'He's painting.'

And I said, 'What's he doing, painting all these walls?'– the perimeter walls.

7 Gusty Spence, founder member of the UVF, who served nineteen years in prison and was credited with turning a section of loyalism towards a more radical political ideology. This radicalism culminated in the formation of the Progressive Unionist Party (PUP).

And she said, 'Yes.'

And I said, 'Ma, he's going to be here for years.' It turned out he was!

I think my da was only twenty, twenty-one whenever he got arrested after the Oxford Street bombing:[8] that was the catalyst that gave him the impetus to become involved. It would have been hard for kids not to get involved. It would have been harder given your peers were becoming involved; it's seen as defending your community because that's what it was propagated as. You have to look at what unionism was propagating in the people at that time: 'ethnic cleansing' and 'all-Ireland' and the fear that was being pumped into the working classes only went to fuel the fire. During that era, it was a honey-trap for kids. I don't think he would have been mature enough to fully think through what he was doing, or maybe he thought he wouldn't get caught. I'm not sure that he devoted the thought to it that it deserved at that age. I think he did that in prison. He had time to reflect then how he ended up there and why he ended up there.

I saw him once a week for, I think, it was an hour. I would have taken myself into where the guards would have been, the guard hut, and they let me play darts and made me toast and a wee cup of tea. So I was well looked after whenever I got there, although still with no notion of what the place was or what it was all about. That didn't come until much later. Just prior to my da's release, a man stopped me in the street and said, 'What about your daddy? When's he getting out?'

'What do you mean, when's he getting out?'

'Sure, he's in jail still, isn't he?'

And I was, like, 'What!' Because up to that point, he was a painter and decorator!

I started to inquire then, not off my mother because I knew I was never going to get the truth there, or if I did, it was going to be some sort of jaded version of it. And I found out, yes, he was in prison; he had been a member of the Ulster Volunteer Force who'd been caught in the act, so to speak. My father didn't tell me until I was about fourteen or fifteen; he then divulged it because he was under death threat from the Provisionals and thought it was best I know, not only for his security but the security of the family. Of course,

---

8 In one hour on 21 July 1972, the IRA exploded nineteen bombs in Belfast; this became known as Bloody Friday. One of the bombs, at Oxford Street bus station, killed six people. Three others died in the other bombs. The events of the day are cited by many loyalists as the trigger for their involvement in paramilitary activity.

then I'm asking, 'Why?' So he had to come forth with it. To his astonishment I said, 'Well, I knew this for years. Why didn't you tell me all this before? Why have you waited until now to tell me?'

'Ah, well, I didn't want to burden you.' I think he was afraid to broker it with me. He wasn't sure how I'd take it.

My mum was very, very angry because she didn't know that he was involved. I think she was very hurt by it. But she stuck by him. Early on in his incarceration, he told her, 'Listen, just you get on with your life. We'll just cut our ties.' He didn't want to have that hold over her where she's going to be sitting waiting on him. He'd got sentenced to eleven years and subsequently he ended up doing about six and a half or seven. He didn't want that eating into her life. But she was much bigger than that and she was willing to wait and to sacrifice that part of her life. It was almost like a jail sentence for her as well.

We lived with my grandparents. They would have been very supporting of my mum. I don't think she liked staying in the house on her own. They'd bought their own house, and she would have gone round and checked it, made sure that it was okay. The grandparents only lived two streets away. My grandparents featured in my early years and I would have looked to my grandfather as sort of the father figure. I saw my other grandmother every other day. She lived on the Albertbridge Road, within walking distance. We were all pretty close.

My da was something I never really spoke about among my friends, although whenever he did get out of prison, some of my friends wondered who this man was who was running about with my ma. And then you had to explain, 'Well, this is my da and he was away working.' It was normal. And from such a young age for that to be a fact of life! I just viewed it: this is normality. Because you didn't know any different. I can't say that I found it stressful.

I found it more stressful once he actually got released. It was late 1980 and I was eight. Up until then, my da was God to me. I loved my da. I only saw him once a week and that hour that I did see him was full of laughter and full of love and hugs and kisses; it was all great. Until he got out of jail, and then he was the disciplinarian. It was a big adjustment for him from being institutionalised into a family. 'Who are you to tell me? Sure you weren't here.'

Being used to him not being there, it was a big adjustment for everyone. And once the discipline started, slowly but surely I started to resent him, especially in my teenage years. I think I rebelled a wee bit more than what might have been normal. We were highly confrontational. And it wasn't just a one-way thing. I found that my da was sometimes pretty dismissive and I don't know if it was born out of frustration, but it almost seemed like a lot of the time he had no time. Maybe it was because he had other things on his mind. About pretty much everything: football, girls, who my friends were, what I was doing with my spare time, not trying in school, probably all the things that would be normal in a normal sort of setting, but it was like lighting the blue touchpaper with both of us, which would have resulted in confrontation. And at that age, I did bear a grudge, and I wouldn't have let a thing go. I never forgot it. And I'd have been saying, 'You said this, or you said that.' Just basically doing whatever I could to make his life a living hell, because I felt that that was what he was doing to me. It was only later that I stopped resenting that: resenting him as a person.

For me, it was strange; took a whole lot of getting used to. And I've no doubt that for my father it was strange, coming into a house and there's a kid running about, going mad when you're used to a bit more quiet than that and a bit more time to collect your own thoughts. My mother told me he had trouble even getting onto a bus where he was freaked out surrounded by a crowd. He didn't like being in crowds because of being in prison. It was a big adjustment for him to make and it was only later that I appreciated that. Whenever you're a kid and your da's telling you what to do and what not to do, it's hard to look beyond that.

It took a long time for me to calm myself down and try to get my life back on track. I wouldn't have been bad, but I would have been pretty wayward and done my own thing. In fact, my da used to call me 'the child of the mist' because you'd have seen me and then not see me for days, and nobody knew what I was doing or where I was. I was pretty much a free spirit and just did whatever the hell I wanted. I never went out to harm anybody or hurt anybody but just pretty much did my own thing.

I've a younger brother, eight years younger. He came along not long after my father got out of prison. I think I never really got the chance to know my da during my childhood, because he was always caught up with other things, ie my young brother, playing happy families. Maybe I felt my nose was out of joint and resented it. By the time the brother came, I was starting into the rebellion and I saw that my da didn't have as much time for me as he had for him. So there was a resentment there. I don't know whether it was right or it was wrong, but I'm not going to sit and tell lies that it wasn't there. It was very much so until I hit my mid-twenties, early twenties anyway.

The politics didn't take up so much of his time in the early years of it. That came much later, just prior to the ceasefires, the IRA ceasefire.[9] A lot of his time was taken up with formulating political strategies. I was a 'hate-the-world' at that stage; too young, didn't have a clue, UVF-mad at fourteen or fifteen. The area would have been pretty impoverished, a working-class loyalist area. I was never taught anything like that in the house.

One thing my father was never, he was never a bigot and I was never taught bigotry. A lot of the friends I had would have been Catholic. In fact, my first steady girlfriend was a Catholic; we went on to have a son together. So it wasn't bigotry towards the Catholic populace; it was towards republicanism. And it was heavily propagated throughout the area that I lived in. By adults and by kids. You'd hear it on the street, you'd hear it in school, pretty much everywhere. That was pretty much the heyday of the Troubles, the early '80s. But politics would never have really featured much in any conversations that I had with my da. I remember him telling me that one in the family was enough; we didn't need any more. The UVF didn't need me and I didn't need them – words to that effect. He would never have actively encouraged me to become involved in anything. I thought he was talking out of his arse! At that age, fourteen or fifteen, I'm saying, 'It's a bit like the pot calling the kettle black.' I didn't see it that he was telling me from experience; I just saw it that this is the rod of rule again, and I'm not having it.

A lot of my friends would have been the same. We would have hung about in the lower Woodstock Road and kids from the Strand[10] would have been shouting over about the Provos[11] and next minute there would have been rioting. So at that age, when you're surrounded by that, it was hard to see where my da was coming from. I can remember one time whenever we were rioting down the road, the UVF came down and told us all to get off the road because I don't think they wanted the police coming into the area. We were told to get off the road or else; the rioting needs to stop. Of course, it didn't. To be honest with you, there wasn't much else to do. Most of it was done out of boredom. It wasn't because you hated the people in

9 The IRA ceasefire was declared on 31 August 1994. Six weeks later, the main loyalist paramilitary groups also announced a ceasefire.

10 Short Strand, a working-class area in East Belfast with strong republican sympathies.

11 Provisional IRA.

the Strand. In fact, a lot of the times the fights would have started because we were sitting having a carry-out together and then somebody would have said something about Celtic or Rangers[12] and the next minute there'd have been fists flying. I don't think there was any real hatred or animosity, because I don't think any of us were old enough to understand what was going on.

I wasn't happy about my da's heavy political involvement, because I felt it put myself, my brother and others in the family into a position where we had to watch what we did for fear of bringing shame to my da or blackening his name. Being a typical young fellow, I felt it was being put in a straitjacket almost. I didn't appreciate what he was doing for the people round me or how he might have been helping the community. I don't think I was still old enough to understand the bigger picture. I'm a slow learner! But I think it was maybe just a carry-on from the resentment that had built up through the conflict with him throughout the teenage years.

Later, I would have been actively involved in canvassing and helping out the party in whatever capacity that I could. It just took me a while to get there and by that stage, politics would have been a heavy feature of the conversation, and we still would have had conflict! That never changed. I carry a lot of my father's traits regarding temper and lack of patience, so the two of us would still have been at loggerheads at times. But we weren't going to let it get in the way of our relationship 'cause there'd already been enough of that with the teenage thing. I think he saw the changes in me and whenever I did become active in trying to assist him, I think maybe then he realised, or I hope that he realised without me having to tell him, because he wasn't a stupid man.

He would have encouraged me in sporting endeavours and any sort of academic endeavour. He would have pushed and pushed at me to go into education and I didn't want to. He tried to get me to go to art college and I didn't want to. But he always encouraged me in any aspect of what I was doing artistically because he had great faith in my ability; I'm not sure I share it! I painted my first mural whenever I was about six, in Ravenhill Street, and I was never able to put the brushes down since. I would have been considered a vandal during the early '80s. I never painted paramilitary murals; in my eyes, there was enough of that on our walls. What was a big concern to me was, the

12 Celtic and Rangers: rival Scottish football teams supported by nationalists and unionists in Northern Ireland respectively.

people of my community knew nothing of themselves beyond the Twelfth of July.[13] A large amount of them within working-class areas didn't know their own history because they weren't taught it. They were taught about the Vikings and the Romans and 1066 and all this crap and never, ever taught their own. Maybe it was viewed by the establishment as being divisive, but I think that it was even more divisive within the community that the people didn't know. So what I would have liked to have done would have been to address that and use the murals as a means of education about people's history, about their culture, because we were constantly being told we didn't have a history, we didn't have a culture. The gunmen on the wall were plentiful, yet there was nothing that really addressed who we were and what we were about and where we came from. You're propagating an idea; you're putting it out there for people to chew on and hopefully they'll come away with not a different mindset but an ever so slightly changed one, maybe not as right-wing or as bigoted. I think the murals can be used not just as propaganda but as a means of education and addressing social issues rather than political issues, you know, like alcohol abuse, racism.

I'm not sure that I'll ever be able to get out of his shadow. I'm always 'David Ervine's son'. That can be sort of tedious sometimes, because in the back of my mind there's always, 'well, I'm not my da'. And then fear of doing something wrong, and then it's 'David Ervine's son'. You're not Mark Ervine anymore. I'm not sure that I'll ever be able to get out from underneath him, but it'll not be for the want of trying. You're always sort of mindful of the esteem that your father was held in, how your actions might jade that in some way. Are you a free man? I'm not so sure. I'm not sure that's a shadow I'll ever be able to get out from under, because when you look at it, he was known throughout the world. He has spoken in universities all over the world and newspapers and on TV.

There'll not be as many people know Mark Ervine as David, so I think I'm always going to be David Ervine's son. Maybe not to my friends or to those close to me, but to the bigger, wider world, I think that's unavoidable. I can't say that I like it or that I enjoy it. You're always fearful that if you say something and it doesn't go down well, it's always going to reflect in some way on my da, which isn't right. I should be held accountable as being me and not somebody's son. Or judged because you're somebody's son or people having a

13 The annual celebration of the Battle of the Boyne in 1690 when Protestant Prince William of Orange defeated Catholic King James to become King of England.

preconceived idea of you because of who your da was. In a good way or a bad way. Sometimes people can expect too much.

When I look back on it and see what my da was able to accomplish given the background he came from, not only did he move on light years but he helped the community to move on. A lot of people within the community who would have been entrenched in their ideas now, thank God, embrace a different ideology from the one they did prior. So for that, it's much bigger than just about me.

I think he moved my community on light years. If he hadn't had the life experience that he did have, then there'd have been no PUP, there would have been no left-wing politics within unionism. When you look at the bigger picture and how it affects more lives than just my own, maybe it all worked out for the best. Because it's not just about me. I would be more content as a person if my community was doing well, if they were moving forward, rather than just me on an individual basis. So maybe I think that that sacrifice was something that worked out for the greater good. But it took years for me to come to that. And it was only when I started to see the effects of it that I started to formulate that opinion.

Dan McCann's Daughter

Name withheld

Daniel McCann was a member of an IRA unit which went to Gibraltar in March 1988. Their intention was to bomb a British Army parade. Two days before the event, while probably on a practice run, they were confronted by a British Army undercover squad which opened fire, killing McCann and two colleagues, Mairéad Farrell and Seán Savage. All three were unarmed at the time, and the vehicle which they had left in place near the site of the army parade contained no explosives. Dan McCann's daughter was born in 1985. She has requested her name be withheld.

To me, he's just a parent, someone who has contributed to half my DNA. Unlike most other people who have a voice and a smell and an association, I have nothing. I have a name, but I don't have anything to go with it. So I rely totally on what other people tell me to build up a picture. What I know is what I have been told. I only have my emotional attachment, which is based on information which has been fed to me. Sometimes it's very strong and other times it can be fleeting and weak, and if someone asks me, it would actually take me a while to recall something to tell them, because it has no impact on my life in terms of an association of 'oh, that day, that memory; I was there and I created it myself'. There's that disconnectedness to it.

But although he's just a parent to me, to the outside world he's something different. I'm the child of someone who chose a very different way of living, which, to people who agree with him, is something that should be remembered and commemorated, and to someone who's left to pick up the pieces, it's a very stupid, silly thing to do. If you're a single person, full steam ahead, but if you make the decision to get married and have a family, not so good. I don't like the word 'famous' or 'notable', but his life is that. It is taken away from the family circle and put into the general, so therefore you have to share the person with everyone else. And maybe they have more claim over the memory than I do because they were there. I don't have any of my own recollections. As I said before, I don't like the word 'famous', but it is something historical; I can live with 'historical', something that has happened in a series of events, and because it happened, it had impacts on how other things played out.

Out of the three of them,[14] he was the only person who had a family. And some people would say it must have made him more committed to it. If you're willing to make the choice, you shouldn't be making it because you're not just making it for yourself as a single person, as an individual, you're making it for other people. My brother Daniel and I never had the choice; we were never asked our opinion. I see the other side, the kind of the abandonment of everything else to do this one thing. One idea – that in the end didn't even turn out to be successful – overrides every other thing in your life.

I don't think people ever think they're going to die: that's the problem. But I think there was an element of wanting both, but wanting both in a 60/40 kind of a way. Have a family and all the rest, because that's what you do, and that keeps you normal. And then you have this extraordinary 'hobby'. I think if they thought that they were going to die, they wouldn't. But somehow, when you think right's on your side, people think they're invincible and nothing's going to ever happen to them. But if you're not successful and we have to muddle on like we've had to without you, show me where it was good, show me how it benefited.

As a girl, women the world over have fought for my right to vote, for my right to work. I understand that. I don't think throwing yourself under a racehorse actually helps your cause. I don't see how that made any impact whatsoever. What a waste of such a creative, inspired mind! What could you have done with those years you have now sacrificed? You could have changed society forever, but no – for a point, for a one-off, for an event! If you're choosing a road that has a very high probability that that is going to be the outcome, which it did, why not become a political activist? No! You had to do something gung-ho. To me, it's a simple choice. For God's sake, sit down, look at your own situation and make a choice that actually benefits your whole family in the long run. Don't make one that suits you at the time you made it and then not alter it for the rest of your life, which turned out to be very short. There's 1,001 things you could have done, but no, you had to choose the most risky.

I can't see how the Gibraltar plan had any impact at all. I see it as a delaying mechanism to where we are now. I see it as something that makes getting to

14 The Gibraltar 3 is the collective name given to McCann, Savage and Farrell.

anywhere successful politically in a harmonious manner much more difficult. As events like that happened, the amount of hurt and pain and the amount invested in it grew. Then to turn round and say, 'Possibly, the outcome they wanted is never going to happen. This is Plan B. Let's go for this,' makes that more difficult to accept. Prior to all that, Plan B might have been more palatable to a lot more people.

This was an empire on which the sun never set. And when they wanted to go, they went. You fought them to a standstill? You know, they have a national army. They could have imposed any sanctions they wanted and they imposed quite a few while they were here. When they want to do it, they'll do it. When they get fed up with it, they'll do it. It's not because you have amassed some kind of military power over them. Gibraltar didn't push their hand so far to go, 'Right, now we need to employ a political solution.'

There's a year and ten months between Daniel and me. Daniel has a memory of Mummy having to tell him about the killing, but I have no memory. I really didn't see it as an issue until I got much older. I didn't feel that there was a void there, so I really didn't associate that with 'oh, I must find out where this person is'. So it wasn't till I got much older that it kind of snapped with me that there is something actually missing here and your situation is different from other people. I suppose when I was younger and at school, I was friends with other children where it was just their mum and them. And I don't know if that was a subconscious thing of matching up family situations with my own so that when you were together, everyone's all the same; there is no difference at all. And you're never going to be in a situation where someone goes, 'Oh, Mum's picking me up and then Dad and I are going somewhere', because it's always going to be their mum.

Mummy did such an excellent job in shielding us from everything. She had to cope at the time because Dan and I were so tiny that we needed her constant care and attention as any child would at that age. But when that started to lessen slightly, I think the enormity of it hit her like a brick wall. Sometimes either you have to start to plough through it or you put it in a box and put it away and say, 'Right, that can come out later on.' I think she saw that it was a dangerous pathway if that was fed into our lives constantly and in a way control would have been taken out of the situation entirely and it would be placed into the hands of fate or into another organisation that she wanted nothing to do with anymore. It was better if it was hidden away, but also it fitted in with the childhood and the way our lives were to pan out, the vision Mum had in her head of schooling, educational achievement, job prospects –

Mum had that planned out and that didn't fit with it, so it had to go. You can say what you want about it, but it worked. That was the choice; either you plough through it at the time and see how the wheels come off or you leave it.

I don't want to find out the whole truth of what happened, because I don't think I'd like what I would find. I think I'd find someone who's so alien to me I would find it very hard to make any connection at all. What I know, I don't like, and I think there's more of the same … or worse. I find it very hard to reconcile with … that people applaud someone who maybe left someone else in the same state we're in. I can't get on board. It doesn't matter how bad things are, how awful it is – that doesn't achieve anything, only makes it worse. I can't take that bit out of the equation and just look at the person. Because I couldn't do that to somebody no matter how much they had bombed me or whatever; I just couldn't do it, physically couldn't do it, emotionally couldn't even comprehend doing it. And I think the more I would know, the stronger that would become. I think I would end up hating the person, absolutely hating, to the extent that I couldn't have anything at all to do with the person.

The only thing we have at the moment is Mum and I would hate that to spill over onto her. She's all that's left, really; she's the only person that bridges the gap between the two. So if you hate one, it kind of affects your views of the other. And I know that sounds very like I just described Mum saying, 'Put it in a box, close it and we'll deal with it another day.' In a way, I can understand having a feeling, a principle, and just thinking, 'My God, something dramatic has to be done.' But I can't say that it's okay to hurt someone else because you feel that strongly about it. And you end up hurting everyone else around you.

So in a way, no-one had to say it because it was the elephant in the room. You'd pick up bits and pieces. Mummy would never say. But I think we were in Granny's once and something came on the TV; it was the cemetery scene,[15] and then it started to click. For a long time, I thought everyone who died got a funeral on television. That was logical to me. So there was that, a shape missing, but there was never any kind of emotional response to that from me. I knew he was involved in something, could never really put my finger on what it was. And everyone knew who he was. We used to go over to the shop[16] every Friday. Over there, there were photographs of him everywhere. I started to get

15 When the Gibraltar 3 were being buried in Milltown Cemetery in West Belfast, a loyalist, Michael Stone, attacked the mourners with a gun and grenades, killing three of them.

16 Dan McCann's parents owned a shop on the Falls Road in West Belfast.

a visual image then. That would have been maybe around seven. Then people at school would start, 'Oh, yes, your father's dead.'

But there was that hesitance about it which meant something is funny about this. They had been told: 'Don't say to her! For God's sake, don't say!' It wouldn't be until around seven that I started to get an image in my head and a realisation that the person wasn't there and something funny was going on, that it wasn't a cut-and-dry thing, because there was sympathy, but there wasn't that empathy from people. This is a sad thing, but it is not something that you can openly discuss. You get that sense that there was something dodgy about the whole thing. Didn't know what it was, but there was something funny about it.

When I was growing up, people like Paddy McGrory[17] being in the house, meeting him at Mass, people like Gerry Adams[18] coming to the house, this was normal to me. Mummy is just the most straight-down-the line, unimpressed by anyone in the world kind of person and she's so straightforward I think sometimes she bamboozles people. 'Okay, Mr Adams is coming. Be polite.' That's it. She doesn't attach an importance to people either because of what they do or their persona, so to us, it was the man that came in that you saw on the news, but knew Mummy and knew Daddy, and came to see Mummy; it wasn't about seeing us, it was to see her. And we got the feeling that it was a superficial kind of thing. So we were there to be polite children as when any adult came into the house; we behaved in the same way, to say 'please' and 'thank you' and be courteous. They would leave and our lives would carry on as normal.

By about ten, we had a full understanding of everything and it was in between those years that it all kind of started to slot into place.

At the time of the tenth anniversary of Gibraltar, I remember people calling to see Mum. They always come with some kind of marble or Belleek boxed thing;[19] always in a hideous green box. Like, be original! And it gets put in the cabinet with the others. And then the commemoration gets televised; there was, like, a five-minute broadcast from the cemetery. That's his friends doing that. I suppose the best way to describe it is that it's like having a birthday and going out to dinner with your family and then going out to a big event and it's

17 Paddy McGrory, a well-known Belfast solicitor, appeared at the inquest into the deaths of the three IRA personnel in Gibraltar and later became a family friend of the McCanns.

18 President of Sinn Féin and former MP for West Belfast.

19 A world-famous pottery produced in Belleek, County Tyrone.

public and it's televised and it's a hoo-hah. And we sit together like every other day, go to Mass and maybe feel a bit more concerned for Mum around that time and make sure everything's steady. And then that passes and you go on. For, as soon as it's off TV, the day is over and it's back to the same cycle again.

And then the Good Friday Agreement[20] kicked in and our house became really busy. It was actually when the conflict was winding to an end that we realised, because people were coming in that Mummy wouldn't really tell us who they were, were coming in to talk to Mummy. And later on, you'd hear her talking to her friends, and then it would appear in the news. They were keeping her informed, so that she wouldn't turn the TV on and realise, 'Oh, God!'

At the twentieth anniversary, they came with all the posters and the bumph. They got these hideous portraits done that looked like all the faces had melted. They were going to stick them onto old pieces of two-by-four and parade them up and down the Falls Road at rush-hour traffic, shoving it in everyone's face. They're being battered by the wind and elements on some little piece of waste ground in West Belfast. And then they all go off to some kind of function. And you're, like, 'Really, is that the only way you can think about commemorating them? Having this?'

Everything's a hoopla. I don't think there's anything personal about that. They come and say, 'We need to do this because they're friends,' but there's nothing personal. It's about how they died, and that's it. So to me it's not about the person. I know that if it was, God forbid, any of *my* friends, I would not want to be continually going over how they died. I find that so bizarre. If your wife or partner was riddled with cancer, was in excruciating pain and was being given morphine around the clock, would you then recall that and retell it every time her anniversary came up to your children? And yet they're so shocked, that it's some kind of betrayal that you're not bloodthirsty for all these little bits of information. I mean, tell me something lovely by all means if you want. But you're not going to, are you? You're going to tell me your part in that story, and that's all you have to offer me. Because that's what's important to them, but they don't think that as a family you would have a different idea of what's important.

Purely for selfish reasons, I would have something more to do with the person, more to do with the music they were interested in, the art they liked, the books they read, the comedians they found funny, their favourite food, those

20 An all-party agreement signed in 1998 which led to the establishment of a power-sharing devolved administration in Northern Ireland.

kinds of silly things. But if I was doing it for the person that died, then I can't erase that part of their personality that found that desire to have this godforsaken piece of land re-united under one government – you would have to have something about that in it. He found that more important than his commitment as a father and a husband. So I'd have to put that first because he did.

We don't go to the public commemorations because we don't like the other people that are there. It's not for us. That doesn't help my grief. They're commemorating not the person but the deed. I can't get on board with the deed.

When I meet some political colleague of my dad, we've nothing to share. It's just information being told to me. It isn't, like, 'God, did I tell you about the time your dad and I were arrested. Oh, the laugh!' There are no stories like that. You can't trivialise those kinds of criminal acts into some kind of gap-year adventure. I don't find them funny, because they're still there telling the story, but my dad isn't. It's like someone trying to tell a funny story about concentration camps.

There's a great line that's used a lot; I find it hard to take: 'This is what he would have wanted.'

I don't think anyone can know and I don't like people presuming, and kind of coming in and saying, 'I really know better than you.' How dare you say that to me, you patronising person! I find it very hard to take and very difficult to be polite to them after that. It's, like, 'I'm trying to be nice to you, but really, it's so much better that you don't have any connection, because that gives me the upper hand and I can tell you what I think you need to know.'

People who talk about him want to impress you by their knowledge of something, and it's never nice knowledge; it's never some kind of personal story. It's how they were involved in 'the Gibraltar event'. It's like a *Lord of the Rings* epic. That is the ground and the basis of any interaction. Anyone who's been here who would be republican minded, very high-ranking people, they find it very difficult to interact with us. Even pleasantries are laboured. And you're trying your best to find something because it's your parent's friend.

What he did made my life worse. First of all, you have a void where someone else has a person. The interaction of members of your family becomes distorted because of that. It makes you either over-dependent on the other parent, over-dependent on the other sibling, or it distances you from them at the same time. You're always trying to protect someone from the same emotions you're feeling, so you never actually display them. You lose time; this is very hard to get across to people, this loss of time. You never get it back. Childhood's gone, that's it finished, because you're constantly trying to protect other people from yourself. We have to protect Mum. So we don't look sad and we don't look upset so that when she looks, she thinks she's doing okay because she thinks the kids are fine. And she's trying not to look sad so the kids will think she's fine. It's this constant, vicious circle; but time's lost doing that.

You also lose out with other people socially as well. Like, a male photographer came into the nursery school and I freaked out. 'Oh, my God! There's a man and a camera.' I just couldn't cope with it. I still find men's voices very alarming. I don't like the sound of a man's voice in another room, because the house is filled with a female tone. So that seems alien to me; I'm not comfortable with it. I've got better at it. I'm so used to having a practically totally female environment – going to a female school and coming home.

And obviously you have it financially as well. You have one major breadwinner down. You're already starting from minus and kind of fighting your way back up to zero again.

I always have a sense of what my life could have been. You're living two lives in one. You're living one you could have been if that event had never happened, and one where you are now. So there's always a sense of longing for something that was never realised but should have been. It's a terrible position to be in, to be thinking: *I wonder would I have made the same choices if that hadn't happened?* It's a terrible thing to impose on people. And it is imposed, because that wasn't an accident, that wasn't a terrible disease; that was imposed, that was a choice.

People expect you to be sad, but I'm not sad at all, just terribly annoyed. Sometimes that's a socially acceptable emotion to have; that's okay for the stages of grief, then you get over it and go back to being sad occasionally. But to be livid for that length of time isn't, because it's not a normal cycle in life. Mum was robbed of those last minutes, of that goodbye, robbed of all that for one person's decision.

I'm mad at the person, obviously, but I'm also mad at the people who put him there and the hierarchy of brainwashing that's gone on. Because I do believe, people who join those things, they're always very dumb, mostly male, impressionable. And there are people pulling strings, never actually do anything themselves, and I don't like organisations like that, that end up in people's deaths, asking people to go and do things like that and portraying it as some kind of grand act. And saying that anyone left behind would be looked after because we're all in it together, boys. And we're clearly not.

I'm disappointed at anyone who feels they need to kill anybody, but I can't be mad at those who shot him. If you want to be in the army, whenever somebody shoots at you, you shoot back. They could have arrested them, but they could have not been there to bomb somewhere.

Some people would think that the way I can talk about it is cold, but I think it's because I've no fond memories. So I'm just looking at a person as if I were reading a job application form and the personal details at the front. And for a long time, there wasn't even a photo attached. So I'm working from ground zero up. That's all I know from what I pieced together myself and how Mummy raised us to be very independent. If I had an opinion that differed, all the better. That is mine to own and mine to have and mine to justify rather than Mummy feeding us stuff and then us wondering, 'Why do I think that?' I know why, because I have formulated it myself. Whether it's right, wrong, cold, whatever, it is mine. I own it. And I'm very protective of it, because you feel that you don't own the person.

Because I've no memory, I feel I have no claim. And it is a person that, because of the way in which he died rather than in the way in which he lived his life, parts of him are divided up. Somebody claims one bit and somebody claims another and another. And there's only a very tiny bit left. And those are memories Mummy has prior to the event that are her own, that she guards for herself. Daniel has a few memories. Everyone took their bits before I got a chance. So I just surmised from what I have heard, from what I have thought and the person I was while that realisation was happening. Because I had a personality and opinion, a way of looking at the world while that was happening and it didn't dawn on me until that was quite well established. So it was almost as if I was looking on at the event, made my opinions of it, and some have changed and some haven't. It's the objectivity I have from not having an emotional attachment – which is something I would have loved to have had. I would trade all these opinions for one, but I don't have it; I'll never have it. So therefore the only thing I'm left with are the opinions. That's what I have left; that's what I have to safeguard.

David McMaster

Son of David McMaster

David McMaster senior is a former UDA life-sentence prisoner. He was jailed in 1976 for the murder of a Catholic schoolteacher. David McMaster junior was born in 1968.

My dad is Davey McMaster, probably better known as Davey Mac. He did life in jail, seventeen years. I think he was the commander of the H Blocks. Apparently, he could have been out sooner only he wouldn't renounce violence; that's what I've been told.

Growing up was hard for my mother, with four kids, bringing them up on her own with no help from his organisation. He was the one who was the so-called hero on the Woodstock Road, around the pubs and clubs. To me, he wasn't the hero; my mum was the hero. My mum was the one did all the hard work bringing four of us up.

The murder that he got sentenced for, it happened on the Cregagh Road. I could take you to the entry now. When the forensics were out that day, my mum had actually walked past it with a neighbour and went, 'What dirty bastard could do something like that?' not knowing that it was her husband that done it. This man was stabbed twenty-odd, twenty-eight, twenty-seven, I don't know how many times. She did know about Davey's involvement; she married him. She probably didn't know in depth because then, the paramilitaries had only started.

We came from the Woodstock Road, Malcolm Street. We lived there for three years, then we moved up to Grillagh Way. I was only four, five, six when we lived up there. I can remember the peelers hitting the house all the time, looking for guns. We got tortured because of him. It was time for my ma to get out. She took the beatings, she took everything else. She got out. She moved from there, from a three-bedroom house to a two-bedroom house so she could get away. Four kids, and she moved into a two-bedroom house, and she's lived there for the last thirty-odd years. My mum to me is the hero. I've always been close to her. She's come through bad times, hard times, but it's paid off for her, for all her sons love her; they all talk to her. We don't all speak to our so-called da.

When my mum was twenty-eight, she had cancer. She's sixty-two now. She's still alive. She's a fighter. She was the youngest person in Northern Ireland then ever to have a hysterectomy. Twelve years ago, she got three aneurisms in her head, three brain haemorrhages. She's still living. She just fights and fights. She's a walking time bomb, but she's still living. She could never be where she is now if she was still with him. She has her own car, she owns her own house. She worked for ten, twelve years. She used to try and work, a wee bit of work on the side to get us a few quid. A few times, she was squealed on because she was on benefits; God knows who squealed on her. She was doing nightshift. My uncle used to mind us, who was my dad's brother, a brilliant uncle; he's the closest out of them all. There's a big family of them. She got the chance of getting this job in the railway station to cover for a girl for two weeks. Then she got a job cleaning the toilets. She went from cleaning the toilets to cleaning the offices, from cleaning the offices to being a porter, from being a porter to being a senior porter, from a senior porter to being a conductor, from being a conductor to driving the trains, all in the space of ten years. She was the second woman train driver in Northern Ireland. But then obviously with the brain haemorrhages she had to stop work. She has no love for my dad. If she wanted to talk about him, it would be to run him down. She's had hard times with him. She would never have been where she is now being with him. Her four sons, when it's Christmas, we go to her house. We don't go to his house.

We grew up with a family name everybody knew, even the police. We got harassed by the police because of who our so-called dad was. I can remember the police, I remember the army, I remember the sniffer dogs up on top of our bed in the early hours of the morning, us getting wakened up all the time, him getting lifted all the time. I remember seeing photos in the house of him, mugshots from Castlereagh. I was told that it was very rarely he got out of the estate without being stopped by the police. My mum used to have to get up and leave the house when his men came in and they had their meetings. 'Right, Margaret, you've to go for a walk. Take the kids.' Whatever happened in there, she didn't know. She was a married woman being told. That's what they did in those days. When we lived in Malcolm Street, I can't remember the peelers hitting the house then. My da was in the TA[21] then.

There was a UDR[22] woman who lived in the next street to my mum, which was down the road. She actually got the UDR ones to grab my older brother

21 Territorial Army.

22 Ulster Defence Regiment, a locally raised regiment of the British Army.

Robert and shake the living daylights out of him. They started shouting 'your da this' and 'your da that'. So my mum went round and boxed the head off her.

My mum went to visit my so-called dad at the start of his sentence and that was for the simple reason to take the sons up to see him. I wouldn't go unless she was there. If she was there, I was going. When she put in for the divorce, he took it bad.

My mum didn't have a good life with Davey; we didn't have a good life with him. He'll always put other people in front of his family. I've always said he can be a gentleman, as long as you're not his family. He's going to die a lonely man, because anywhere outside his family he's a gentleman. He can be brilliant with people, but see in his family, he treats them like shit. I think it's a lot to do with him being away for all those years. Maybe I'm just making excuses for something that I don't know, but I think it's to do with him being incarcerated. If you go to jail, and you get life, you've lost your family, you've lost your kids. He never saw them growing up. He might have seen us when we went up to the jail, getting a half-hour visit. But yet of all, when he got out, he was back into the same shit, the same cronies, the same people. The UDA owes us; they owe me and they owe my family. My mum struggled at Christmas; she got nothing. We heard of other people's kids getting sorted out for Christmas, but we never got nothing.

At the start I didn't go to see him unless my mum went with me because I didn't really have much time for him because of things that I remembered that he'd done to my mum. I didn't want to go up and see him where my other brothers did want to go and see him. I stayed out of his life for quite a while. I don't know whether it was a good thing or a bad thing, but I would say through the years I didn't have a good relationship with my dad. As I say, I didn't go up to see him in the early days. I did once go up to see him without my mum and that's after I ended up in jail.

Myself and my wee brother John did a jail sentence. When you grow up without a dad in the house, if somebody hits my brother, I'm going to hit them. If somebody hits me, my brother's going to hit them. That's just the way the four of us were. You hit one of us, you hit all. So me and my wee brother ended up in jail for beating a fellow who beat my wee brother. I'm not proud of us going out beating people. I knew the fellow. That's just because we grew up close. My wee brother was in Hydebank.[23] I did eighteen months in Crumlin Road and Magilligan. Me and Davey Mac started writing; he

23 Hydebank Wood Young Offenders' Centre, near Belfast.

wrote a letter to me. I was in the Crum.[24] And I thought, I'll write one back. I never wrote him letters; I think that was probably the first letter I'd ever written to him, and that was 1990. I was born in 1968. It was only a matter of time before the dirty washing came out, and we stopped writing because it turned into an argument because I told him the truth. Why? Because my ma wasn't sticking around seventeen years to a life sentence waiting for him. Anyway, he was already with someone else.

When I put in for a visit with my young brother, they took me down to the Maze to see Davey Mac because he had requested a visit for my young brother. That would have probably been the only time I went up to see him without my mum. And it was an uncomfortable visit because I only got five minutes with my wee brother and half an hour with him. I just didn't like it. When he started getting his paroles, I did meet up with him. I met up with him in the bar that I had drunk in for a few years and I wasn't willing to give my Friday or Saturday night up because he was getting out. When I did meet him, we had a talk. He did hug me; he dropped what he was doing and he came over and hugged me. We had a talk and we tried to get things back on track. We did get things back on track for a while, but I still didn't go up to the jail to see him. He did ask me when he was going back after his parole. He said to me, 'I'll get a pass out for you.'

I said to his face, 'Don't be sending me a pass; I won't be going up to the jail to visit you.'

And this set him back, this big meant-to-be-hard man. I didn't know this at the time, but he had actually said to my older brother, 'You know, David hurt me. He's very straight to the point.'

The day came when he got out and he was out on licence. I did take to him and him and me got very close and we were like friends. He was never a father figure 'cause he was never there. I drank in the same bars as him and I wasn't going out of the bars 'cause he was out. We did get close, but then we had a fall-out where he put other people in front of me. We're now fell out, it must be six or seven years.

My older brother fell out with him fourteen years, maybe fifteen years ago. But then, my older brother idolised him. He was my older brother's hero many years ago. Unfortunately, Robert's dead now, September 2008. He took his own life. He idolised him, and that was part of the problem why he took his own life, I believe.

---

24 Crumlin Road Jail, in Belfast.

Robert joined the paramilitaries, but he joined the other paramilitary; he never joined the UDA; all his friends were in the UVF. He went to the UVF from a very young age. He was the only one in the family to do it and we're going, 'Why?' But he had already committed himself when he was fifteen.

My mum found out and she went ballistic. She said, 'I've been through all this before. What the f— are you at? What made you do it?'

But by then it was too late. When these boys get their claws into you when you're fifteen, you don't get out. I have two daughters and a son; my girlfriend's got two sons. And I have them tortured. I'm at them all the time: 'If anyone asks you to join anything, tell them to come and see me. Do not say yes for one minute. Don't go near them because you'll only get sucked in.' My brother got sucked in and he went to jail. My da got sucked in, he went to jail. My brother was in for petrol-bombing a policeman's house, but my so-called dad was in for murder.

My brother Robert had got some sort of threat put on him by one of Davey Mac's friends, but not in the same organisation. This is a top UVF man. My brother put his hand on this fella's shoulder and went to say something to him. Your man was full of coke and he turned round and said, 'Get your fuckin' hands off me! Your da was right – fuckin' kill you.'

On that night I was out separately from my older brother and I nipped into the bar and I saw my brother's wife, my sister-in-law. And I said, 'What happened to Robert?'

And she said, 'Away over and get him. He's away over to the bar.'

So I ran over and my brother was standing outside the bar, talking to my uncle. I let the two of them talk and I stood talking to my uncle's wife, and I still didn't know what this was about. So my uncle says, 'Right, come down and see me tomorrow. We'll get it sorted out.'

So I said to my brother, 'What's going on?'

And he told me what had happened. He said he'd been to the bar and this threat was put on him and he says, 'I'm getting done here.' So he made it for the door, got his wife and away he went. He went over to the bar, looking for his da to see about this threat, but his da wasn't there.

When Robert was telling me this, we were walking back to another bar. So I said, 'Hold on, there. Away you in there.' I went back over on my own. I went over looking Davey Mac, but I was told he had left.

So to cut a long story short, we went down the next day and met my uncle. He wanted this top UVF man and Davey Mac together to see where the threat came from. My uncle phoned Davey Mac and said, 'Davey, your Robert's down here. He was in a bit of bother last night with —.'

My brother had already taken a nervous breakdown, and part of the problem was the fallout with his dad. And Davey Mac said, 'It's got fuck all to do with me. Do you see if he comes near my door, I'll kick him up and down the street.' And I watched my brother falling to bits and crying. My brother was reaching out to his da and his da turned his back on him again. So we never got the two people together to find out where the threat came from. It just so happened that the fellow that made the threat took himself off on holiday and obviously when he got back, it had all blown over.

As I said, my brother was a paramilitary and he belonged to the UVF. But there was a split in the UVF in East Belfast and my brother belonged to one side and the fellow who made the threat belonged to the other. But this fellow is very close to Davey Mac. So this is only me thinking: when talking about the feud situation, the UVF man has probably said to Davey Mac, 'If we shoot them, what happens to your Robert?'

And he's turned around and said, 'Fuckin' shoot him.'

That's what we think; we've never found out.

My brother fell to bits and he was never the same. When it came to his funeral, the family told Davey Mac, 'We don't want you near it.'

Sam, a friend of Davey Mac, phoned me and said, 'Sweep, very sorry to hear about Robert. Where are you?'

And I said, 'I'm in the house.'

'Can I come up and see you?'

I said, 'Where are you?'

And he said, 'We're in the bar.'

I said, 'Do you want me to come down and see you?'

He said, 'You don't mind?'

And I said, 'I don't mind,' because I knew what it was for. I went down to the bar.

Sam said to me, 'I've been up with your da there. He's in bits.'

And I said, 'My heart goes out to him.'

And he said, 'What's the craic about the funeral?'

And I said, 'Sam, tell him to stay away.'

And he said, 'Your da doesn't know I'm down here. I'm asking you, is there any way we can resolve this?'

And I said, 'No. This is not my decision solely. This is a family decision.'

I have a lot of hatred for Davey Mac, especially because of my brother, and

I couldn't sit in the same room as him now. When the brother died, it ate away at me, because I wanted to say things that my brother didn't get saying. And I wanted to do things, as in go face to face with my so-called dad. After the funeral, I was just full of everything. My younger brother Steven is the only one who has anything to do with him. He gave me the minister Gary Mason's phone number and says, 'Phone Gary and we'll set a date up and we'll all go and we'll talk and we'll try to sort this out.'

And I didn't. I just went, 'Do I need to go and talk with him?'

Gary Mason wanted to get us all together in a neutral environment that was out of the bar, somewhere where we would all feel comfortable and where no-one felt intimidated. It was for us to sit down and for me to talk to Davey Mac and ask him questions, ask him why he did this and why he did that.

But then my wee brother John says, 'What's it going to achieve? Are you going to turn round and accept him as who he is?'

And I just went, 'He's going to stay the same; he'll never change. I don't want anything to do with him'.

And he said, 'Well, do you think there's any point?'

And I said, 'I think the point is I can speak on behalf of Robert because I know what my brother was thinking, and I know a lot of things that you don't know'.

It was only last week I actually thought about it. The thought just came through my head and I asked myself the same question: do you need to get this off your chest, or do you just go on? Because I know he's not getting any younger and probably when he does die, I might kick myself and go, *I should have*. I should have asked him the questions. I should have gone face to face. But I think that if we do go face to face, it'll probably end up getting worse.

My brother Robert died not speaking to him. I'll probably die not speaking to him. My younger brother John, he couldn't give a toss. But the youngest one, Steven, he's the one who'll go and have a drink with him; he's the one who'll keep in touch with him. But I can understand; he's the youngest of the family; he never really knew his dad.

Robert idolised him and at the end of it, he got nothing out of it. John, if he sees him on the street, he'll pass himself. But he doesn't go looking for him. He doesn't go have a drink with him. Steven, he would make a point of going to the bar to have a pint with him. But even at present now, he doesn't see any of his grandchildren.

I have no love for him, but I would never try and stop my kids. It's up to them to find out for themselves. He has no time for them. He gets his girlfriend to take their Christmas cards round and birthday cards. My daughter is twenty and I've a son of eighteen; my other daughter is seventeen. But when they were young, it was photos after photos down in his house; it was all about the grandchildren. But as they got older, he didn't want to know them. My son would drink in the bar. Well, he doesn't now, but he used to when he was sixteen.

He actually barred his grandson from the bar that he runs for not speaking to him in front of a UVF man, snubbing him. This wee lad, my nephew, had just lost his dad, my brother Robert. My nephew knows about the threat. And a few months later, this UVF man was drinking in the bar. My nephew walks into the bar and sees your man. His granda tried to speak to him. My wee nephew said, 'I heard him calling me, Uncle Sweep. I wouldn't turn round because your man was there.' The next minute, my nephew got barred from the bar. He was barred because he snubbed Davey Mac in front of a top UVF man. Davey Mac lost face.

I think Davey Mac – I don't call him Dad – has been affected big time by being in jail. I don't think he can handle family life, I don't think he can handle social life. His life is his paramilitaries. He put paramilitaries in front of his family and he would still put paramilitaries in front of his family – apart from the daughter that he's got now; she's about seven, maybe eight. I don't see her. I used to be close to her until we had the big fallout. That would be the thing now that has calmed him down, settled him down from the paramilitaries. He's not settled, but it's sort of mellowed him out a bit, this daughter that he's got.

One thing I did notice about him – it was then, not now – but he always had a lot of time for his grandchildren. When he got out, there were boxes of photos – just him and his grandchildren. And me and my brothers used to talk about it. We knew that he missed out on us growing up. He missed out on our childhood and he was giving all this affection to the grandchildren. If my kids ask me anything, I'll tell them the truth. I don't hide anything from them. They did go up and see him in jail. Their mum took them up. My dad and my ex were close. She used to take them up in the UDA bus. They don't know what he's about now. They don't go down to the bar to see him. They don't go round to his house to see him. He's a strange man. As I say, if you're outside the family, he's a gentleman; but he's a Jekyll and Hyde.

I would say towards him I have a lot of hatred now, especially for what happened with my brother and him turning his back on me when I was there for him. I got put under death threats for him just because I was associated with him, during the feuds. I'm not even in anything. I never was in anything.

Because I was associated with him, and because of my name, I've been put under death threats. And then he went and turned his back on me because of who he's living with. And that really gutted me. And it gutted a lot of people, a lot of his friends, and he lost a lot of respect from his own friends, or comrades, if you want to call them that. Because they all came to me individually and they told me. But he's the sort of person you can't tell him he's wrong. He wouldn't listen. And that's part of his problem, because down that road they don't tell him he's wrong. I told him he was wrong and he didn't like it. And we fell out over it. But there's a lot of people down that road don't tell him he's wrong. He's been through jail where he ran the Maze, so you're not going to get people going, 'You're wrong, Davey.' They're going to go, 'Aye, we agree with you,' but maybe do things otherwise. I stood up to him, because I don't fear him and he didn't like it.

I've got … can you call them friends? People that I know … school friends. I've watched my school friends growing up. For instance, two brothers were going to join the UDA. I talked them out of it. Lifelong friends of mine, I went through school with them. I said, 'Catch yourselves on.' Talked the two of them out of it and about a month later they joined the UVF. About a year later, the two of them ended up in jail. I watched people jumping into the paramilitary ranks. I've told all the family, 'Stay away from them. They get their fingers into you, that's it.' There's no call for them now, but they don't know how to wind it up. And there's too much money in it for them.

I have never joined any paramilitary organisation and I have no intentions of joining any paramilitary organisation. I've received death threats and all, all down to him. I've never done anything for a paramilitary in my life, but because of him … my name being passed about because being associated with him. He lived three doors away from me. I would give him a lift down to the bar so he's not standing at bus stops. And the more he was seen in my car, my name got thrown about. I actually got stopped in a different bar and a UVF man said to me, 'You know the best thing you ever did was stop drinking in that bar.'

And I said, 'Why? I've got friends down there.'

And he said, 'You were getting the blame for everything that happened about that road.'

That was news to me.

He said, 'Everybody thinks you're in the UDA.'

Steven McMaster

Son of David McMaster

David McMaster is a former UDA life-sentence prisoner. Steven McMaster was born in 1974.

My father is Joseph David McMaster. He served about seventeen years of a twenty-five-year sentence for murder. I think he was only about twenty-one at the time.

I was about six months old when my father went to prison. The first time I actually saw my father walking the street was when I was fourteen. It was his first parole. That was weird. However, I had a lot of contact with him as a child. My mum sent me up probably every visit that was going, which meant I had to stay in my grandmother's house, my father's mother, every week and get up on a Saturday morning, probably about half five, six o'clock, go down to the UDA headquarters, which used to be on the Newtownards Road in East Belfast, and wait there, get on the minibus. The guy who drove the minibus, John, he used to put me on his knee. How unsafe is that while driving a minibus!

But as a child, this was great, this was fantastic. I suppose it took away from the whole experience of having to go down to the prison, which, looking back on it, isn't a very nice experience. I went to see this man who gave me sweets and spoke in code to other people who I'd never seen before in my life. There would have been one other family member there, my father's brother or somebody like that, somebody who I would have recognised. But as far as I was concerned, it was a place to go and you got sweets and you ran around with the other kids that were there and you went home and that was it. And this person that you knew as 'Dad' didn't really pay any attention to you. Looking back on it now as an adult, it was all codes, passing messages across and so forth. I called him Dad, I didn't know why I was there, I didn't know why he was there, I didn't understand the whole thing, but the bus driving was great on the way down. Visiting prison was familiar but alien at the same time: it was familiar just because of the repetition; every week you had to go and do this. But it was really alien as well because of the gates of the prison and it really looked draconian, with the barbed-wire fences, but at the same time, it was fascinating. These big, tall, giant men in dark blue uniforms, they all looked really massive, just as police officers all seemed really massive. To be honest, they were always really nice, would always talk to you and pat you on the head. I've never had a bad experience with any of the prison officers whilst visiting prisons. I've visited a few of them over the years.

On the outside, living with a father who was in prison for paramilitary involvement, in a weird sense, had benefits. I used to hear people say: 'The UDA bought us Christmas presents.' I can't remember getting anything off the UDA, to be honest. I don't think we ever got any Christmas presents. But as a family, we had a kind of kudos having a father who's been in for 'the cause'. Your father was put on a pedestal. If you got into trouble, well, 'That's Davey Mac's son. Leave him alone,' a kind of protection. As you get older, you realise this is no benefit at all, this is wrong; but as a young person growing up, it did benefit me as a protective measure. It kept me out of a lot of trouble. I believe that people were less likely to ask me to join a paramilitary group because of that. There was only one time in my life that I've ever been asked to be part of a paramilitary organisation. The guy who asked me to join found out who I was and retracted that very quickly for some reason or other.

I joined the army straight from school; I was just sixteen and a half. I was in the army for six years. That was a conscious decision to try and get away from stuff in Northern Ireland. I suppose I was running away from things and at the same time justifying it by trying to make a life for myself. At that stage, it was so embroiled in paramilitaries. My eldest brother was involved in paramilitaries, and to a certain degree I think at times we have sympathised with a lot of what was going on, whether knowingly or unknowingly.

When I came home on leave from the army, the friends that I had left behind either were in prison or had been in prison or were at risk of being in prison. They had all joined paramilitary groups. I felt a million dollars. I felt like I had achieved something in life. I was coming home, a wad of cash in my pocket, sun tan – I was living in Cyprus – coming home for about three weeks and throwing the money about and these people were in jail or running about, not a penny to their name, not working. And I was, like, 'God, I've achieved something here.'

As a child, I had a lot of bad experiences with the police. There was one day I was playing and this police Land Rover pulled up. I must have been no more than eight years old. In fascination and in awe, we kids were over talking to the police. Even at a young age, I had this fascination with guns and uniforms. So I was asking this police officer, a big mountain of a man I can vividly remember; it was a Sterling submachine gun. And I made a remark: 'That's a smashing gun you have there.'

He put it to the side of my head and pushed me and said, 'You're going to end up like your da.'

I was shocked and stunned; I couldn't make sense of what was going on, because I was, like, 'What have I got to do with my dad? I don't even know what's going on here.' It was so intimidating. That sticks in my mind. As an adult and when I was in the army and training with guns, I'm thinking to myself, 'How unethical was that, of him to do that, to stick that machine gun in the side of my head as an eight-year-old child?'

I experienced the police raiding our house. This wasn't because of my father. This was my eldest brother Robert. They came in and they were looking for him. This was about four o'clock in the morning, three o'clock in the morning. We were all in bed. He wasn't in at the time. It was chaos. I didn't realise what was going on. There was an age gap there; I was the youngest in the family. I didn't really know what he was doing. To be honest, I wouldn't have made sense of what was going on. I was really naive to it all; it was all just so normal.

I didn't recognise the real dangerous aspect of it. That was taken out of it because when I went down to the minibus to go to the prison, the men that I was greeted by were all, 'All right, Stevie, Young Mac.' It was all very friendly, very open. They were all friendly; camaraderie was there. I felt really part of this and there was no threat.

And then I went into the prison and the prison officers were really nice. So where was the danger aspect there? It's only looking back on it as an adult, you go, 'Wow! Those people were killing each other, they were killing people, they were passing over intelligence.'

It's crazy to think about it now, to put a child in that situation. Then to have this other element to it: 'Why are the police picking on us? We're all really friendly.' You look on it now and you realise that these police officers were the kind of people who were getting their houses burnt out. My brother Robert was in prison for petrol bombing a police officer's house while the police officer was in it, and this was about six streets away from where we lived. Having been a member of the security forces myself, it's really difficult not to build up resentment for people who are trying to burn you or your work colleagues out of their home. As an adult, you look at that now and go, 'It's not right to do that as a police officer.'

But it's also not right to have people burn you out of your home or feel so scared and intimidated that you may be forced into doing something like that or feel that that's the right course of action to do. 'I'll put fear into you, because when you grow up, you're probably going to put fear back into me.' That's the endless, vicious circle that went on in Northern Ireland.

My mum got beaten up by the police, beaten very severely. She had staples on top of her head and was left lying outside the police station with her clothes ripped off, lying in her bra. She was dragged into the police station by the hair. I think she broke her nose as well. This was a policewoman and two male officers, RUC.[25] She was coming home from out drinking one night. The police officer lady called her over and there was a bit of an altercation. Two police officers came out of the station and beat her unconscious. There was a male with her; he ran. She woke up in the police station reception with her clothes ripped off. My mum got done for breach of the peace or drunk and disorderly and got fined. I'm not saying it's right, but you've got to put it into context. My brother had just petrol bombed one of their colleagues' houses. I don't know how I would feel if somebody tried to burn me out of my home with my family and kids in it. There's no way I can justify what went on. Violence breeds violence.

They had taken photos of my mum when she was lying there unconscious, bleeding. My brother was in Castlereagh[26] at the time; he had just been arrested. My brother was seventeen. They came to him and threw photographs down of my mum and told him this would happen every single weekend if he didn't co-operate. It's really difficult to believe that that would ever happen, but I think I would be naive to think that it hadn't happened. I remember my brother when he was in Castlereagh, he had to go and see the doctor. When he came out of there, he was black and blue. I grew up with no animosity towards police officers and actually worked closely alongside them when I was in the army. Even today, I have no animosity to any member of the security forces, police included. There are some bad people out there. I don't think it was a bad organisation.

My mother was really influential and contradictory. I grew up in this whole contradiction of things. I went to the prison to visit my father who I called Dad. My mum had a partner in the house, Dixie, who acted like a father: took

25 Royal Ulster Constabulary.

26 A police holding centre where interrogation of suspects was conducted.

me and bought me shoes, took me to the park, took me out on walks. He worked in the shipyard and every Friday we used to go down there to collect his wages. I can remember the shipyard when it *was* the shipyard. And yet of all, he's not my dad. Why is this? The whole contradiction you get: this is your dad in prison and this is your father figure outside, but you can't call him Dad. That really affected me during early adulthood and in some ways still does now. I'm thirty-four and I'm still trying to make sense of it all.

I grew up in a home where violence was accepted. I have had brushes with violence in the past and have struggled with anger throughout my life. So I joined the army, and I had this notion: it's violence, but it's controlled.

I grew up in a household where domestic violence was prevalent, every single week. It was always every Thursday night, say, would have been drink night, maybe a Saturday. It was like a ritual; they got vodka and they sat and drank. And it was all happy, it was all a brilliant atmosphere, and then it was just, like, boom, that was it. I'm sitting there; I was a child; I just couldn't go somewhere else, like my brothers used to take themselves off. So I witnessed this every single week for most of my adolescent life.

My mum seemed to hate men. Men were awful; men were terrible. But we were men. The whole focus of that hate was my dad. Who did we go to talk to when we were kids? I didn't feel we were allowed to go and talk to Dixie, because Dixie wasn't our dad. To me, he was a father figure. When I look back on it now, I'm going, 'You know what? Things would have been a hell of a lot easier if I was able to call him Dad and forgotten all about what was going on in that prison.' If I could go back and change things, I would. That's the main thing in my whole life that I would change.

My mum used to tell me: 'Your da's a bastard.' It still goes on. I'm thirty-four. I got a phone call from my mum a couple of weeks ago. My brother Robert passed away last year, and she was really teary and really crying about it. I was, like, 'I'll go over,' because she was on her own.

I went over and it was like I was transported back to a child. I was sitting there as an adult hearing the same stuff again and again. I was told all this as a child. As an adult, I never had the opportunity to ask the actual person who's actually being blamed.

When I got out of the army, I went on this soul-searching mission with my father. I went to live with him. It was, like, 'Right, what do I do now?' I moved back to East Belfast. I had no job. My father got me a job in the shipyard. Again, jobs for the boys. I went down there to work and it was all UDA men. They seemed to have their own contractor that took them all on. I was happy enough to fit into that. I wasn't working, didn't have any money, and I was, like, 'It is what it is. I know what I'm going to do; I'm going to earn money. I'm not going down here to talk shop. I've nothing in common with any of the people that's here.' And actually it would be quite interesting and weird at the same time to work with my father, which brought on a range of emotions and thoughts. The shipyard was such close quarters; I was with him in a confined space. I was working with him and thinking to myself, 'Right, there are loads of questions I want to ask him. When is it appropriate to ask, or is it appropriate at all? What do I say? What do I do? Who is this man? Why did he do the things he did?'

I always wanted to know did he just suddenly sprout up one day and go, 'I want to kill people.' Is that what happened, or was there a process behind it? Would he have killed if there was no Troubles?

Before I actually asked him, I took a step back and went, right, I get on with my dad. I don't really know him as a person, but he's never, ever done anything bad against me and I've never heard him say a bad word about anybody. Why do I want to ask these questions? Do I want to prove my mum wrong? Or do I just want to hear another side of it? And would that change my perception of my dad? If it's a conflicting answer, who am I going to believe? Am I going to believe my mum or believe my dad? And if I believe my dad, I believe then my mum to be a liar. And if I believe my mum, I believe my dad to be a liar.

But at the end of the day, if he says, 'No, that's not what happened,' will it ever affect me? No. It's none of my business. Even if he turns round and says, 'Yeah, I kicked the shit out of her seven days a week for years,' well, that's not my problem. It's not my relationship; it's not my marriage.

So I did get to ask him these questions. I can remember going over it, you know, you're getting butterflies in your stomach, and in my mind I was going, 'Just ask him, just ask him.' I just blurted it out: 'Did you ever hit my mum?'

And he looked at me with such surprise. And to be honest, I'm sitting here today and I still don't know whether he did or not. He was so convincing, although I've got no reason to disbelieve either of them. He said to me, no, he didn't, and he was very surprised that my mum had said anything like that.

As time went on, I went, right, there's other questions I want to know about, like: what was your motivation? I suppose I was trying to get his political view. Did he have a belief that what he was doing was right and could he convince me? I believe that if somebody believes strongly in something and does that for those reasons and can stand by those convictions, it's really difficult to tell them that they're wrong. I suppose I was trying to find out could he justify what he had done and what he was still involved in when he got back out of prison.

When he told me about some of the things he had done in the UDA, it was disturbing. And afterwards, I was, like, 'I wish to God I hadn't asked that question.' I wasn't prepared for the answer.

I have two choices: I'm kinda stuck between a rock and a hard place. My morals and values totally go against everything that he was telling me and I couldn't in any way, shape or form justify anything that went on. But how can I accept this man as a father if I can't accept what went on before? That wrecked me for a lot of years. Now I do have a relationship with him, but it's not any kind of meaningful relationship. The relationship I have with him is that if anything goes wrong in my family, I'm the intermediary. I'm the go-between because I have this relationship with him. I have accepted this relationship. I sat back and said, 'If I want a relationship with my father, it can't involve paramilitaries, it can't involve the bar which he frequents and it can't involve the kind of people that he associates with.'

But how do I do that? Because he is so entangled in all that and without that I believe that he thinks that he is nothing. Who is Davey McMaster without power and control? He is Davey, unemployed, been in jail for seventeen years, kids don't associate with him – what is that? How as a man can you accept that when the easy way is, 'Well, I'm Davey McMaster, I have power, I have control; what I say goes.'

There are very few people that'll tell my dad that he's wrong. He works through fear. It's not respect. He thinks it's respect, but it's not; it's fear. I also had to accept that because that was so precious to him he wasn't going to have any kind of meaningful father-son relationship with me. Not that he wasn't: I don't believe that he's capable of it. I had to factor in seventeen years in prison; I don't know what that would do to your mind, to be honest. He was surrounded for seventeen years by people who did say 'yes' to him and didn't say 'no', including prison officers. How can you take that away? I've never tried to take that away. I would never put him in a position where, 'Look, if you want a relationship with me, you've got to get rid of all this.' You couldn't do that. The only way you could do that with my father is probably with a gun. I had to accept that and, do you know what, it's really, really difficult as a human being having to accept all of that with very little in return.

With my father, I have always had to compromise, and it's difficult sometimes. It takes me a while to take a step back and say, 'Look, if I don't compromise, I'm going to jeopardise this relationship because I don't believe that he has the capacity to understand what's going on.' I do believe that he doesn't have the capacity to understand the whole relationship side of life, because that was cut short from him. I don't know what his family life was like before he went to prison. It was very much like my own family life: the very strong mother figure. My granny was a mountain of a woman, but she was like nothing. What she said went, and she had mostly sons. There were nine brothers and three sisters, I think, in the family. My grandfather died in 1969. My eldest brother was the only grandchild to see him. So she took over as head of the family, like my own family. There were men there; the men didn't get a say, because it was her way or the highway.

I have a seventeen-year-old son. He knows about my dad. He and my dad have a really good relationship. I have always encouraged that. He goes round to his granda's, calls round and sees him. I've always tried to keep him away from reaping the benefits of having a grandfather like that, because with those benefits, you have a responsibility as well, like I have found out over the years. The benefits of protection come with the consequences of being blamed for being in the UDA. You're restricted in the choice of bars you can drink in as a young man and you're restricted in the people you can hang about with. I think my dad has spoken to him about his time in prison. I don't think he would be glorifying it or romanticising it. I would certainly put a very abrupt end to it if that was ever happening. My son isn't involved in any paramilitaries. He's actually in the process of joining the army himself. I talked him out of it for a couple of years. He's seventeen, going on eighteen. If he's going to join, he's going to join. I've done my best to talk him out of it and try to push him down the education route. He has no interest whatsoever in education. You just gotta hope that things turn out okay for him.

My brother Robert was better known as Sticky – he got 'Robert McMaster, Sticky Plaster' as a kid. The impact that the Troubles had on him were catastrophic to the point where Robert took his own life. He joined the Ulster Volunteer Force at around fourteen or fifteen years of age. He'd been in prison and there were certain things he'd done that probably weighed heavily on his mind. He idolised my father as a child. There was a real split between one sibling and the other. My brother David was Mother's protégé and Robert was Father's protégé. Robert went up to see Dad, and David went up to see him probably three times in seventeen years. David was also told 'your dad's a bastard' and he believed it very strongly.

To Robert, my dad might as well have been seven feet tall, shoots thunderbolts out of his ass, this brilliant man. My dad was seventeen years in prison; he came out; he had women on the go. Who wouldn't do after that? Something happened with one of these women and it was really basic. My understanding of it was, Robert asked my dad a question: 'Are you going with this girl?'

He answered, 'No,' and he was.

And Robert fell apart. 'This is lying. My dad is lying to me.'

And I was, like, 'What business is that of yours? And if he's lying to you and you know the right way of it, just drop it. That's more about him than it is about you.'

He couldn't let it go. That escalated then into violence between the two of them. I've heard both sides of the argument and I really couldn't tell you which is true. What I do know, the facts are they came to blows and the relationship became irreparable, in part due to others' involvement.

We expected a hell of a lot from our father and didn't give much in return. You can't want somebody to act like a father, but when they do, you tell them to, 'Fuck off, you're not my da.' You can't keep somebody at arm's length and expect them to come and hug you. I think that was the whole expectation thing that was going on with all our family, all the siblings, me included. I did that and I had to realise my own part in it. Unfortunately, I don't think my brothers have actually realised their part in it.

Not having a relationship with my father, I had to take responsibility for my part in it and I suppose that was part of the compromise. That was my own personal development and I think I'm a better person for it. But my brothers, I don't think they understood their part in it. My dad gets the blame for more than his fair share of wrongs in our family. I think David to this day blames Dad for Robert taking his own life. I don't. I don't blame him whatsoever. I think Robert's problems were his own and a lot of them were self-made and a lot of them were fallout from the conflict in Northern Ireland. I do believe that there's a lot of that that goes on. Robert by no means was any kind of a hard man; he was a very genuine person who would do you a good turn before a bad turn. But how do you keep that image when you're hanging around with people who are out murdering people, shooting people, beating people up, robbing banks? How can you present yourself as any kind of soft, kind and caring man when you're surrounded by that, and how do you live up to my da? That broke him. Robert went searching on many occasions for his father and never found him. All he found was this person who saw Robert as an aggressor and didn't see Robert as someone who wanted a loving father. That really took its toll on him. I think that's where David comes to blame Dad where I don't think Dad had anything to do with it. There's a role to play there, but I think it can be equally shared with other people.

Would my dad be a murderer if it wasn't for the Troubles? I don't know. Would life have been very much different if the Troubles hadn't been around? I would really like to think so. I would like to think, you know, *Sliding Doors*,[27] that things would have turned out very much different if the Troubles hadn't been around.

I work with young people nowadays and I see such a change. Their experiences of it are what their mums and dads are telling them. And you know what? Three of four generations, there's nothing going to be around. Who's going to be a first-hand eyewitness of accounts like that to muddy somebody else's views of the things that are going on? Once my dad dies, in two weeks' time they'll be, 'Davey who?' All his friends, they'll all be there at the funeral, you know, 'Stevie, I'm sorry.' He'll be no sooner in the ground than they'll be fighting for his position.

27 A 1998 film staring Gwyneth Paltrow. A woman loses her job and heads to the tube to go home. The film follows two possible versions of what happens next; in one, she catches the train and in the other, misses it, and her life turns out to be totally different in each scenario.

Liz Rea

Daughter of Gusty Spence

Gusty Spence, a former British soldier from the Shankill Road in Belfast, joined the UVF in the mid-1960s and was sentenced to life imprisonment for murder in 1967. In prison, he became the UVF commander and was credited with instilling discipline and arranging political education for the mostly younger UVF prisoners. He increasingly took a more political route and after his release in 1978 became involved in the organisation of the Progressive Unionist Party. The grand old man of loyalism, he was selected by the Combined Loyalist Military Command, comprising the UVF, UDA and RHC (Red Hand Commando), to read out the loyalist ceasefire announcement in 1994. Liz Rea was born in 1954.

My father is Gusty Spence, the former leader of the UVF. When I was eleven years of age, my father was arrested. He was charged on his birthday, and he was sentenced on my twelfth birthday, 14 October. That was 1966. It was hard for my mummy. I was the oldest and my brother was only four. So Mummy had to rear four of us on her own. My mum had a nervous breakdown. In fact, she had a couple of nervous breakdowns. But she had four of us and she had to carry on.

It was hard for us at school as well. We got taunted about my daddy being a jailbird. But we managed to rise above it; we had to.

We were all in the house when he was arrested. It was a wee tiny kitchen-house we lived in. I remember the police coming in and us having to get up out of our beds and just searching all of the house. It's funny now; my mummy laughed at it years later. My mummy hadn't a clue what was going on. She says, 'What are you looking for?'

And they said, 'Guns.'

And my mummy said, 'Well, hold on a minute,' and she went and got this wee bucket; it was my brother's toy guns. And she actually brought them out to them and said, 'There you are.' And she was genuinely serious, because she hadn't got a clue what was going on. They took my daddy away and my mummy and my aunt tried to keep everything quiet from us. But I could read the papers, so I saw what was going on. For years and years, up until my daddy got out for my wedding, my brother and sister thought that my daddy was in a military hospital; the Crumlin Road Jail was a military hospital.

In those days, you only got a visit once a month. I'll never forget the first time we went up. It was a wee tiny room, the table up against the wall; my daddy was at this side and we were at that side and the screw was sitting at the end of the table. We bent over to kiss my daddy, but we weren't allowed. You weren't allowed to touch him, you weren't allowed to kiss him, and the screw could have butted into the conversation if you were saying something that you shouldn't have been saying. My mummy was never political minded. She would let the screw into the conversation; she asked him into the conversation. But it was one of those things, you got used to it; that's just the way it was. Our visits were like that for years. Before my daddy got out for my wedding, we had open visits. You could have touched him then, but you weren't allowed round the same side of the table as him. My mummy always gave up one of her visits to let one of my daddy's family up.

She was taking the whole four of us, and with us living on the Grosvenor Road, it was either walk it up and get the bus back or get the bus and walk back because she couldn't afford the bus fare both ways. Then me and my sister went and got jobs. I worked in the wee sweetie shop around the corner and my sister – she was just coming up to twelve and I was just coming up to thirteen – she got a job in the chippie on the Grosvenor Road. We gave every halfpenny to my mummy because it was the only way my mummy could have survived. My mummy never got nothing from nobody. In later years, when he got out for the wedding and went back in again, he had set up a welfare system for the prisoners' wives to get money for their parcels. But in the early days, no, my mummy got no help from nobody.

I'll never forget the night of the fire in Long Kesh.[28] My mummy couldn't drive, so we had to get a neighbour. And we drove down to Long Kesh that night, but the police and the army stopped us. There were rumours going about that people were dead and nobody knew at that stage who set the fire. They weren't able to get word out through the welfare officers because all the lines were down. So for days, we didn't know what was happening. And I had

28 In October 1974, republican prisoners set fire to Long Kesh Prison. This was the end of a protracted struggle over prison conditions which came to a head when a republican prisoner and a prison guard were involved in a physical fight. Much of the camp, which housed 1,500 prisoners and internees, including some loyalists, was destroyed.

my husband and my father in at that time. In the end, my daddy got word out through the welfare officer that they were okay. My daddy went on all the protests in Crumlin Road Jail to get political status. He went on hunger strike after hunger strike. It was through my daddy that they got the political status right at the very beginning.

We would never have denied my daddy. Never denied where he was, what he was in for, never. My mummy never once in her whole life ever said, 'Your daddy shouldn't have been in there. Your daddy should have been here with us.' She just stuck by him. Even though she wasn't political, she stuck by him. Never once did she say, 'If your da had've been here,' or 'your da shouldn't have been in jail.' In all those years, never once did my mummy say, 'He should be here with me.' Never once did she criticise him. She just got on with life, no matter how hard it was for her.

He was a great dad. I remember one time – he wasn't very good at papering and decorating – but he was papering the living room, and my younger sister, she was mucking about; I think she was only about three or four at the time. She ended up in the bucket of paste. So that was it up in the air. My mummy ended up finishing it herself. He was in the Orange Order at that time and he took us to see the bands. We thought it was a treat when he took us up the Shankill to see my granny, because we always got money from all of them, maybe sixpence or a shilling if you were lucky. So we went round collecting from all the aunts and uncles. He worked in the Post Office. And then he was a stager in the shipyard. He was always a worker. My mummy worked in the railways; she cleaned on the trains. Our family always stayed close, always.

When we were misbehaving, all she had to do was threaten us: 'Right, you're going up to see your da next month.' My mummy would have written him a letter saying such-and-such a one was misbehaving or such a one was doing this and we got trooped up and we'd be told off like any other child. We got brought up there to be told off. And we had respect. If he was telling us off, we just stood there and took it. Still do till this day!

My daddy came first. Never once did we question him: 'Why are you here, Daddy?' We knew what his politics were. We knew it through the papers. We knew it through people talking on the street. My mummy never spoke about it. It's what he believed in. And to this day none of us would ever ask him to explain. When the Troubles started, we knew it through that. Gusty Spence's name was written all over the Shankill. People were calling their bloomin' dog after him! And calling their kids after him. So we knew who he was. And what he was there for, but we never, ever questioned him.

I've seen people over the years going into bars, clubs, and they'd say, 'Do you know who I am? I'm such-and-such a person.'

We would never, ever have done that. If someone had said to you, 'Are you Gusty Spence's daughter?'

'Yeah, I am.' It didn't matter who it was; 'Yes, I am.' But we never, ever went to tell anybody who we were. To us, he was our daddy; he was just our daddy. And we would never use my daddy's name for anything. We could have, but we didn't.

The younger ones, the grandchildren, would have boasted about it more than we ever would have. They would probably go to somebody and say, 'Do you know who my granda is?'

Well, we would never have done that; still never would. If someone asked us, yeah, but my mummy never, ever went around saying, you know, 'I'm Gusty Spence's wife.'

We were born and reared on the Grosvenor Road, which was a mixed area. I went to Kelvin School off Roden Street. I have to say that our neighbours were very, very kind to us. In 1969, the Troubles started and our Catholic neighbours came out and stood in front of our houses. But we got burned out of there. All the Protestants moved off the Grosvenor Road then. We ended up staying with relatives up in the Shankill. I remember my mummy went to the City Hall for a house. It was all unionist councillors then. My mummy, for some reason she got it into her head she wanted to go to Silverstream. I don't even think she knew where Silverstream was. 'See when I told those councillors who I was, not one of them would give me a house.' In the end, they had to re-house us, so they stuck us in this tip of a house in Highfield. Whoever had lived there must have worked in the shipyard, because it was all red-lead paint or green. Eventually, we got a house round in Springmartin and that's where I got married from when my daddy got out for my wedding. He was out officially for two days but he didn't get arrested again until October or November.[29] It was the first of July I got married and I think it was the end of October, beginning of November he got caught and was flown to Long Kesh.

They searched the whole of Northern Ireland for him and where was he most of the time? Either in my mummy's house or my house. They looked, but any time they looked, he wasn't there at that particular stage. We dyed his hair every other week, changed it all different colours. It was a lot of ducking and diving, but we did it. He was caught coming out of

29 While on parole for Liz's wedding in July 1972, Gusty Spence was 'kidnapped' by the UVF.

Glencairn. It was the two tattoos on his hands gave him away: my name and our Sandra's name. It was a wee eighteen-year-old soldier.

Whenever he was out on the run and they were staying in a place up in Glencairn, my daddy took ill. My mummy had to run the whole way down the road to get help because there were no mobile phones in those days. That's when my daddy said, 'Right, that's it; you're going to learn to drive.' A few times we had to go in the prisoners' bus, but once my mummy got her own car, we were able to go down ourselves. I was lucky when Winkie[30] went into jail; we always made sure the two visits were the same day. I was eight months married and four months pregnant when Winkie went in. I brought my son up to see his granda and his daddy; I got out of the hospital on the Thursday with him and in the car we went straight to Crumlin Road Jail to see his daddy and the next day there was a visit set up to go to Long Kesh to see his granda. He grew up thinking they were living there, building houses; he didn't know any different. We told him they were in there working; there was no work outside so they had to build houses. So he never knew until his dad got out. He never knew what his daddy was in for. The kids in the street would have told him what Long Kesh was, but we never told him.

My daddy did nineteen years. I'll never forget that day he got out. He hadn't been well; his heart was playing him up and he'd already had his gall bladder out. Me and my mummy and my sister Catherine, we went up on a visit that day. They accepted the parcel off us when we went and handed our visitors' pass in and went and sat in the waiting room as usual. The next thing, a screw came out and said, 'Mrs Spence, the PO[31] wants you in his office.'

Well, we nearly collapsed. We went to sit outside, but he said, 'No, the whole three of you.'

Me and Catherine's looking at each other: *there's something wrong here.* So we were put into a room and the door was locked. It was only about five or ten minutes, but we seemed to be sitting there forever before the PO came in. And then the door was locked again. My mummy said, 'What's wrong? Is he not well?'

He said, 'No, he's actually being released today, but we can't let you out of this room until we have him in the car park and into your car.'

It was in case we went and got the press. And we sat there completely gobsmacked, just looking at each other. We couldn't believe it. We drove to

30 Winkie Rea, a leading member of the Red Hand Commando, a small paramilitary group linked to the UVF, and later Liz's husband.

31 Principal Officer.

our house in Denmark Street. Winkie had the chip van at the time. There he was, cooking everything; it was just outside my door. My daddy said, 'Don't say anything.' My daddy got out of the car and went over and leaned over; I thought Winkie would die! Then we had to try and contact my brother; he was working for the council. My sister worked in Gallaher's.[32]

We didn't want this coming to them through the press. We wanted to get to them before they did. At that stage, there were whispers coming out. In the end up, I don't know how they got my number, but they started contacting my house. In the end, I think it was the next day, I gave them an interview to get them off our back. 'Just leave us alone. Just go away and let him lead his life and leave us alone.' We hadn't got a clue that he was going to get out. Me and my mummy had gone to meet the Secretary of State about two months before it along with Peter Robinson[33] – at that time he was on our side – to get him out, but not an inkling did we have that he was getting out. Neither did he. He was just told that morning to pack up his stuff. If he had known, he would have got word out to us.

We just didn't question my daddy. Like going on hunger strike: if my daddy thought it was the right thing to do, then to us, that was the right thing to do. I'm not saying we always agreed on it, because it brought my mummy down a lot. My mummy worried about him a lot. I know it sounds stupid, but that's just the relationship we had with my daddy. We had absolutely the greatest respect. I couldn't say I respected anybody more in this world more than I respected my mummy and daddy.

My dad didn't try to put me off marrying Winkie. He never expressed anything like that; it was my decision. And I was only seventeen when I got married. Somebody just told him Winkie was a headcase. 'You're not going to let your daughter marry him; he's a header.' I remember when my daddy met him; I'll never forget that day. We went up to the Crumlin Road and we arranged that Winkie went in first. Me and my mummy stayed in the waiting room and then we went in for the second half of the visit. Winkie was actually going into the lion's den; he was going in to meet him without anybody with him. But by the time we got in, the two of them were getting on all right.

With my daddy and my husband in jail at the same time, it was double trouble. But sure we got through it, didn't we? You had to. If I could change my life,

---

32 Gallaher's, a tobacco factory in Belfast.

33 Peter Robinson, a founder member of the Democratic Unionist Party, councillor and MP in East Belfast over three decades and who succeeded Ian Paisley as First Minister of the devolved Northern Ireland Assembly in 2008.

would I do it? No. Don't get me wrong; I'd have loved for my daddy to be there when I was growing up. But I wouldn't change the life that I had. It's the same, like, if you say, 'If you had your life to live again, would you marry at seventeen?' Yeah, I would. Even if I knew what was in front of me, yeah, I would; I would do it all over again. I didn't know when I got married my husband was going to end up in jail and I was going to be left to rear a child on my own. But I wouldn't change my life. Yes, I would have loved to have my father there when I was growing up, but circumstances were that he wasn't and we accepted it. He thought it was worth it. My husband thought it was worth it. And in those days, I did think it was worth it. I don't know about it looking back now. Maybe because we've got the taste of peace now. In those days, you had the Troubles and people went out and did what they sincerely believed in. But not any more.

My daddy was a smart man before he went in, but he self-educated himself in there. He got exams. If the Troubles hadn't come to Northern Ireland it would have been totally different. He always got the blame for starting the Troubles and that's why he read the ceasefire statement out; hopefully, he was ending the Troubles. And it happened to be read out on my birthday – again! The fourteenth of October.

I wouldn't change my life, I wouldn't change my parents, I wouldn't change my husband, I wouldn't change any of my family. If circumstances had been different, of course, I would love to have grown up where my mummy didn't have to worry about money and to live and to be able to bring four of us up. But it wasn't to be, so we just accepted it and got on with it. All of us, the whole family did. Can I say that the Troubles were all worth it? No, I don't think it was all worth it. And it's the same with the marching thing;[34] I don't think any road is worth a life. It's just what people believed in in those days, but was it worth it? No. No life was worth being lost.

It's great for the young ones now because they're getting to meet each other and they're all going into the town together; it doesn't matter what religion you are. Yes, you will get the odd headcases everywhere, but most of the young ones are all getting on well together.

The grandkids thought it was brilliant: 'My granda's Gusty Spence. Head of the UVF. He was in jail.' But they didn't follow him down that route, thank

34 Periodically, there is tension, sometimes leading to rioting, over loyalist parades during the months either side of the annual celebration of the Battle of the Boyne on 12 July. The conflict centres around parade routes, with march organisers demanding the right to 'walk the Queen's highway' and local nationalists objecting to loyalist marches in the proximity of their streets.

goodness. It's different when it's your own child. My brother was in and it nearly killed my mummy, nearly tore her apart. It was worse my brother being in than my daddy being in. My daddy was out by that time. My brother was in the Blocks.[35] She got through nineteen years with my daddy and she could hardly get through three years with my brother. It nearly tore my daddy apart, too. But it was circumstances led people to it. It's the same with Alistair,[36] Louise's husband; it was circumstances. And it's the same on the Falls Road. Ninety-nine per cent of those republican prisoners would never have been in only for the circumstances of the Troubles.

My uncle Bobby died in prison. My uncle died in my daddy's arms. Heart attack. They were jogging round the compound. My daddy's brother's son, Ronnie Spence, he was in the IRA compound at the same time as they were all in. My daddy didn't speak to his brother for years, but not over that. It was only in the last fifteen years the two of them fell out. I haven't seen any of them for years. I don't even know if I would know them again. You know the Price sisters?[37] My daddy's brother married their cousin. She was a Catholic and the kids were brought up Catholic. My mummy's sister married a Catholic. One of my cousins was married to Gerry Adams' nephew. We're very close to my mummy's side. One of them lives in Beechmount and one of them lives in Stewartstown. We go to their houses all the time and they come to us. We've stuck together through the Troubles and they've never asked no questions; we've never asked them no questions.

In Mountcashel Street on the Springfield Road, my cousin was only married, she was Catholic, she was pregnant, and the loyalists were putting her out. Me and my mummy went shoulder to shoulder and stood beside her and helped her to move. We stayed very close through everything. We are a strange family! Family means a lot to us. You fall out with one of us, you fall out with all of us. Half of them don't know what they fell out for! My mummy was very family oriented. She loved getting her photograph taken with all the grandchildren around her.

---

35 H Blocks, Long Kesh/the Maze Prison, so called because of their shape.

36 Alistair Little, sentenced for the murder of a Catholic when he was a teenage member of the UVF. He is now involved in conflict transformation work, especially with ex-combatants, globally. He is married to Louise Spence, Gusty's granddaughter.

37 Marian and Dolours Price were imprisoned for IRA car bombs in England in 1973. After a long hunger strike during which they were force fed, they were repatriated to Northern Ireland in 1981 to serve out the rest of their sentences.

My daddy was seventy-seven in June. His health is not very good. He has lost a powerful lot of weight and his eyesight has gone. He has macular degeneration; he can only see a bit out of the side of the eye. He went down badly since my mummy died. My mummy will be dead eight years in December. He just misses her.

The 2000 feud near killed him.[38] That was the finish of my mummy. My mummy was only sixty-eight when she died. You knew something was brewing in the estate the whole week. We just tried to keep ourselves to ourselves. There were kids running around with Johnny Adair[39] T-shirts on. My wee girl was only nine, and she was, 'Why can I not wear one of them?'

And I said, 'Get in, you're not wearing one.'

'Can I not go to this festival?'[40]

'No, we're going to the caravan.'

My mummy and daddy had already gone down to their caravan the day previous to it. On the Saturday morning, there was an awful atmosphere. Winkie and Eddie, they went out to collect the coal money. I'll never forget; I saw them coming down the street again and he said, 'Come on, get yourselves gathered up. They're starting to block this estate off. Get you and her out.'

So away I goes, down to the caravan. It was my daughter's hen night. I had made all the stuff and took it all up into her house. A gorgeous day it was. I went round to see my mummy round at her caravan and came back round. I fell asleep out in the sun, then woke up. Mobile phones had just come out. And I remember ringing my daughter: 'Have you everything all ready for the party?' But unknown to me, she knew what was happening to our house and she's trying to talk to me normal and cry at the same time 'cause her daddy warned her not to tell me. She's holding everything back.

And then I got a phone call from Winkie and he says, 'Now, I don't want you up in arms and I don't want you coming up here, but the UDA's in our house now, burning it. I need you to go and tell your daddy.'

By that stage, word had come through there was trouble on the Shankill. We'd heard that people were dead and that there was shooting in the Rex.[41]

38 A feud erupted in the lower Shankill area in August 2000 between the UDA and the UVF. In the following weeks, seven people were killed and 200 families with links to the UVF were intimidated out of the area.

39 Johnny Adair, leader of C Company of the UDA in the lower Shankill area.

40 A festival organised by Johnny Adair around the unveiling of some militaristic murals.

41 A bar on the Shankill Road frequented by UVF members.

I warned my mummy; I said, 'Mummy, don't you be going up to Belfast.' Unknown to me – I had gone on to my own caravan – my mummy and my son had gone up to Belfast. My daddy had been out for a pint with his friends and he came round. The hardest thing I had to do that day was tell my daddy that he didn't really have a house.

Our Louise and Sandra were on the phone to me, crying 'What do you want us to save out of your house?' It sounds stupid now, looking back. As I said, it was my daughter's wedding and I had to wear a stupid hat at the wedding. I didn't want to wear it, but the first thing I said to our Sandra was, 'Get my hat out.' It didn't matter about anything else in the house. Louise and Sandra went through a terrible time, trying to get the police. Louise was cut to bits in her bare feet, trying to get help from the police, jumping in front of police Land Rovers. They were at her granda's house but couldn't get anybody to help. The police stood at the top of the street and watched it being done. My brother and Catherine and their husband and wife, they were in Benidorm and they knew something was up when their son went up to the airport to pick them up. We all ended up, I think there were about thirty of us, in one caravan. My mummy and daddy couldn't go back to their house; it was wrecked. They set mine on fire and his was wrecked. What they couldn't wreck, they stole. I was homeless for eight months. Mummy and Daddy were homeless; that was in August, and they didn't get re-housed until December. They got a wee bungalow, but my mummy never accepted it as her home. Sherbrook was her home.

The next day, we all met up at the Northern Ireland Club. It was funny afterwards. We all decided: 'Right, my daddy's going to do a press conference outside his house.' All our cars met on the Crumlin Road, just at the Mater Hospital, and went into Denmark Street in a convoy, right up the middle of the road. Ivan Little[42] was doing the interview; he was petrified doing the interview. At that stage, Johnny Adair's mob were about, he was still there and heard we were out. So the police and army got us all out. That's when my daddy pleaded with the good men in the UDA to stop this. It didn't stop for a couple of months. There were 1,600 people lost their homes. I started off a group with Plum Smyth[43] called FODDD, Families of Displaced, Dispersed and Distressed, to get people re-housed. I was getting

42 Ivan Little, a reporter with Ulster Television.

43 William 'Plum' Smyth, a founder member of the Red Hand Commando, an ex-prisoner and long-time community activist.

everybody re-housed and I still wasn't re-housed myself. I was still stuck in my daughter's house.

I never blamed it on every UDA man. UDA men offered me a roof over my head. I blamed it on one squad of UDA men, but I never, ever held it against any other UDA man. We knew the people who did what they did to us, and to this day, I hate them. I would be telling lies if I said any different.

I had two nervous breakdowns. Our Christine is coming up to twenty, and it was about five years before she was born. It was just after the IRA tried to shoot Winkie and just missed him. For five years I had it and I ended up pregnant, and I think that was the first thing that helped me, brought me round. When the feud first started, here's me, 'Nothing's going to bring me down here again. I've been there.' And I didn't let it bring me back down. I started up the Shankill Stress Group[44] along with my daddy and Mina Wardle. I've come through and out the other end.

People found it strange with us, 'cause even when we were young, we were never bigots. We were never brought up as bigots. When people found out we were Gusty Spence's children, they couldn't understand. But we were born and reared in a mixed area. Our best friends were our cousins, who were Catholics. Before my daddy went in, Sunday mornings he got us up, and we were sent round to Christ Church and the others were sent round to St Peter's. He never went to church, but he sent us!

I didn't hate Catholics; none of us hated Catholics. People expected us to. Yes, we were against the IRA because of the atrocities. But I could see two sides to the story. People on the Shankill were going mad whenever your man Seán Kelly[45] got out, but I'd say, 'Hold on a wee minute; you have to take a step back here. One of the worst atrocities was McGurk's Bar,[46] caused by loyalists. So if one's getting out, the other one has to get out.' But some people have blinkers on and can't see that.

---

44 Shankill Stress and Trauma Group, a counselling service based in North Belfast.

45 Seán Kelly was one of two IRA men who carried a bomb into a crowded fish shop on the Shankill Road in October 1993 with a view to killing those at a UDA meeting allegedly taking place on the first floor of the building. The bomb exploded prematurely, killing Kelly's companion and nine other people, including two children, and seriously injuring Kelly. He was arrested at the scene.

46 In December 1971, a bomb exploded in McGurk's Bar, North Queen Street, Belfast, killing fifteen people, including two children. The British Army blamed the explosion on an IRA 'own goal', but a later court case, which led to a prison sentence for a UVF member, proved what republicans and nationalists claimed all along: that it had been a loyalist bomb.

Absent Fathers

I was afraid and started to wonder if I was ever going to see my daddy again. I remember it being very strange and unsettling, and looking back, I would call it separation anxiety ...

Jeanette Keenan

Jeanette Keenan

Daughter of Brian Keenan

Brian Keenan was a leading republican for most of his adult life. He was the IRA's quartermaster general in the early 1970s when the IRA was involved in bombings in England. Influenced by his trade union background and his admiration of anti-colonial movements in Africa and Latin America, he was consistently on the left of the IRA's army council. In his final years, he was the intermediary between the IRA and the International Commission on Decommissioning and as such negotiated the IRA's dumping of weapons. He died in 2008, aged sixty-six. Jeanette Keenan was born in 1964.

My daddy's name was Brian Keenan. He was a television engineer. He and my mammy started off their married life in England but came home to live in Belfast. There were six kids born between 1962 and 1968. He had a strong background as a trade unionist. I think he realised very early on that working-class people got a raw deal and the people at the top of the chain looked out for themselves and didn't get a raw deal. He was a self-educated man. He came from a family where his father was a civil servant; he had been in the RAF.[47] That meant that there was a perceived higher status, access to education that maybe other Catholic people didn't have. My daddy dropped out of school early; he was very headstrong. That led him to educating himself. He was a very avid reader. You would hear him talking about how people shouldn't have to fight to be a citizen; that people are citizens and are equal.

My earliest memory of him being involved in standing up for things was coming home from a civil rights march. At the time I was only five, so I didn't know he was coming home from a civil rights march. There was a commotion in the house when he came home and said to my mammy they were beating everybody. He was talking about the police, but I didn't know that then. They were beating everybody and there was this guy that he knew and there was blood pouring out of his head.

47 Royal Air Force.

What can I tell you about him as a man? A very, very strong personality. Incredibly articulate, which he didn't pass on to us because we probably didn't spend enough time with him. He could take something that was really complex, particularly to do with world politics, injustice, racism, very strong subjects, and he could turn that into something simple that a child could understand. And for me, that was where I developed my very fundamental beliefs in human rights. I didn't understand what was happening in Palestine as a child, or Angola, but when he explained things in very simple terms, I understood what was right and wrong. I think that those were great messages to grow up with.

We lived in Turf Lodge until 1970. One day, we all just moved without any warning. Now, we only moved across the road into New Barnsley, but to us, it was miles away. And after that, we never really saw much of him. He went on the run; we didn't call it that back then and I don't even know if it was meant to be on the run forever, because at that time, it was a crisis situation.

In that little interim period between civil rights and us moving, I remember being in the back of his little television repair van a lot; I think we might have been decoys! When he moved to New Barnsley, we very rarely saw him; maybe he would manage to sneak home overnight.

There was a lot of activity in New Barnsley in the early '70s and there was a lot of soldiers in the streets with guns. And there were gun battles which you didn't see but you heard all the time. I can remember him then during that time, but he was always in a hurry.

The earliest memory I have where there was a really strong impact was during internment.[48] I knew what internment was, funny for a child of that age to understand it, but we knew that the British soldiers were coming in and taking away all the men and all the boys. We were all kind of evacuated. My mammy was very sick at the time, and I think, looking back on it, she was under huge stress and my daddy asked her to go and stay with her sister in England. My daddy knew that internment was coming, because people who were involved knew what the British Government was going to do next. She went to England and he looked after us.

We were evacuated, believe it or not, first to Ardoyne![49] He just came in the darkness and brought us all to Ardoyne. It must have been a safe place at

48 In August 1971, the Northern Ireland Government introduced internment without trial. Approximately 350 men were interned in the first instance in Long Kesh, a former air base outside Belfast. Over the next four years, almost 2,000 men and women were interned, about 100 of whom were loyalists.

49 Ardoyne, a working-class nationalist area in North Belfast.

that time. Then we went to my granny's house in Jonesborough;[50] that's where they had gone to live when the Troubles started, because my grandfather had a heart attack and my daddy got them somewhere else to live. We stayed there overnight, I think, and when he came back, he obviously had plans. He split us into twos, and we all went off in twos to live in different people's homes. Me and my sister Anne Marie went to Dundalk.[51] Obviously, we went to families who supported the struggle. And that was brilliant.

But looking back on it, I was afraid and started to wonder if I was ever going to see my daddy again. I remember it being very strange and unsettling, and looking back, I would call it separation anxiety, because it had been going on for maybe eighteen months. And my mammy wasn't there. And because she was always our stability, not having either of them there was really weird. And the woman we stayed with at the time – a lovely young woman and her older parents – I remember getting into bed every night with her; I didn't sleep until she got into bed and I held onto her really, really tight.

I knew back home things were bad, because people watched the news all the time. You could see the raids on TV where they were taking away the men and the boys, and I knew about Long Kesh. I don't remember stopping to think, 'Well, thank God my daddy isn't there,' – I just remember feeling anxiety. We were safe, and that was fine. We had some great times there in the South, and we got to see a lot more of him during that time, that initial time when internment started.

Some of our Christmas, Easter and summer holidays were spent in the south of Ireland, because that was where people believed that it was safer. And we saw him for loads of that time, and they're all the good, happy memories. But they are coupled with a memory of sitting in the car on the way home and nobody speaking.

I don't know what all my family were thinking about, because we never spoke about it at the time. And I don't know how my mammy felt about it. We talk about it more now, but we didn't talk about it then. It was absolutely like having your heart and stomach ripped out; you are just sitting there in the car in silence. You don't cry, even though there's a lump in your throat and you really feel like crying. You don't cry, because nobody else is crying.

During the holidays, we'd be in the back of the car like sardines and my mammy in the front, and my daddy saying, 'Be quiet! Be quiet!' But not when

50 Jonesborough, a village in South Armagh on the border with the Republic of Ireland.

51 Dundalk, a town in the Republic of Ireland, close to the border.

we were going home back to Belfast, because we knew that was it; we were leaving him behind.

In late '73 or '74, Brian was arrested, just for membership of the IRA; that's how they got people into prison then. He might have done just nine months out of a year because you served three quarters of a sentence. We visited him in Portlaoise.[52] We went on the bus from Sevastopol Street[53] and travelled to Portlaoise. We didn't see him very often, but just seeing him was fantastic – access to your daddy, and with your mammy, because you'd travel with her. But we only went one or two at a time, because it was a very gruelling journey. And it was in a tiny minibus that always broke down. I think we left the house at four in the morning.

We went straight back to New Barnsley after internment had settled down. We went back on our own, obviously, without my daddy.

The British soldiers would come to the house and they would check everyone in the house, take us out of bed. Usually, that was early morning, maybe five, six o'clock, and we'd all be taken out of bed. Meanwhile, they'd be going around the house doing a check and we would have to sit in the living room. And that would go on anything between half an hour and an hour and a half.

We went to St Bernadette's Primary School and the teachers would ask things like, 'What does your daddy do?'

Obviously, we didn't tell the teacher anything. My daddy used to laugh and say, 'You tell them that I'm a brain surgeon and they'll not ask any questions.' So I remember going in one day and saying it, and the teacher just smiling. Years later, the primary school teacher – she was actually at my daddy's funeral – said she didn't have a clue because most of the kids in the school either had a daddy in prison or a daddy who wasn't there during those years. So it was all around us and there were never really any questions asked that I remember.

My mammy was very strong. She was our stability; her job was to look after her children. But she lived in a constant state of worry about the knock at the front door. She watched the news all the time as well. God love her, she had in one way a really mundane life because she had six kids and hardly any money; she lived under constant pressure. She never was privy to information, because my daddy wanted to protect her. But obviously from the news, she knew when things were bad and when things were dangerous for him and she

52 Portlaoise Prison in the Republic of Ireland.

53 Sinn Féin's headquarters in West Belfast. Minibuses brought relatives from there to visit prisoners in jails in Northern Ireland and the Republic.

would be very stressed. She had a short temper at times. But she was always consistent about caring for us, and that was our saving grace.

My mammy was very active in the local community during those years. At times, we would all help out, all the kids gathered at the table and the floors writing out leaflets by hand – in the days before photocopiers – if there was going to be a protest. The women used to chain themselves to the railings at the Henry Taggart[54] for rights for prisoners, rights for internees. She always was very similar to my daddy in that she believed that standing up for your rights and other people's rights was worth doing. One of the big differences between them was that she had strong religious beliefs. She was a Catholic. She didn't go to Mass, but she still has strong religious beliefs. And he didn't, although he never prevented us from practising it. She wanted us to go to Mass and she got really cross if we didn't.

I knew we had a different life. I always knew that. We even had a different life to many other republicans' children because we spent a lot of the time on the busman's holiday, in the summer time, on the run, with my da. Obviously, *we* didn't go on the run, but we always went to a place of secrecy. Every year we had a different surname – whatever ID my daddy had. We used to be stopped by the Guards[55] and he would tell us, 'You think they're your own, but the Guards are worse.'[56] We'd find out our surname, usually in the car on the way down or when we got there: for example, O'Neill.

He'd ask us: 'What's your name?'

'Seán O'Neill, Daddy.'

'What's your name?'

'Bernadette O'Neill, Daddy.'

'Yes, that's right.'

He wasn't that kind of daddy; it was just for those particular things he had to be very strict. We didn't have false IDs, but he did. And it did happen, if there was a road check in the south of Ireland, he would get stopped and he would give his name. And they'd always look at the back at these six kids squeezed into the back and they'd usually say, 'Go ahead.' Those holidays were fabulous. Sometimes it was in a farm, an isolated farm; sometimes it was on a caravan site. The life was a different life. I don't know if other

---

54 Henry Taggart, a former Protestant church hall in West Belfast, later turned into a highly fortified base for the British Army.

55 Garda Síochána, the police force in the Irish Republic.

56 Worse than the police in the North, the RUC, notoriously anti-republican.

republican children travelled round the way that we did, but I guess lots must have.

The heartache was strong; it's as strong even now. The pain of leaving my daddy behind, every summer, every Easter. And that followed on to when he went to prison. That pain's the same now as it was then; I don't understand; it shouldn't be, but it is very strong. And it causes anxiety. We dealt with it back then in silence; you didn't talk to your family about it. The difference is I can tell my kids about it now, and tell funny stories and make it sound humorous. And I tell them about the pain and the words are coming out and I'm still feeling the pain, but at least I can talk about it. At least the silence is gone.

He was arrested when I was fourteen at a road check in Banbridge. He had a driver. They were both arrested and brought to Castlereagh and they were held there for three days being questioned. Then he was taken by helicopter to London. He was remanded in custody to Brixton Prison. I think he was there on remand for about two years before he was sentenced.

When we came home from school that day, we got to the top of the Whiterock – we went to St Louise's – and my mammy was standing across the road at the Credit Union. She told us, 'Go on over to the house. Your daddy's been arrested.'

So we just went, 'Oh, right. Okay.' It wasn't a shock; I don't even remember talking about it on the way over to the house.

We just went over to the house and put the dinner on. That's not a normal reaction! My mammy was standing around because people were coming to her to give her information and fill her in on what was going on and what might happen next. Then she said, 'Your daddy's been taken to England.' I remember I didn't like that because my memory of Portlaoise was you could visit him; I didn't know what this would mean to us. But I was fourteen this time; I obviously understood a lot more. I don't remember being as frightened as I had been when I was a lot younger.

He was in for two years at the beginning. That was very difficult for my mammy at that time, because we did live in poverty in that my mammy had to sustain six children with virtually no money. She didn't know how she was going to get all of us over to England on visits.

The only person my mammy knew in those days who visited England was Lily Hill, Paul Hill's mother.[57] She had an awful time; she had to borrow

57 Paul Hill, one of the Guildford Four, was a victim of a miscarriage of justice. Jailed in 1975 for bombing bars in Guildford, Surrey, the sentence was finally quashed and he and his co-accused released in 1989.

money. She was always in debt from visiting Paul. My mammy and Lily started having meetings and talking about the situation. I remember them saying, 'What are we going to do about this? This isn't on. These children are entitled to see their father. It's not our fault that they're over there. You're entitled to see your son. What are we going to do about it?'

Together, the two of them pushed the Social Services, the DHSS,[58] to create a system to make it easier for people to access money. They were brilliant women. I remember then the DHSS put in a system whereby you were entitled to visit your daddy or your husband once a month. You went down: you told them you were going on a visit; there were forms to fill in; there was a procedure to go through and that was down to my mammy and Lily. So that's how we then started going to visit my daddy. In the initial times, I think she got some sort of emergency money to go and visit him.

The first prison we visited in England was Brixton; it was in the middle of an area we didn't know. I suppose it was exciting. You had to go on the boat – you had to go on the cheapest way – it was also the longest way. So it might have been a boat and two trains or three trains, depending on where you were going. He was in for fourteen years. During his second year, Mammy went to visit him one time; I think it was for their wedding anniversary in October. The security forces in London arrested twenty-one people, three of whom were women; one was my mammy. She was accused of trying to aid an escape; the twenty-one people were all arrested for that. The women's prison was in Holloway Road in North London, but my mammy was put into Brixton. There weren't any women in Brixton Prison at that time. But the three women were put together into Brixton on a different floor above where my daddy was being held on remand.

I was fifteen. We were able to stay on our own in our family home because my eldest brother had turned seventeen and legally could be responsible for us. When my mammy went on prison visits, we all knew how to run the house; she had taught us that. We had a family friend to help keep house and we managed the budget, shopping and cleaning between ourselves. My sister was sixteen; she got pregnant; my mammy was devastated. Her child was having a child and my mammy wasn't allowed to come home.

To cut a long story short, when it came to trial, she was allowed out on bail; she wasn't allowed to leave London. My daddy's sister lived in London. They were an RAF family, like my daddy's. They gave huge support to my mammy

58 Department of Health and Social Services.

and daddy. My da's brother-in-law was Irish, from the south of Ireland, and they'd lived with discrimination and jibes about being Irish all their lives because of being in the RAF. So Mammy came to live with them in London and signed on at their local police station twice a day at the beginning, or three times a day – it was something ridiculous.

The judge threw the case out of court. He did make some kind of a little speech, saying how wrong it was that a woman was taken away from her children with no evidence. Lots of the other people had been convicted but had already served whatever time. The three women were released. Mammy was completely acquitted.

My mammy was away about a year. And when she came home she got stuck right in and became the doting granny and helped my sister, encouraged her to go back to school. Having a baby in the house was great; I suppose we all behaved a bit like mothers during the time my mammy was in prison. There were very rough times in the house; there was a lot of arguments, but they were kids' arguments; they weren't anything serious. But at the time it seemed like, 'This is terrible. If Mammy was here, she would sort this out.' If you look back on it, we had the life where you had to deal with whatever was there, and I think that was part of making you strong.

Some people in the community thought that we were privileged in some way because our dad was seen as a senior republican and he was in prison. But that's completely the opposite of the truth. We were not privileged.

We had to live in secrecy and children shouldn't have to live in secrecy. There was massive financial hardship and a huge stress. Maybe people just made assumptions because of who our father was. Maybe that's a working-class thing: because people have low self-esteem, they don't have a lot, so they start to pick on other people's lives. I know that went on and I felt that. And when we got older, I felt it, too. I was labelled as Brian Keenan's daughter. I was not the person I was; I was Brian Keenan's daughter. When I was older, I became heavily involved in community work, although not necessarily where people would know who I was and be more likely to make assumptions about me.

I started to work in the community as a volunteer at first, in youth centres and on ACE[59] schemes. But at the same time, I could see that there were people not from the community coming in and getting the good jobs, well-paid jobs, jobs that were more important in terms of how decisions were being

59 Action for Community Employment, a government training scheme for the long-term unemployed.

made. But at the same time, there were local people who would have done the jobs much better. They were more motivated and more connected to what was needed, yet they weren't getting the jobs because they didn't have a bit of paper from university.

I went to university as a mature student. My daddy had always taught us that if you educate yourself you won't surrender power to other people, people who don't necessarily have your best interests at heart, the misguided do-gooders or people who have different agendas. I remember saying to people when I was a voluntary worker in the community, 'I'm pissed off. I want to be the one who comes in with the piece of paper with the view to change things.'

And I absolutely believed that when I went to university. And it hurts that people in the community thought, 'Sure, look at her. Her dad's Brian Keenan. Sure, they all went to university.'

They didn't all go to university; only I went. We never had any more than what they had; in fact, we had less than a lot of people. My mammy never went looking. She was very proud that way.

My dad went into prison when I was fourteen; he got out when I was twenty-eight. His homecoming was a whole story in itself. He was totally paranoid about getting out. He was getting out into this world – he had no idea. Yes, he was a very intelligent man; he knew all about the world, but he didn't know about coming home in the 1990s – how to get on a bus, silly things like that. We were all up to a million when he was coming home; because he was so paranoid, he made us jumpy. He hadn't been home since the '70s and the world had changed. He had been away for fourteen years.

The house in New Barnsley was all fitted out with stair gates and bars on the doors, camera, alarm bells; we did all that for him coming home. He was handcuffed on the way home, I think, because he was deported, escorted from England. When he got out of the airport, he just got on the bus himself. And when the man told him what the fare was into Belfast, he said, 'I don't want to fucking buy the bus; I just want to go to Belfast.' He hadn't a clue about costs! He landed at the door of our house when we were supposed to be at the airport.

We all went to my house and we had a party. It was secret – again! We waited until we had food on the table and then we invited a couple of close friends and family, but we didn't want a big one of those homecoming things and he didn't want it, either. We were all grown up, but there were all these children, Brian's grandchildren, running around, too. And that was lovely.

My dad went straight back to 'work'. He could have held back for a couple of days but he had a meeting on that first day. We were raging and my sister

Bernadette told him off and sent the visitors packing. But apart from that time, I don't remember criticising him, because we never said anything back then; we never challenged him. I never said to him, 'Have you not stopped to think about how this will affect the rest of us?' To the day he died, I never said it to him. We did have conversations about how we were affected, but I never challenged him on it. We both had regrets about not having time together or having talked about it. But it wasn't worth it. Near the end, he was very ill and it wasn't worth doing at that time. I just wanted to enjoy what we had left.

I went to work with Tar Anall[60] in the youth project to support children of prisoners. I wanted to encourage young people to be more assertive about their needs and their lives and leave all that anguish behind. A lot of parents' relationships break up after prison. My mammy and daddy lived separately because he just couldn't live a settled life; certainly not in Belfast, where security was still an issue. It broke my heart when he left and our whole family was devastated. We were more devastated because we had been looking forward to him coming home for so long. Communication between him and my mum was very difficult and caused a lot of stress within the family. In those days, republicans didn't talk about the consequences of war, so we didn't benefit from other people's experiences, and we always found that people kept things close to their chests. There was a lot of taboo around talking about the emotional effects on relationships and families. Those feelings are still destructive for children and families today. You get people who say, 'What do they want to get that money for prisoners for? That's all over now.'

And I'm thinking, 'You don't know the half of it.' The feelings are still there. My hurt and anxiety from being ripped away is still as new to me today as it was then. We have a generation, two generations, of children who were directly affected by the war and by parents not being there, being away in prison and parents who now can't come to terms with being out. And lots of parents and their children who can't talk about how they feel or cope with their feelings, and this affects their relationships now.

My daddy believed very much in family life, and part of his political struggle was that he was trying to create the best possible life for families, where people could be nurtured. But he wasn't doing that with his own family, and there was a lot of resentment. When he came out of prison, the shit hit the

60 Tar Anall (Irish for 'come hither'), a support group in West Belfast for republican prisoners, ex-prisoners and their families.

fan, because we then were adults, we were building relationships with him as adults. Right up until he got out of prison and I was twenty-eight, where he was concerned, I felt like a little girl and I related to him like a little girl. When I went to visit him in England, even in my twenties, I still felt my heart ripping out when we were leaving. I cried and felt like hanging on to his leg; it was ridiculous!

When he came out, it was still like that. But within two years, things changed. I'd started university then, as well, so my whole life had changed and opened up and I was having a great life. I was getting a great sense of who I was, and I never had that growing up. I got married. Before then, my reference point had always been him, the struggle and our parents. It wasn't about finding out 'who am I?' and I never knew who I was. I had that anxiety and uncertainty about identity because I didn't really know what my identity was. I knew the things I loved to do, I had strong beliefs, I knew what I wanted to do in life, but until he got out of prison, I never had a reference point as being Jeanette. It was really worth working out, but I didn't realise I'd have to work at it; it came as a shock. And when the light bulb came on, I couldn't turn it off; I had to go with it. And that meant challenging lots and lots of things about the life that I had had. At the same time, I was evaluating the things that were very unique and very special about that life, too.

We went through a period of resentment, and this is where me and my sisters would talk a lot. Bernadette had already moved to America a long time ago. My mammy, me and my two sisters would often make comments like, 'Sure, you know he's not going to get involved with family things.'

He owed us something and he wasn't willing to pay up. Back then, I was also angry at both of my parents. I felt that they both owed it to us to at least try and communicate and work it out. It was only when we got out of that negative cycle of resentment that I sort of came to terms with the fact that they only ever communicated by writing, by fourteen years of letters – no-one to share children, life, love and human contact; they didn't know how to be together after fourteen years apart, and it wasn't their fault. Nobody came up to you when your husband was getting out of prison and said, 'This is going to be a rocky road, there's a lot to work out!' When he was getting out of prison, my mammy was totally anxious. But we never thought about it, we never thought that this woman has a stranger coming to live with her.

I don't know where we would have been as a community if people hadn't gone out and done what my daddy did. How long would it have taken me to get a place at university? I was twenty-eight when I went to university; I couldn't have gone at eighteen. I could have and struggled through. I'm using university just as an example. There are lots of things I couldn't have had the opportunity to do. In 1964 when I was born, people were fighting for things like voting rights. That's only in my lifetime! That's how I can manage to say it was worth it.

My daddy used to come home sometimes and I knew he was in pain and I knew he was tired and I knew it was all too much, too exhausting. He'd be talking to my mammy and he'd be talking to us, too, and he'd say thing like, 'I don't want you to do it. It's not fair that it has to carry on for another generation of children.'

I believed that and I still believe it. I do think that the war was worth having as a necessary evil and I do believe that it had to become an armed struggle because nobody was going to give me those rights. Somebody had to have the conviction, the commitment to do that. I knew he wasn't a warmonger and he didn't approve of killing; he believed in humanity. I'm absolutely sure, because he told us so. It was a very intense time, the armed struggle, and what women went through! I would never live with someone who was a soldier. My mammy was second-best in my daddy's life. I wouldn't settle for that.

Having kids changed my view about life. It made me think, 'How did he ever leave his kids? I could never do that. How did he ever leave my mammy to bring six children up on her own? I could never do that.' And I could never be with someone who would not put me first and my kids. My daddy preached about gender equality in relationships, but he didn't have the opportunity to practise it – another sacrifice made by the family for the war.

He died in May 2008. I miss him more as the time goes on. It's too soon for me to feel that he's not coming back, because I don't feel that. I feel that he still lives round the corner from me in South Armagh. I feel his presence every minute of the day because that's the effect he had on my life, throughout my life. His inspiration was very strong.

I moved to South Armagh a year ago and a month later, my daddy came to be cared for in a house very near to me. I didn't visit him all the time, because that would have been overkill, after years of having no access to him. But I could visit him every day if I wanted, or every two days. I'd been studying holistic therapies during that time, so I used them on him. And that was our way of communicating; it was powerful because of that touch, that human touch. And he would get really relaxed. He would tell me wee stories. And those were the times when he told me how he really felt. He was very good at letting you know: 'You've done really well; you've done great, and I wasn't around for you.' He was telling the family in his own way that he recognised that he wasn't around for us.

He made remarks to friends, knowing that they would tell us, about being proud of us all. So he did give us little messages. And he said: 'I didn't do right. Your mammy didn't deserve the life that I gave her.' He took full responsibility for it in his own way. 'She didn't deserve the life that I gave her. She deserved more. You know, she was an amazing woman throughout our lives and I didn't repay her the way I should have. But I didn't know how to and there wasn't the opportunity to. And it's too late now to start.' I feel sad that he never told her those things directly, but such was the nature of their communication.

In the last couple of months of his life, he told every one of us how happy he was. He said: 'I'm very, very happy. I've done everything that I need to do. I'm very happy that you have your children and they're healthy.' If you were to write it in a novel it would sound soppy, but when it was spoken to you, it was very sincere. He really meant it. He wanted each and every one of us to feel that we had nothing to feel bad about. In the last few months of his life, he told us all the time that he loved us. And he always told us in letters from prison. The letters were lovely.

If he was here now, I think he would be glad that I'm remembering those things, that I know that he knew and we knew that we all loved each other. He would be happy about that, because he was a very simple man. He never talked about or ever needed money. He always talked about humanity.

Fiona Bunting

Daughter of Ronnie Bunting

Ronnie Bunting was a republican socialist activist. Formerly a member of the Official IRA in Belfast, he went on to become one of the founder members of the Irish National Liberation Army. He was shot dead in his own home by loyalists in 1980 along with fellow INLA member Noel Little. Fiona Bunting was born in 1973.

My father was Ronnie Bunting. I've very, very clear, vivid memories of him, but I can't remember day-to-day life. I remember a lot of different incidents and I remember what it felt like being with him. When I was younger, he used to bring me everywhere with him. I remember going on the train to Dublin with him. I used to feel safe when I was with my daddy. I remember the feeling of his leather coat. And I remember in the mornings Mum used to send us in to wake him up if he wouldn't get out of bed and we'd be bouncing on him, playing. I have a lot of ordinary memories like that, like everybody else would have. I have one brother and one sister; I'm the eldest. When my father was murdered in 1980, I was seven, Deirdre was three and Ronan was a year and a half. Daddy was a big softie with us. He also used to do lots of things with me, like reading. My brother and sister don't have memories like that.

I remember another time, travelling up the road with him in a car with other guys – some of them are dead now as well – and they had a weapon in the car. There was a checkpoint and they said to me, 'Here, hide that up your coat.' I remember being told, 'Listen, it's not a real gun, but the Brits would try to get me in trouble.' So I knew things were different. My father was in the INLA.

He came from a Protestant background. He grew up in East Belfast. Then he married my mum. He had a teaching job. They'd got a house but they had to leave when he was interned because they were living in a loyalist area. So they moved over to West Belfast and that's where I was born. Mum jokes about internment babies; all the guys got out and I was born nine months later. I think I was about three when we moved to Downfine Gardens. That's where my father was killed. There was also another man killed in the house, Noel Little, and my mum was seriously injured.

My grandfather was a major in the army.[61] My father and my grandfather stayed close. I remember hearing when my daddy was arrested that they used to take his clothes for forensics, or just badness; probably a mixture of both. They'd throw him out in a boiler suit. My grandfather would have driven across to the police station and picked him up. My grandfather spoke at the inquest about a year later and he said that while their political views were at opposite ends of the spectrum, he always upheld my dad's right to have them. He was very close to Paisley at one stage. Me and my granny would be very close. She says my daddy and my grandfather used to sit and have debates. And they'd say to her, 'What do you think?' and she was, like, 'I'm not getting involved in this.' So they maintained their relationship, which is unusual, given the vast differences.

The house used to get raided a couple of times a week. So you'd wake up in the middle of the night and you'd just hear voices and lights on. I remember waking up one night and there were Brits in the bedroom and they were at the bottom of my bed, searching the bed. I was talking to Mum about it recently and she said, 'Yeah, I said to them, "I'm not lifting the kids out of the bed."' So I don't know what was more scary! I remember at that stage that I knew that they were the enemy.

The other thing that used to happen was my daddy would have been arrested, and as I said earlier on, he took me everywhere with him. So they used to bring me into the station, too, with him. I don't know how legal it was, but I remember one time in the Springfield Road station, they had me in a separate room and they were, like, 'Is your daddy a bad man? Where does he hide the guns?'

I remember Mum telling me that, as a baby, they shot through our window during a feud. I think my dad was staying out of the house, trying to keep things away from the house and also for his own protection. I was thrown on the floor and somebody lay on top of me. We also had to move to Wales at one stage because my daddy was shot in the neck. Mum talked him into moving away to Wales. There's a photograph of it and I'm in the picture, but I can't remember. We also lived in Dublin for a while. I have very vague memories of Dublin.

---

61 Ronnie Bunting was a Protestant, the son of Major Ronald Bunting, a former British Army officer. Bunting senior had begun his political activities in Northern Ireland with the Republican Labour Party but later switched allegiance to Ian Paisley. He was a leading light in Paisley's Protestant Unionist Party in the late 1960s. He died in 1984.

My mum says he didn't come home at night sometimes; she was sitting, worrying herself sick, and she couldn't exactly start phoning round. It's not like you phone the police station and say, 'Has there been an accident reported? My husband's Ronnie Bunting and he hasn't come home.' She'd just have to wait.

On the night he was killed, Mummy and Daddy were both in bed, and when he heard them coming up, he tried to block the door. They started shooting and he was shot seven to nine times. He was shot three times in the head. My mum snapped then and she dived on one of them. They were on their way out at this stage. One of them apparently shouted, 'Come on, Geordie,' or something to that effect, and the other one turned around, and Mum was on his back and he shot her in the mouth. Noel was still alive, from what I understand, but he died in the house before he got to hospital. Noel was a good friend of my daddy's. It was really unfortunate, because I don't think it was even planned he was staying there that night. It just happened. That was just a bonus to them.

The first thing I remember is a lot of noise and wakening up and hearing the screaming and noises. I can't remember what the noises were; obviously they were shots. Me and my sister were in the bedroom. I remember my sister going to walk out the door and I must have had some idea what was happening because of the screams. I told my sister to wait; I made her come back in the room. And then things went quiet and I went out. Mum was lying there. It's funny, because I can remember Mummy's face really clearly. I remember she was lying in a big pool of blood and I thought it was coming from her back, but it wasn't; she had been shot in the mouth and it was coming out of her mouth. Noel Little was there, too. I looked at him; I know he was hanging half out of the bed because my mum told me, but in my memory, I can't see his face; I just know there's somebody over there. My dad was lying at the top of the stairs. I remember turning my head, looking towards him, but the images have been repressed – they must have been, because I can't remember. I remember asking my mummy one time, 'Where was my daddy's body?' She said, 'It was at the top of the stairs. You had to step over him.' I remember finding it awkward to get down the stairs, but I can't remember. It's almost like I did it with my eyes closed or something. I had to step over him, but all those things are gone. He was dead at that point, but I didn't know.

I didn't know what to do. I leaned down and said to my mum, 'Mummy, what'll I do?' She had a couple of teeth shot out and she lost a chunk of her tongue, so she found it hard to speak, but she was saying, 'Go and get help.'

So I went next door. I went downstairs; I took my sister with me. My brother was in the cot. I remember going outside, it was cold, climbing down over the wall – we had wee walls between us and the house next door – and rapping their door. They seemed to take ages coming to the door. I think I probably said to them, 'My mum and dad have been shot.' I knew that something like that happened. Next thing I remember is going into their house and being upstairs in the bedroom and looking out the window and there were ambulances and white tape and they were trying to get me away from the window. I can't remember much after that that night. I can't remember what I felt. I think I must have been in shock.

I know I slept in that house and I think one of the other neighbours took my sister. I went down early next morning and got my sister and we walked down to people my daddy was friendly with. They lived about fifteen minutes' walk away. And I remember staying with them. I don't know how long we stayed with them, if we even stayed overnight or not. My grandmother, my mother's mother, came in the car to collect me and the other kids. At that stage I thought my daddy was in the hospital. I remember asking her, 'When are we going to see my mummy and my daddy?' And I don't know if she said it like this or not, but it's what I heard. She said, 'Your dad's dead.'

We went to stay in my grandparents' then. I stayed with my mother's mother. I can't remember my brother being there. My sister stayed with my daddy's mummy. We never went to the funeral.

I remember going to the hospital and visiting Mum. She was still at risk. She was in the Royal[62] and there was always security at the doors, the RUC. When Mum got out, we moved back into Downfine.

They never found the guns, never found the car. You know those big security gates[63] they used to have? They were lifted that night, and they got down, I think it was Kennedy Way; they made their escape there. So there was collusion. The gates were lifted and they were normally closed at night. The other thing was they knew exactly which rooms to go into; they didn't go around searching rooms. They went straight into my daddy's room. And they didn't come into our room. Neighbours reported that just before it happened, the

62 Royal Victoria Hospital, on the Falls Road in West Belfast.

63 Most of the entrances into West Belfast had barriers which had been erected by the British Army. Some were closed permanently or at times of trouble or potential trouble. Others were closed at night. The effect was to channel traffic towards a limited number of roads where soldiers could set up road blocks for the surveillance of everyone entering or leaving.

place was swamped with soldiers. They disappeared then, and they came in, carried out the murders and then vanished. No-one was ever charged. I've also heard rumours – it's never been verified – that they used some UDR[64] man's pass to get through a checkpoint.

I would like to know who was involved, but nothing's going to bring him back. Somebody came into my house and murdered my father. I have a right to know who it was. At this stage of things, you can't go prosecuting people; that's not going to happen. What I would like, although I don't think it's going to happen, is for acknowledgement of the level of collusion that was going on. How did they know where to go in that house? Why was that gate lifted that night for the getaway car? I would like those things to be made public.

Mum was arrested once during the supergrass[65] trials. Harry Kirkpatrick had mentioned her name. She was arrested and questioned but she was released. I remember one day I was walking down the road with her and they came up from Northumberland Street[66] in a van coming across from the Shankill, and they shouted out the window, 'Do you want to buy a ballot for West Belfast Football Club?' And what they were alluding to was a couple of nights before that, our door got knocked. We had a lodger at the time, a young guy with a Southern accent. You didn't answer the door at night; you used to have to shout out, 'Who is it?' So Francis had shouted out and I think it must have confused them, because they went away. But what they had said was that they were selling ballots for West Belfast Football Club, which didn't even exist. So he said, 'No, thanks.' Mum checked next day in the street and they only went to one other house in the street, a house position the same as ours but in a different row. I remember Mum going down and applying for a weapon for self-protection. So my mum thinks they'd come back for her, to kill her. And I knew all this at the time.

---

64 Ulster Defence Regiment, a locally raised regiment of the British Army, some of whose members had proven links with loyalist paramilitary groups.

65 In 1982, in return for inducements, members of a range of combatant groups in Northern Ireland named former colleagues who were then charged and imprisoned. In effect, the policy operated as a form of internment. At its peak, twenty-five 'supergrasses' ensured that more than 600 people were in prison awaiting trial. Some of the trials collapsed when the supergrass withdrew evidence, and many of those sentenced were later released on appeal. In 1985, the last supergrass trial saw INLA man Harry Kirkpatrick used to jail twenty-five people.

66 A street linking the loyalist Shankill Road to the republican Falls Road. Security gates blocked off the street by night, but it was open during the daytime.

I remember being very, very anxious about my mum. I don't recollect this, but she said whenever the Brits used to come into the street, I would run in and cling to her.

I think my mum was pretty much left on her own to get on with it afterwards. She would have had her friends, but I can't remember people being round. I remember one guy used to come round; I can't remember his name now. He came every Christmas and he used to bring us gifts. But he was shot dead.

Because my mother and father both came from a Protestant background in East Belfast, we had no surrounding family. We were quite isolated in that way. Mummy wouldn't have had support. My grandparents took us some weekends. Where I live now, my mum lives ten minutes away and my sister's close by, and my brother; we drop in and see each other. But Mum wouldn't have had that. I remember going to meet my granny in the town, Granny Murphy. We kept in touch; I still see Granny Bunting. Granda Bunting died a few years after my daddy died. He never recovered; he took a stroke about a year afterwards. He was bed-bound for quite a while and then eventually he passed on.

My daddy died in 1980 and soon after was the hunger strike. There was a lot of rioting. You couldn't just travel. Granny Murphy used to come over and visit us, and then one day masked men got on the bus before she did because they were taking the bus. She never came back.

Whenever I cried, Mummy would comfort me and would tell me my daddy wouldn't want me to be upset. So I didn't want to cry. But I remember I used to go into the cupboard underneath the stairs; my daddy's coats were still there. I used to go in there and cry or in my bed at night. But I remember I used to feel his leather coat and feel close to him.

I remember being really angry. I would have lashed out. I used to hit my brother and sister. Part of that fighting would have been about me feeling I had to take care of them: 'No, that's wrong. You'll get in trouble if you do that.' And I in my own way disciplined them. I'm sure we put my mum's head away because we were constantly fighting. I was just a wee ball of anger. I used to think that when I was older I was going to join up and go and kill them. I nearly did, but thankfully I didn't. I kept my nose clean. I think I partly shut down, because I stopped crying. I think I focused my energies as I got older on education. But I was full of overdrive energy. Thankfully, I used it positively. Part of me was in a rage and I just took every day as it came.

For years I'd been really angry. Mummy used to joke and say some people have a short fuse, but with me it was spontaneous combustion. I used to be with my friends and just feel really, really depressed and sad and start crying and wouldn't know why. I knew something was wrong. But it was more the temper that was the issue. I met my husband a month before my eighteenth birthday. I struggled a wee bit in the relationship because, you know when you start feeling close to somebody, I felt myself pulling back. I would start arguing with him; it was because he was getting too close and you know that if you get too close to people, they die or go away. So I went for counselling then. That helped me a great deal. I went for quite a long time. I started to realise then how much I'd been affected by the things that had happened over the years, especially that night. I remember sitting with my counsellor and she said to me, 'You know your daddy's not coming back.' And I remember feeling like calling her a liar. I hadn't at some level accepted it and I think I was still waiting for him coming back.

The other thing that used to happen to me is I used to get flashbacks, images. Occasionally, something would have reminded me and nightmares would start. It wouldn't be a re-run of that night, but loyalists would be chasing me, or there would be bloody images, that kind of thing. It would be as if you were back in 1980. A smell could set it off. Like burnt tyres would bring you back to the time of the hunger strikes. If I close my eyes I can visualise everything in the house just the way it was, very, very clearly. Or you'd just be sitting there and an image would flash up in front of you. It hasn't happened me in a long time now.

I'm a different person. I'm really relaxed now. I have two boys. I'm thirty-five. I don't think it's any coincidence that I waited until I was thirty, because I wouldn't have had the patience. It wouldn't have been fair on the kids. Having kids definitely changes what is important in life. I'm sure I spoil the kids a lot as well because I think it's great that they have what I would see as a normal life now, in terms of not having Brits walking down the street and not having to live through a war. My kids haven't got a clue. My wee lad said the other day, 'I want to be a policeman,' and I was, like, 'Son, you can be whatever you want.' I don't know how I'd actually feel about it, but you know what I mean. I would never have said that I wanted to join the police or I wanted to join the army; he's in a different world. He doesn't know anything about different religions; maybe it's because he's quite young. He's starting P1 now; he's going to an integrated school. I want him to make his own mind up about things and live his own life.

It may be difficult to try to explain to the boys what happened their grandfather because I still try and make sense of it all sometimes. What was it all about? It's the big question. I would talk to them about why my daddy got involved and why he was killed; it may not make any sense to them.

I look at my own kids and I think, they're my priority, and I would never put myself at risk where I would disappear on them. There's times when I felt angry with my daddy and I thought, *hold on a wee second, he was shot before, and he knew*. Six months before he was killed, he was visiting somebody in jail and he said, 'I have a bad feeling I'm either going to be in here in jail with you or I'm going to be dead.' Part of the reason is that he had been arrested and they said to him, 'We've tried everything to get you locked up, but there's only one thing left for you and that's a bullet in the head.' He knew the risks and he continued on. And I sort of think, if that was me, I would put my kids first, take them out of the situation.

I was talking to a friend and she said something; it really struck me. She said to me it was just so different then. I have now come through the experience and I'm looking back with hindsight. He was living it. I don't think I'll come to the point where I'll go, 'Well, that's okay. All right; that makes sense.' I think of myself in that situation at the time, with his strong belief system about social injustice and about our country being occupied and the inequalities and discrimination; from his perspective, what does he do? Sit back and let someone else take that fight forward because he has a family? So have other people. So what do you do? Do you lie down and take it? I don't think he would have had any idea of the impact, because he wouldn't have had the experiences to look back on, to reflect upon as I have had, and he was living in the middle of a very different world.

I've mixed feelings. There's part of me is a child that's going, 'You should have looked after me, taken me away and made sure you'd still be here and be a grandfather to my children.' And then there's a more adult part of me understands why he got involved and why he needed to continue that fight. Because this was a war and he was a soldier, and I can understand it in that sense, while there's part of me at a more selfish level thinks, 'But you're my daddy.' He was a soldier and it was a war and I don't think where he was coming from was a selfish place. He was fighting a struggle for what he believed in and what other people believed in.

I look at the situation now and I think, 'Did he die for nothing? What was it about?' Did my father and all those other people die for Sinn Féin to sit in parliament in a Northern Ireland executive? I don't think that's the case and that pisses me off. Although at the same time, I can understand the argument. What's the alternative? I don't know if it was worth over 3,000 lives.

Seán Ó hÁdhmaill

Son of Féilim Ó hÁdhmaill

Féilim Ó hÁdhmaill was arrested in Lancashire in 1994 in possession of a car containing explosives, weapons and ammunition. He was sentenced to twenty-five years in prison and was released early under the terms of the Good Friday Agreement. Seán Ó hÁdhmaill was born in 1981.

I didn't have a clue that my dad was involved. It came as a complete surprise and shock to us. I just thought he went on a lot of business trips. We always knew we lived in a republican area. We'd have gone to commemorations and parades, but we didn't know he was involved until my father was on the news. And even then, when they read out his name and what happened was, we didn't hear the first part of it. We heard his middle name and his surname. His name is Féilim Pádraic Ó hÁdhmaill. We heard Patrick Ó hÁdhmaill. So we asked, 'Mum, who's Patrick Ó hÁdhmaill?'

We were brought out into the kitchen; myself and my younger brother were very inquisitive. 'Who's this fellow who's just been arrested?' We'd never heard of anyone else with that surname, especially the Ó hÁdhmaill. We'd heard of Hamills, and there's a Hamill Street in Belfast, but never an Ó hÁdhmaill. My mum was distraught, trying to be as composed as she could and saying, 'Your father has been arrested.' This was all in Irish. I'm thinking back in Irish and translating it in my head presently. Especially with emotive things, it's easier to convey my emotions in Irish. So it came as a huge surprise to us and a whole other world opened up. Like, I remember we were driving down the Falls Road in a taxi, and all of a sudden my mum started pointing out who else had spent time in jail, with internment and people's involvement. 'He was in jail, and he was in jail. Your uncle, or whatever, spent time in jail.'

It got to the stage where I turned round to my mother and said, 'Was everybody in jail at some stage?'

My dad was arrested in February 1994. I would have been thirteen at the time, second year in school. Éamonn was two and a half years younger, so he would have been in P7. He was still a youngster, ten years of age.

My dad grew up on the Shore Road, which was a mixed area at the time, and gradually, as we came closer to the onslaught of the Troubles, it became a much more segregated area. What happened was a process of either burning people out or intimidating people out of their homes. My da has mentioned on a few occasions that, coming back from school, his school uniform would have been different. There would have been a crowd of lads waiting for him. Sometimes he could run away and sometimes he wouldn't be able to. My da's nose is a testament to a bit of a hard childhood. He was beaten occasionally by people who didn't like who he was and his nose has been broken a few times. The simple fact of wearing a school uniform can mean the difference between a safe walk home and not.

My da also mentioned that their house was constantly under attack and a Catholic got killed down the street. After a while, things got so bad they abandoned the house and ended up as refugees in Bombay Street. They couldn't sell the empty house.

The British press would maintain that kids are brainwashed from a young age to hate the British, whereas the opposite was true in our case. We were told that, even though there was a British soldier in your garden or pointing a gun at you when you were playing in the street, they're following orders and that it's the British establishment that's the problem; the people in power giving the orders are the problem, not the ordinary people. And a lot of them are Irish or of Irish descent. If we would have heard kids in the street saying 'Fuck the Brits' or 'the English', if that had been said, it would have been aimed at the British Army rather than ordinary British people. Politics wasn't really discussed in our house and it wasn't forced upon us. My da's involvement wasn't known to me. I even thought he was a bit of a pencil pusher because he was always wearing a shirt and tie and carried a briefcase.

The most difficult thing for the British press was that he is educated. This wasn't a fool who had been brainwashed or some thug who was tricked into doing these jobs. It's true; had he not been in Ireland, he would have been involved with some other NGO[67] because he would have seen injustice and wanted to do something against it. I think he got that from his own da. His mother died when he was fairly young.

Before his arrest, he had got a job as a lecturer in England. We didn't see him that often during that period – I think it was only about six months. Although he was actually caught with gear – explosives and targets – he was

67 NGO: non-governmental organisation.

done for conspiracy 'with persons unknown'. The reason that was done was to give him a much longer sentence.

All of a sudden, I went from being an early teen to family members or friends of the family all telling me that I had to look after my mother. I had to be strong for her and look out for her and look out for Éamonn, something I would have been doing anyway as an older brother. My mum was doing the same; she was trying to act as two parents. Whenever there's a certain unit of the family who's taken out of the equation for a while, something has to fill that void. And in a way, my mother filled it; but in a way, I felt that I had to fill it as well. It kind of knocked out any rebellious streak I would have had; it probably made things slightly easier that way. And in a way, it brought us closer as a family; most teens would have been arguing about silly things in comparison. I had to grow up very quickly. I don't regret having to grow up. I know some people might look back and say 'lost youth' or whatever. I could have done one of two things: I could have rebelled completely against my family, my dad, everything; instead, I chose to embrace it. And I think things have turned out beneficial as a result. I would hope that I would do the same again, given the chance, knowing what I know.

Visiting my dad in jail in England was surreal! I'd been in England before, but this was the first time visiting a jail in England. I was still only thirteen, fourteen years of age and Éamonn was only ten. The jails in England are in the middle of nowhere. They're not accessible. They're put there because if anyone tries to escape, it's a lot more difficult for them to get away. What that meant for us was that we had to get a plane over there, to get a train or the metro to the nearest train station, to the nearest town, from the nearest town get a taxi from there to the jail. What you'd have was a day or a two-day visit. You get the flight on the Friday morning and by the time we got ourselves sorted, you might have an afternoon visit on the Friday. We'd go back then and stay where we were staying – friends of the family or a B&B.

The interesting thing about the remoteness of the areas in which the jails were, the prison would have been the biggest employer. So you'd get a taxi out and the taxi driver would know who you were – the Irish accent. Then at lunchtime, you'd have to go back into the small village; of course, that's where all the prison officers were and they'd know as soon as you opened your mouth who you were and why you were there. And then it wouldn't take long for it to travel around. There was an atmosphere that wasn't great, for someone to look down at you from a young age. I don't remember any specific incident, to be honest. If there had been something, my mum would have done a very good job of shielding us from it.

I remember one instance after we were visiting my da, we were stopped at Manchester Airport. We were taken for questioning. We were led away just before we were about to board the plane, having arrived in England, having visited, them knowing full well that we'd visited and knowing full well we were on our way home. So there was no information that they didn't already know. To my mind and to my mum's mind, it was purely intimidation. But because we have Irish, my mum was very cute. She said that she wouldn't let us leave her sight. They kept the doors open. She came in. She said, 'Listen, boys,' – all in Irish – 'as soon as they find an Irish language translator, we'll talk Spanish!' A year or two before then, we had gone over to Spain to live for about seven months because my mum was doing a mature student's degree in Spanish. I'm fluent in Spanish as a result of the immersion we got there. She went in and asked for a pen and a piece of paper. She started writing in Irish: *Is breá liom an ghrian ar lá breá samhraidh* – I love the sun on a summer's day. Gibberish! That was the only incident where someone had gone out of their way in England to intimidate us. I thought that my mum's response was very positive in that we never saw any aggression or anything negative coming from her end. Any intimidation that we felt against us, as long as we stayed together, it bounced back, it didn't affect us.

There was a British Government policy whereby after a person had been convicted they'd spend their jail sentence close to their family. That was British Government policy. Now, it took a few years for them to implement that policy! What they did was move him around almost every single jail in England.[68] Making it more difficult for us to visit was a by-product of this; whether they did that on purpose or not is a question for them. Even though the ceasefire had happened just after he was arrested, the situation actually got worse for the prisoners over there. So that made things worse for us as his family. We would have had a fairly close relationship as a family. It was stressful for my mother. She is one of the strongest lobbyists I've ever come across. I remember going over our phone bill; it was in the hundreds of pounds. Before he was arrested, it was £20 or whatever. She had written a letter to every single MEP, MP, TD,[69] senator in the US and in Australia, contacted them all in relation to getting him transferred over. As a result, within two and a half years, he had been transferred from England, a feat that had rarely happened before

68 This policy, known as 'ghosting', was common for Irish republican prisoners in Britain.

69 MEP, Member of the European Parliament; MP, Member of Parliament; TD, Teachta Dála, a member of the Dáil, the lower house of the Irish parliament.

in our recent history. People had been left over there for twenty-odd years in different jails in England, but within two and a half years he was moved over. I think that is in no small part because of the work my mum did. It's a shame that it took so much effort and stress on her part when it was already British Government policy.

My respect for her grew immensely. You think of your mum as someone who's always there; you take her for granted. Seeing this other side to her gave me another opportunity to sit back and see her as the fantastic woman she is. She was getting up and speaking at marches, spokesperson for the transfer committee, Saoirse,[70] and all the rest of it because she believed she had to. This isn't somebody who would normally have been involved in politics; her main interest was to rear her family. But she took on this other role because she had to. And that's the same as we all did. I suppose it gave me a bit of an impetus to make sure that I didn't cause her any trouble. It's not that easy when you're a teenager; sometimes you just want to go fucking mental. Luckily, I went and did a lot of sports and got a lot of pent-up aggression out with a hurley stick and a football and focused on schoolwork.

I remember we were in the Gaeltacht[71] in 1997 when we heard he was being transferred back to the North, myself and my younger brother, on a summer course. My mum phoned the house where we were staying – no mobile phones in those days. We got the message that she would call us later on that night. It was the only time we were allowed to watch TV. The family we were staying with were all happy. That was a huge sigh of relief; even though he was still in jail, it was ten miles down the road from us and conditions were much better. I remember my mum telling me one of the first things he said on the first visit in Long Kesh: he mentioned how beautiful it was to see the sky, because for three months, he hadn't seen the sky; he was in solitary confinement on a no-wash protest. Conditions worsened for prisoners over there, so they responded by not co-operating.

I remember one of the first times we went visiting my da on our own in Long Kesh. Before then, we'd been with my mum. It would have been on a Saturday. You go into the visiting area; there's a few screws sitting and they have a book of all the visits of the day. They check that you're down in the

70 Saoirse, the Irish word for 'freedom', was a Sinn Féin organisation set up in the 1990s to work for the early release of politically motivated prisoners and the repatriation of republican prisoners from English jails back to Northern Ireland.

71 Gaeltacht, an Irish-speaking area where children go to improve their Irish on residentials.

book. You say your name and they give you a sheet. They have my da's surname and then our surname down on it. You've to hold on to the sheet until you're called. They open this Chubb-locked door and you go into one of the small rooms where there are two other screws that search you. There's this very important piece of the process whereby they get a tiny little piece of white paper with a space on it for the prisoner's name again. So they write down the prisoner's surname and staple it to the piece of paper that you came in with. There's no new information going on it. It's probably to make sure you've gone through the searching process. So that's one person's job, and the other person is there to search you. So we're in this cubicle, two grown men and myself and my younger brother and they search us; no problem.

And he says, 'What's the name?' The name's in front of him.

So I say, 'Ó hÁdhmaill. I'll tell you how it's spelt.' I start spelling it out.

He says, 'It's grand.'

He hands me the piece of paper with the staple on it and it's spelt wrong, even though it's spelt correctly underneath on the other piece of paper. So I say, 'I'm sorry, but that's spelt wrong.'

He says, 'That's all right.'

I say, 'It's not all right; it's spelt wrong.'

He said, 'No-one will see it.'

I said, 'I'll see it. You know, it's supposed to be my name; it's not my name.'

So I take it off, put it in the bin and say to him, 'Will you please write it again? I'll spell it out for you if there's a problem.'

He didn't like that very much, obviously – a fifteen-year-old telling him how to spell a word he had in front of him. I was trying my utmost not to be cheeky, even though every bone in my body was telling me to, but because my younger brother was there, I couldn't let someone bully me and I couldn't let him see that it was all right to let someone bully you. I'm not sure if I would have stood up to the two men if I was on my own, but I had to because of my younger brother.

So he wrote it down again. And even though I spelt it out to him, he wrote it incorrectly again, at which point I said, 'Listen, I want to speak to your superior.'

Now, you're in an area about half the size of a prison cell; it's padlocked. Eventually, they opened the door and we were left waiting there. Everyone else has gone through on the visit. We're waiting there, not knowing what's going to happen next. Anyway, the head PO[72] comes out of the visiting centre and says, 'What seems to be the problem here?'

72 Prison officer.

So I said, 'There's a problem with one of your prison officers. They have difficulty spelling my name despite me spelling it out for them and it being spelt correctly on the visitor's sheet.' He said he'd look into it. We went through and a different person searched us and we had no difficulty with him. So it was only one person who had a bit of a chip on his shoulder.

We went through and we were half an hour, forty minutes late for our visit. My da was concerned. Around that time, there would have been a fair amount of freedom inside the jail; they ran a lot of the wings themselves. But the one weakness in the place was with the visitors. The POs knew that and the prisoners knew that and it was an unwritten rule that you don't harass the visitors. It was the first time I actually saw my da angry, really angry, because it was probably the first time we'd ever been intimidated, or an attempt made to intimidate us. So he went up to the prison officer, the screw who was up watching the visits, and said he wanted to get the head PO down. Most of the visit was wasted because of this one person. But it turned out that a week later he was moved away from the visiting area. That showed us as well that it can work. You can go up against the system and you can win, even if it's just a small battle and even if it's just with one small, bigoted person. Had we not stood up to him, he probably would have intimidated other kids and that may have had an effect on them down the road in terms of their self-esteem. It taught me it was important to stand up for yourself and for others.

My grandfather had a gold fáinne.[73] By the time we were born, he had lost a lot of his Irish; he'd learnt it in jail and that would have been thirty, forty years earlier. But he did make an effort and definitely was supportive, which I think is as important for people who don't speak it. It's extremely important that you show young people that it's a good and a valuable thing to speak Irish and to have an appreciation for your culture. And he helped along with my parents to set up the naíscoil.[74] My mum hadn't a word of Irish growing up. My dad did a little bit in school in St Mary's,[75] but he only became fluent after school, at night classes and running around with Irish speakers. I was told later that he taught an Irish class while he was remanded in Crumlin Jail in 1978. My parents met through the Irish language and they took a decision to become fluent and to make Irish the family language.

---

73 Fáinne, a ring, worn as a badge, indicating that the wearer is an Irish speaker. A gold fáinne indicates greater fluency than a silver fáinne.

74 Naíscoil, a pre-school where the Irish language is spoken.

75 St Mary's, a post-primary school in Belfast.

They took a decision. Around that time, the hunger strikers and Bobby Sands would have been writing in Irish and speaking Irish and trying to promote it. I was actually born 'Sean Hamill' – the English spelling of it – whereas Éamonn was born 'Éamonn Ó hÁdhmaill'. My father was working in mixed areas when I was born and it would have been dangerous for him to have an Irish surname, whereas Hamill, it could have been anything. And Féilim, they wouldn't have known what Féilim was, just a strange name. So even to this day, if I want to transfer to a different GAA[76] club or whatever, I need to bring my birth certificate and a deed poll to show that I'm Seán Ó hÁdhmaill.

The Irish language was a huge part of our upbringing. A lot of my generation, and especially Éamonn's generation, would have been sent to gaelscoil,[77] although very few people spoke Irish in the home. Even though some parents would have been taking classes, their main language would have been English. So that was a huge thing for us. And my name was a huge thing for me. I think that also helped us, because there was a support structure there for prisoners in our area. But there was also an Irish-language community that mightn't have been republican but that would have felt a lot of sympathy for what was being done to us as an Irish-speaking family. Éamon Ó Cuív, then Minister for Community, Rural and Gaeltacht Affairs in the Dáil, came over to visit my da, the reason being that they refused to let us have a visit through Irish. They refused to let us speak to each other in Irish. That was one of the main things that bothered me more than anything else.

One memory that comes to mind very vividly was on Christmas Day. Whenever my father called on Christmas morning, my younger brother answered the phone. He said, '*Dia duit, Éamonn. Nollaig shona.*'[78] That was all he heard. They cut the line. It was a security risk for a father to tell his eleven-year-old son Merry Christmas. Some people can be very small.

My mother went over to Belmarsh,[79] did the whole journey, knowing full well that the visit would be called off because she would refuse to speak in English to my dad. I have a huge amount of respect for her for that. We didn't actually see my da for maybe nine months because he was away working in

76 Gaelic Athletic Association, which promotes a range of Irish sports and athletic activities.

77 Gaelscoil, a school in which all teaching is done through the Irish language.

78 'Hello, Éamonn. Happy Christmas.'

79 Belmarsh, a prison in London which holds, among others, Category A prisoners. IRA prisoners were Category A.

England and then when he was arrested, it took a few months for that to get sorted. So we hadn't seen our father in a long time, hadn't even spoken to him, because any time we tried to speak, they cut the phones off. Every time we had a phone call, it was recorded. So now and again we'd throw in 'the red car is coming over the sea'.

It was a bit strange, especially at the beginning, knowing someone was listening to your conversation with your da, especially intimate things. It was their job to try to gather intelligence. I don't blame them for recording. But I do blame them for refusing to allow us to speak our own language. I just think that was very small of them. The more I think of it, the more of an effect that had on us. Anyone who knows me now sees me as an Irish-language activist; you could say the British establishment has influenced me. I live most of my life through Irish: I work, socialise and intend bringing up a family through Irish. If anything, they've made that determination even stronger in my mind.

There was a peer education programme organised for prisoners' kids in Tar Anall,[80] and I attended it, and so did my younger brother. It was extremely beneficial to us. It taught us how to be assertive. But the main aim was about getting young people, especially young men, to talk about the situation and to get it out, to discuss it. It helped me a lot to see how it affected other people and I planned on not making the same mistakes again. We put together a document as prisoners' kids[81] and the prisoners themselves put together a document and both were circulated and discussed.

For the first time, there was something there from our experience that discussed the whole situation. It gave us a certain amount of empathy about how each of the participants involved felt. One of the young lads, his father had just got out of jail and there was a bit of conflict there between him and his da because his da saw him as much younger, saw him as the age he was when he went into jail and he was obviously much older and had taken on responsibilities in the home and felt much older than maybe even his own age. One thing we never thought about before was that whenever a prisoner gets out, their constant fear is that because of the loyalists, their family is a target, that they could attack the house.

Before that, people thought that my parents were separated, which helped and meant that our house was never raided. My father was living abroad.

80 Tar Anall, a support group, based in West Belfast, for republican prisoners, ex-prisoners and their families.

81 *Left in Limbo: the Experience of Prisoners' Children*, 2000.

When he was arrested, he said that he was married but he was separated. They believed that. They'd actually watched our house and they realised that there was nothing happening in or around it. So there was no reason to raid it, which in and of itself kept a very negative memory out of our heads. It meant we didn't have to experience that. I know people who have experienced it – doors getting kicked in at four in the morning and people in riot gear coming in and wrecking and going through all your valuables. So we were lucky in that sense. And we were lucky in a lot of senses in that my da's still around. A lot of people's fathers and mothers aren't around. And the time that he did spend in jail was fairly short in comparison to some others. People have come out of the Troubles a lot worse than either I or any of my family have. I have no regrets.

I'd taken on a different role in the family than a normal role of a child – in my head anyway – a kind of protector, trying to keep the family together. When my father got out in 2000, there could have been tensions there about who is the alpha male in the family. But it came at a very opportune time. I'm not saying that there would have been tensions, but even if there would have been, we had the honeymoon period for about a month and then I moved down to Dublin to do a specific degree course. So I missed out on all that. Éamonn didn't. Although Éamonn didn't have as much of the role as I did, there was still a time – for a period anyway that he was around sixteen, going out with his mates – when my da was worried about safety. Even five years before then, it wouldn't have been safe to go into town if you were from West Belfast if you had a name like Éamonn. My da was thinking about town as the place where he grew up and what he was thinking: you had to stay in your own area. Safety was a big thing. Whereas Éamonn, a sixteen-year-old, wanted to enjoy himself.

Normally, if there was ever any tension, it probably would have been between the eldest son and the returning dad. We've actually stayed very close as a result of us being separated. Whenever I went back to visit home, we spent time together, me and my da, me and the family. Even though our family is spread across Ireland – Éamonn's in Belfast, I'm in Dublin, my parents are in Cork – we always make the effort to talk to each other on the phone or whenever we are in each other's cities to spend that night together. I suppose it makes you realise that life is short; anything can happen and you may as well use what time you have here with your friends and family to the utmost.

What would Che Guevara's son think of him? Or what would George Washington's son think of him? Or any of those people we would call heroes or revolutionaries? In terms of my da's involvement, I was very proud of him. There were very few people who would have the courage to go into the heart of MI5[82] territory; at one stage there were sixty people following him. Had there been no reason for the war, there would be no reason for the existence of the IRA or any grouping. So in that sense, I can't look down, or in any way negatively, upon the decision my da had taken, especially from where I'm sitting, not having lived through that era. I may well have been in his situation had I grown up in the '70s in West Belfast – people getting burned out of their houses, no real equality, blatant discrimination, not to mention the lack of self-determination, as well as how our language and culture was not respected. I think it was an analysis of the situation which led him into it and it was a decision that he saw that there was something wrong in this part of the world and it was his duty as a decent human being to do something about it.

There were repercussions in that. He spent a fair amount of time in jail, not as much as many other people, and a lot of people have died on all sides as a result of the war. He participated, and if he hadn't participated and if others hadn't participated, we mightn't have had the peace process, we mightn't have had the power-sharing that we have now and hopefully what will come later. Would we have had to wait for unionists to realise that equality is a necessity? If their attitude towards an Irish Language Act[83] is anything to go by, I think we would still be waiting. Until we get to a situation where people can be respected despite their political ideals, where people have the right to self-determination and in my opinion, British influence out of Ireland, then you're always going to have a problem. I think there is a process now that wasn't open to people then. The IRA was reborn out of the failure of the Civil Rights Movement. If it had achieved its aims of equality and civil rights, we mightn't be having this conversation.

Did I feel angry at my dad for his involvement? I can only ever remember feeling anger at one person throughout the whole time, and that was Michael Howard, who was Home Secretary at the time, who was behind the worsening of the conditions. Whenever Howard was interviewed, there just didn't seem to be any humanity in what he said or what he did. He seemed cold and

---

82 MI5, the British intelligence and security agency.

83 Negotiations at St Andrew's in Scotland in 2006, involving the Northern Ireland political parties and the Irish and British governments, led to an agreement for an Irish Language Act for Northern Ireland. It has still not materialised, with republicans blaming unionist ministers for recalcitrance.

ruthless. And when that ruthlessness is put into policies against a member of your family, it can't but bring out feelings of anger. You can let anger get the best of you and you can let anger turn into hatred and hatred rule your life. But it can also spur you on, it can also tell you, 'Do you know what? Fuck you! You're not going to break me, you're not going to break my da or my family. You're not going to ruin my life no matter how hard you try.' So that's what we did. We became stronger. And I made sure that I worked my bollocks off in school (I got three As in my A-Levels). I was there for my younger brother. I tried to be as good a person as I could be.

Some people maybe see the parent's involvement in a negative way. To them, I'd say, 'Listen, don't try and see the world through your eyes only. Try and see it through your parents' eyes in the times in which they lived.' It seems ludicrous for us now to think of a bombing campaign in England, but we're only here now because of it, because of the war that we all went through. How willing would the British Government have been to negotiate with Sinn Féin had there not been an IRA? What I'd also say is: 'Try to see the world in a wider context as well, not just in terms of how it affects me or you, but how people took a decision about how to change the world as it affects us all.'

Abnormality as Normal

It wasn't like I had known anything different for a couple of years and then it started. From I was born, it was happening. So to me, it was normal.

Áine Fryers

Gearóid Adams

Son of Gerry Adams

Gerry Adams was born in West Belfast into a family with a republican history going back three generations. He sided with the Provisional IRA in the 1970 split and was interned on two occasions, in 1972 and 1973. In 1978, he became joint vice-president of Sinn Féin and in 1986 president. He was a key figure in the peace process which emerged in the mid-1990s and abstentionist Member of Parliament for West Belfast during most of the period from 1983 until 2011. In 2011, he was elected to Dáil Éireann, the lower chamber of the parliament in the Republic of Ireland, as TD for the Louth/East Meath constituency. Despite his centrality to the republican movement over three decades, he has consistently denied any military involvement. Gearóid Adams was born in 1973.

I didn't really see my dad in a normal sense until I was five; he was in jail. And I don't have any great recollections of that time. I just remember wee different bits: going up to the Kesh visiting, going up and this man was there, Cleaky Clarke,[84] in the visiting room, winding me up that he was my real da and then all of a sudden when I was five, he came out of jail. I think we went to Omeath, Carlingford, round about there for a week and that's when the relationship started.

Even when I was younger, I was known as 'Wee Gerry'. We used to live in Harrogate Street until I was about ten or eleven and I was also reared with my granny in the Whiterock. When he came out of jail, somebody came rapping the door and asked for Wee Gerry and he said, 'Wee Gerry doesn't live here. It's Gearóid lives here.' So, it was one of those things; all of a sudden there's changes.

I was an only child and he was busy a lot of the time, especially when I was younger. I would see him at times and other times he would take me away.

84 Terence 'Cleaky' Clarke was a veteran republican who from the mid-1980s co-ordinated bodyguard protection for Gerry Adams. He died in 2000 of cancer.

There were times he was away for weeks; there were times he was away for nights. Round Belfast it was very active at the time so it wasn't safe for him to be staying in one place too long. In the situation, he couldn't live in his own house. I lived on and off with my grandmother and mother for years in Whiterock Drive. I'll always remember the Ard Fheis[85] every year being around Halloween and always spending Halloween with my aunts. I'd a big family circle so I was always staying with different relatives. You didn't want to be stuck in the house on your own; you were an only child so you were going up to different places.

But I spent a lot of time with him. If he was going round Ireland, he took me away. I spent plenty of times down in Dublin with him and my mother where he was having Ard Chomairle[86] meetings and different meetings down there. And as a kid I was going down to Dublin for the day or the weekend and I'd go around Dublin city centre with my mother while he was talking. Or I'd have sat in different places, bored stiff while he was finishing off meetings.

Politics never entered into my family life that much. It never dominated, despite all that was going on. It wasn't as if I was having political conversations with my dad on a regular basis. Even to this day, there would be very few political conversations. I think he has had that much politics thrown at him over the last thirty-odd years! Sometimes I would bring things forward – maybe it might be about Ireland, it might be about America or it might be about something else – ask him an opinion, and sometimes he would give an opinion. But very rarely is it the crux of any real conversation. It does come in, of course; I give my opinion on what's happening here; and the way he is, he will either say little or he tells me what he thinks. Very rarely would we have more than a ten-minute conversation on politics. It's probably a strange thing, that people see the politician, but when I'm with him it's always sport, what's happening in the West,[87] what's happening now, what's happening with the kids, things like that.

I was involved in sport that much that it seemed to take over everything. My own personal view: I don't like to be seen as a protégé. I see Ian Paisley junior; I see the way he is referred to as Ian junior and I prefer to be Gearóid Adams in my own right rather than just following the legacy of my father or whoever else came before that.

---

85 Ard Fheis, annual party conference of Sinn Féin.

86 Ard Chomhairle, national executive committee of Sinn Féin.

87 West Belfast.

I am a republican. Living down the Falls in the early '80s during the hunger strikes was a time when many kids my age first started to grasp the politics of what was going on in our areas. I have my own views and beliefs. I actually like just keeping them to myself. I don't think I have to espouse them to everybody. People take for granted, 'He's Gerry Adams' son so he's going to have the exact same views.' There are things I disagree with, there are things I agree with. There are things I think are going well and things I think could be improved on.

I have very solid viewpoints and views very similar because a lot of my cousins, friends and family were all involved politically and with the IRA and so there was maybe an interest there. It wasn't even a conscious decision; it was just the way it was in our house. I would still to this day get a wee bit embarrassed, because a lot of my family made that decision to join up or become politically active; I never did. So sometimes I think, 'Do they think I'm a bit selfish?' My da always says there wasn't one time during the conflict that there wasn't one of them in jail – right through from Sean, Paddy, Liam and Dominic and whoever else. Maybe it's because I spent most of my time with my mother's side of the family when I was young; they were republican but they weren't as active. I've never actually put my finger on it – why I didn't; it wasn't a conscious decision. It was just one of those things; I was doing my A-Levels. As I got older I was going to college; I was trying to be a teacher and it just didn't happen.

There were plenty of times he would give his advice. He wouldn't be didactic. He wouldn't say, 'Do this. Do that.' So when I said I wanted to be a teacher, obviously I could just go down to St Mary's,[88] and everything was still on the Road.[89]

I have not had anyone come over to me and say, 'Your da's this, your da's that.' Nothing negative has been said to my face. When I was younger, everybody thought we were rich because he used to wear a tweed jacket and an ould beat-up tie. The other thing, when I was younger, my name on the Falls Road was the first Gearóid and I just got slagged about it, you know, 'Garage'. Everything I did, even then, was involved in sport. I became my own person that way. I've never felt as if I've been in his shadow because he's never let me be there. Outside of the political domain, he's a quiet person himself who likes to mix with me and mess with the kids. He does his own thing. He likes

88 St Mary's University College, a teacher-training college on the Falls Road.

89 Falls Road.

to go and watch the hurling matches and football matches and I would be with him. If you're from the Falls Road, you're from the Falls Road; it doesn't matter if you're Gearóid Adams or you're anybody else. You're just a normal person. That's the way I've always been treated and the way I'll always want to be treated.

When I was running about it was more the hoods[90] who would give me a bit of stick. In West Belfast then, there was a lot of joyriders, even though the IRA was about; they were doing the kneecappings[91] at that time. I would go places and get terrible stick from them because they thought I was the same as my da. It became physical a couple of times. In West Belfast, it was part and parcel of our lives.

When stopped by the police or army when growing up, I didn't give my name. They did not realise while I was running about as a kid who I was. They probably weren't interested. I remember in Beechmount Avenue during the hunger strikes, it was mad; there was rioting, there was shooting, but every time I was stopped, they didn't know who I was. The peelers started finding out who I was when I started to drive when I was about seventeen. My da bought Tom Hartley's[92] car for fifty quid and I just drove that until it conked out. They would have seen the car, gone straight after it, stopped it, giving me all the usual: 'Where are you going? Where have you been?' But probably no more or no less than anybody else. When they saw the licence, they probably saw the second name, but some of them didn't click. The first name actually put a lot of them off. The first time I ever gave my name, I was about seventeen and the Brit couldn't really understand it. He ended up writing down 'Evans'. There was one particular peeler I used to meet all the time at the bottom of the Whiterock. He was obviously really bitter; he used to bless himself with his left hand and say things about taigs:[93] 'Your da's going to get shot,' and all this mad stuff.

90 Hoods, petty criminals, usually young, involved in activities such as car theft and breaking and entering.

91 The IRA, like the loyalist paramilitaries, was involved in policing anti-social behaviour in the communities in which it was strong. One method of punishment was to shoot alleged offenders in the knees.

92 Tom Hartley, from West Belfast, was active in republicanism from the late 1960s, becoming General Secretary of Sinn Féin in the mid-1980s and Chair in the early 1990s. Imprisoned on two occasions, he later became Belfast's second Sinn Féin lord mayor.

93 A pejorative word for Catholics.

Our house in Harrogate Street, it became a routine it got raided that much. I used to stand and watch so that they wouldn't plant anything. I used to stand at the top of the stairs and there were times I was nearly falling asleep. The first couple of times it happened, you're a kid, you think it's great. It became that regular it was like second nature. 'There's the Brits again.' That was only when he was in jail; when he got out of jail it became even worse. We were getting maybe two or three raids a week. Personally, they didn't give me that much stick.

There was a fellow in St John's[94] who was held by the peelers to check out myself and my cousin to see if I was active. I was in work and he came on the news and said he was paid by the police to check on me. I was shocked. What were they going to find out? 'He plays for Antrim!' That was probably the most personal one and it wasn't even that personal; it was just stupid.

I was in Connolly House the day that Seán Downes[95] was shot and it was really nerve-wracking. I was in the front room when the RUC were shooting and a plastic bullet hit the window, showering everybody in the room including a baby under a year old. I remember Martin Galvin being led through the hall, followed in a matter of seconds by the Brits. We were under the tables when one of them burst into the room. It's almost comical looking back as we were waiting on more shots, but all he did was jump up and down on a pile of *Republican News*[96] papers and then he ran out.

There was a time my neighbour up the street – now living in America – was walking up Divis Drive and was grabbed by a couple of men. They thought he was me. We were told they may have been undercover peelers and he got a bad beating. So I was worried about that, too, whenever I was going home at night.

I got stopped more when I was with my dad and it used to be great craic. My uncle Eamon and Peter Hartley, my da's friend, sat in the front. Peter used to have a black book and he took down all the names of all the peelers he

94 St John's Gaelic Athletic Club in West Belfast.

95 Seán (or John) Downes was killed by a plastic bullet fired by police at close range in August 1984. The incident happened outside Connolly House, Sinn Féin's centre in Andersonstown, West Belfast. New York-based lawyer Martin Galvin, director of Sinn Féin's US support group Noraid, had been banned from Northern Ireland but had entered anyway. As he appeared to address a large crowd commemorating the introduction of internment without trial in August 1971, the police attacked in an unsuccessful attempt to arrest him.

96 *Republican News*, the weekly newspaper of Sinn Féin.

didn't like. They would have been nice to the RUC for the first five minutes to get away quick, but if they knew they were getting stopped for a duration, there used to be an argument back and forth and it was hilarious.

When my da was shot,[97] I think I was in primary six; I was about nine or ten. I went to St Finian's – the same school as my da – and my uncle Paddy came down and gave me this spiel as he took me out of class. Brother Christopher, the teacher, and the other brother, Declan, were looking a bit funny. They just knew something was happening. And Paddy gave me this comical story to try and put me at ease that the Adamses were hard men, and then he told me that my da was shot but that he was okay. It was one of those things. You were that young you waited to see what happened. I went to the Royal[98] to see him. Of course, it was a shock to see your da like that. I met my mother there, but the police wouldn't let us in. A bit of a panic ensued and my mother got all upset and struck out at one of the policemen. Next minute, my da had to actually jump out of the bed with all the drips on him. Eamonn Mallie[99] was in the hospital at the time waiting to do an interview and he witnessed it all. To say that he was shocked was an understatement. At that age, I was still naïve; you obviously knew something was going on in the background but it was just part of life. About four or five years later, they found that from that shooting there was a bullet still in his neck; he had this lump. Then I was a wee bit older and I was thinking to myself, *that doctor could have left the bullet out of badness; didn't want to deal with this so-called bad person.* So that was a wee bit more annoying. It was just one of those things. I'd seen so many things happening, it was just another one. If I had gone in and he was lying unconscious or in a coma, I probably would have taken it differently, but the fact that he was up and about kept it positive for me.

I think the only time it affected me was whenever I was out of the country. I went to America three or four times through Project Children[100] for six weeks, and for some reason when I was away, it came more in my head. Every night you were going to bed, you were going, *something could happen.* It was playing

97 Gerry Adams was shot and injured by loyalists in March 1984 as he was driven away from a Belfast court.

98 Royal Victoria Hospital, Falls Road, West Belfast.

99 Eamonn Mallie, a Belfast-based journalist.

100 Project Children, a US-based organisation formed in 1975 to give children a holiday away from the experience of violence in Northern Ireland.

on my head that time. When I was doing my A-Levels, we got a hand grenade thrown at the house; I was actually studying at the time. But I don't think it really affected me that much. But when you were coming into the house that night, that was a bit more worrying then. I can't remember any time, except when I was in America at twelve or thirteen years of age, where I couldn't get asleep at night due to that wee bit of fear.

I started drinking before I should have been drinking and a friend and I used to go socialising down the town in areas which would have been probably predominantly Protestant. Because nobody knew who I was, I was in having a drink, having a bit of craic there and then coming out. When I went to St Mary's, I started socialising down in the student areas a lot more – Renshaws, the Bot, places like that. I was always more wary if I knew somebody. The problem was if you knew somebody and they said to somebody else, 'There's Gerry Adams' son.' So you'd actually have preferred going into a place where nobody knew you. One time, there was a barman in Robinson's whom I knew well and he gave me a warning. He said, 'A couple of these boys know who you are,' and they were from the Village,[101] so obviously I didn't go back for a while. If I saw somebody I knew in a bar where I maybe shouldn't have been, I wouldn't have been comfortable. I would have left and gone somewhere else. But my younger life, up until I was about seventeen or eighteen, was all West Belfast. I didn't know what was past Castle Street![102]

I have three kids now. If they wanted to be politically involved, it's up to them; it's their opinion. I was never held back doing anything I wanted. I might have been swayed by reason. I would give my opinion, the same as my dad did to me – give my opinion and then it's their choice. Any choice I made was made by me. I'd pass that on.

If they wanted to join up with the dissidents?[103] Not a chance! There's a minority of people who wouldn't have opened their mouths years ago, and that's one of the things that really annoys me – post-ceasefire soldiers coming in and saying, 'They should have done this. They should have done that.' The dissidents, or whatever you want to call them, are sadly lacking in leadership.

101 The Village, a loyalist working-class area in South Belfast.

102 Castle Street marks the demarcation between the centre of Belfast and West Belfast.

103 Dissidents: a generic name given to those republicans – including the 32-County Sovereignty Committee, Republican Sinn Féin, the Real IRA, the Continuity IRA and Óglaigh na hÉireann – who do not agree with the peace process and the position of Sinn Féin in particular.

Whether you agree with everything or not, the place is a lot better now than it was.

And if they want to join the PSNI,[104] I'd say, 'Wait a while.' That's my own personal opinion. I think there's still a lot of trust to be gained. My oldest daughter is ten; my other daughters are five and one. Maybe when my oldest daughter becomes eighteen and she wants to do it then there'd be no problem at that stage – hopefully. West Belfast is sadly lacking in quality policing still. We're getting there, but until we get proper representation on our streets, doing an honest job and not playing politics, it's not going to be good enough. If you'd asked me that question a couple of years ago, I would have said there wouldn't even be a chance. It's ironic that I'd be more against them joining the Real IRA than the peelers!

104 Police Service of Northern Ireland, established in 2001 to replace the Royal Ulster Constabulary (RUC).

Áine Fryers

Daughter of Rab Fryers

As part of an IRA Active Service Unit in Britain, Rab Fryers was arrested for conspiracy to cause explosions. Áine Fryers was born in 1977.

My father was arrested in London in July 1993. He was arrested at a bus stop with a bomb. He got twenty-five years and he was in England for about a year and a half and then transferred back to here. He's important because he's been involved in the war since 1969 and as far back as I can remember. He's my hero because he stepped up and did what he had to do because he had a family and he just believed strongly in what was going on and that he needed to do something. When he was arrested, I was sixteen and he was forty-three. There were five kids; the youngest was nine and the oldest was twenty-one.

I was born in '77, right in the middle of everything. So I was just born into it. It wasn't like I had known anything different for a couple of years and then it started. From I was born, it was happening. So to me, it was normal. Even now, I'm still going, 'Jeez, there's no Brits on the street!' To me, that's not normal!

We were raided every couple of months. One of my earliest memories is getting raided and getting lifted out of bed at three o'clock, four o'clock in the morning. I must have been about three or four and there was a Brit in the room behind my mummy and then the house just getting tore apart. So I knew there was something going on. I hated the Brits because of what they were doing.

Obviously, other kids didn't have to go through the raids and they didn't have to experience all that kind of thing. I used to think it was weird, because some of my friends didn't go through any of that. They would go, 'Oh, what's it like?'

And I'd be, like, 'They just come in and they raid the house and you move from room to room.' And there were some funny stories from it as well. I would tell them the stories and they would laugh. But I would think it was strange that it didn't happen in their houses.

I didn't know about my daddy's involvement; they sort of tried to shield us from that. But I just sort of knew there was something going on; he'd be away for days. Maybe I sort of knew, because he seemed to be an important man in the community. Everybody knew him; so then, everybody knew me. So in that way, I was sort of privileged that people were looking out for me. You just sort of knew there was something important about him. If we were out with him, everyone would have stopped him. People would come to the house, asking him to help them. My mummy is a community worker as well, so I grew up in a community-oriented house. To me, it was normal: you just helped your community. I was shielded in that they didn't force opinions on me; they didn't tell me to support the IRA. They let me make my own decisions. The other side of that was that the house was raided every other month, so I wasn't really shielded.

Every time they raided the house, they arrested him, but this was the first time that he was held. It was hard. I felt it more for my mummy. He had been on the run for a while, so we knew what was going on. Then the day he was arrested, they came up and raided the house. There was something different about this raid, because he was away, and why were they raiding the house if he wasn't here? It was later that night my mummy called me in and told me. I think I felt it more for her at the start because she was saying, 'Look, it's not just like an ordinary arrest. He's looking at going away for twenty, maybe twenty-five years.'

She told me he had been arrested with a bomb. I just went, 'Right, okay,' and walked out. Everybody else was crying. I went round to the youth club and didn't talk about it. It took me a couple of days, but I think it was more shock than anything that made me react that way. 'God, he's not going to get out in seven days.'

He was arrested on 14 July and then he was charged, like, the Wednesday after, and then my mummy went over to see him in Belmarsh.[105] After that, we all had to get security clearance to go and see him. So we'd to go to the cop station and you had to get your photo taken and all your details, even though they already knew everything. She had to do it in shifts because there were so many of us and she didn't have the money. So she brought me and my two younger brothers first. We went for a week. The second time, she took the older ones and my nephew over.

He was in Belmarsh about two or three months before we went over. There was a couple with a family over there who used to live near us. They owned a bar. We went and stayed with them for the week. Because we were staying with people who had Belfast accents, we were okay. I'd never been out of Ireland. It was daunting. You were walking round this city and you knew why you were there and you knew that at some part of the city my daddy had a

105 Belmarsh, a Category A men's prison in Greenwich, London.

bomb and was arrested with it. And people didn't like him and didn't like the accent. There were some who would have stopped you when they heard the accent and put you out of shops.

Belmarsh was a jail within the jail. We were Category A, so the only people who were there were IRA or Mafia, drug barons and all that kind of stuff. When we went into the jail, if you said Category A, you got searched. You went and stood in the line and they searched everybody on the way in; they would have done just a wee pat. When they got to us, because we were Category A, you felt as if you were being made an example of. They nearly tore you apart; they really, really searched you. And then everybody knew. They could hear the accents and they knew what was going on. You felt as if people thought you were dangerous. You went into another building and all the ODCs'[106] visitors would have gone into their visiting room, and we had to wait for an electric car to take us round to Category A because it was literally a jail inside the jail. We had to drive past all of the prisoners, their cells, the ones that were playing football, all the ODCs, to get into the jail. And it was scary, because they were coming up to the wire and looking in and they knew that you were going in to see somebody who obviously had either blown something up or was selling a lot of drugs. But then one day when we were driving through, one of them shouted 'IRA' and we looked round and they all started cheering. And then we found out that apparently whenever they were protesting or something happened in Category A, all the screws went into the jail so the ODCs had a free wing. And that's why they liked the IRA!

In the Category A part they search you again and then they do the metal test. I was the first one and they were searching me. And this man came out to the door and was waving down and I didn't recognise him. I sort of waved up and then turned away. And he kept waving. I looked at Mummy and went, 'Who is he?'

And she went, 'That's your daddy.'

He had lost so much weight and his hair had grown and I didn't recognise him at all. So we went and sat at a wee small table and we had to sit at one side of it and he had to sit at the other side and a screw sat in the room behind him. It wasn't a closed visit, because we had been cleared. We waited until the security clearance came through before we went. The first time my mummy went over, it was a closed visit, with the Perspex, and the holes are at the bottom of the wood so you can't even hear what they're saying.

106 Ordinary Decent Criminals, a term used commonly in Northern Ireland to distinguish non-politically motivated prisoners from politically motivated prisoners.

I think because of the way we are as a family, instead of getting very serious and talking about what's going on and how you feel about stuff, we would joke. At the start it was very tense; no-one really knew what to say. And then he said, 'Do you like my pony tail?'

And Mummy was, like, 'Get it cut off.' And that was the start of it then. He knew it was going to be hard for us, so he started it with a joke and then that was us, talking about where we were and where we were staying, who was showing us about, what we'd seen and all that. I think it was good that he made us feel a wee bit more easy to talk.

We went to see him every day for five days. Because we were only over for the week, you got to go in every single day. We went in in the mornings with my mummy and then somebody would have taken us around London and then my mummy would have gone in again in the afternoon.

The family that we stayed with that owned the bar, we couldn't stay with them the second time because we found out later that the MI5[107] had been following us. And so, after we left, they went into the bar and raided. It was English people that drank in the bar. They held the guy that owned the house and were questioning him about us – what our motives were for staying, even though they knew – and asking about my daddy: did my daddy ever go to the bar with people? So we couldn't go back and stay; they had invited us, but we couldn't do that to them again. In the end, Sister Sarah[108] put us in contact with the Troops Out Movement.[109] So we went and stayed with some of them. They were good to us as well. And Gareth Pierce[110] was really good to us; she was my daddy's solicitor.

Nobody went for the trial. He didn't want any of us there. Coming up to the trial, he had been in court a lot of times. He had a co-accused. And one of

---

107 MI5, the British intelligence and security agency.

108 Sister Sarah Clarke was a tireless human rights activist in Britain. She opposed the Prevention of Terrorism Act and worked on behalf of the many Irish people who had suffered from miscarriages of justice: the Birmingham Six, the Guildford Four, the Maguire family and others. She was also a one-person support institution for relatives of Irish prisoners in English jails. She died in 2002, aged eighty-two.

109 A British-based organisation formed in 1973 to support Irish republican demands for the withdrawal of British troops from Northern Ireland and the reunification of Ireland.

110 Gareth Pierce is an English solicitor noted for her stand on human rights and civil liberties. She has defended a number of high-profile Irish prisoners in Britain, including the Birmingham Six and the Guildford Four.

the times, the two of them, to make a farce of the court, went into the court in their underwear. For the end of the trial, my mummy went over when he was sentenced. He got twenty-five years and his co-accused got twenty. I was in school the day he got sentenced. I rang the house first and then heard it on the radio about two minutes later. It was a real sinking feeling, but I was glad that the trial was over.

He had gone to Full Sutton[111] after he was sentenced. We never went there; my mummy went. He had put in for transfer to the Kesh and they didn't give him it. But then his mummy, my granny, got sick, really sick, so they had to send him home on compassionate. So that's how he got brought back to Maghaberry.[112] Visiting him there was different, because you didn't have to get a plane over; you knew he was just up the road and you could drive up. Also, because the visits weren't segregated, there were loyalist and republican prisoners all visiting in the same room. You could feel the tension in the air; it was there. I remember him saying that there was tension as well on the wings and they wanted them segregated. But he was more content being back here, because he knew that he was closer to home and if anything did happen to my granny or to anyone, he wasn't in another country.

I would have talked to my friends about how I was feeling about the jail and stuff, but they didn't understand because they didn't have a parent in jail. Probably, I leaned on my family more than anything; we talked to each other. I think I got closer to my daddy when he was in jail – writing letters to him when he was in England and then going to visit him when he came back here. I was old enough to travel to the jail on my own; I would have brought my brothers up. I would have asked him questions and talked to him about stuff. It was good for me that I was able to talk to him about what was going on. It was harder for my wee brothers. I had a lot of questions and was able to vocalise them where they couldn't.

I went through a wee phase where I didn't like the IRA because they occupied so much of his time. I knocked about with people at the time who weren't very supportive of the IRA. They would have said, 'Ah, don't be saying anything to her; her dad's in the 'RA.'

---

111 Full Sutton is a maximum-security prison near York.

112 A prison near Lisburn, Northern Ireland, opened in 1986 to house female prisoners. From 1987, it also housed male prisoners. With the closure of Crumlin Road Prison in Belfast in 1996, Maghaberry became the main adult committal prison.

But I would have backed him up and said, 'Well, what's your dad doing? At least he's out doing something.'

And then I started thinking they occupied a lot of his time and maybe things would have been different if he hadn't joined the IRA. If he had been working, there would have been more time in the house. I don't feel like I lost out, because I still had a daddy and I still had a mummy and both of them were very active in the community but also very active in the house. If my mummy was out working, he would have cleaned the house and made the dinner for us coming home from school. Or the other way round, if he was away, you knew that at least there was somebody in the house. When you were younger, you just knew that there was always somebody there. And there were family days out at marches and rallies! And then family holidays, but he was always found; somebody always found him. 'He's away a wee message.'

I had sort of made my mind up at an early age that I just hated the Brits, and because he did what he did, I sort of went, 'Well, I'm backing him to a hundred here.' And I was sixteen and very headstrong, had a lot of very strong opinions. So when he was arrested, I was, like, 'Fair play to him.' Then I started thinking, 'God, that's what was going on. The IRA were taking him out of the house and sending him to do this, sending him to do that.' And that's when I started to resent them. I was thinking, 'They took up so much of his time. They didn't need to take up so much of his time. They didn't need to send him to England.'

I wrote him a letter and he wrote back, basically saying, 'Look, what I did, I did for you, for your mummy. I didn't want you to grow up being a second-class citizen in your own country like I did.' So then when I visited him when he came back, I got to talk to him more because there was no screw sitting behind him. He made the decision. It wasn't the IRA. Nobody joins the IRA to be told what to do; they do it because they're volunteers.

He was released in 2000.[113] It was strange having him back in the house. You would get up in the morning and you would walk out and he'd be standing there. I talked to him a lot more when he was in jail, but when he got out, it was, like, 'You're not sitting behind a table, so I don't really want to ask you that question.' It didn't feel like he was a stranger; it just felt strange that he was back in the house after so long. I think it was hard for Brendan,

113 The Good Friday Agreement of 1998 set in motion a process for the early release of politically motivated prisoners, all of whom were released by July 2000.

my younger brother, the youngest, because he was nine and then when my daddy got released, he was sixteen. My daddy still called him 'the child'. If I was going out for a night out, he would be, like, 'Right, where are you going?'

I'd be, like, 'I'm only going out for a drink.' It was like I was still sixteen to him. I think for a wee while, not that it was uncomfortable, but it was just an adjusting period.

What was good was that we had Tar Anall.[114] Brendan went to Tar Anall and I was doing some work for them. We had the experience of talking with other young people who were going through similar things. Their parents were being released and so we were able to talk about how we felt about him being in jail, how we felt about him being released. And he was doing the same thing in the jail. It was easier for us because of organisations like Tar Anall and Coiste.[115] Not everybody had that experience. I know there were some families that found it too hard to deal with. Probably because we're all so community orientated as well. Out of seven of us, my daddy, my mummy and me, Brendan and Alison all work in the community. And then Niall did a bit, and Mark. So everybody has done something in the community. I remember there were some young people in the group whose parents had got out before my daddy had got out: same thing, teenage boy whose daddy had gone in when he was really young. When his daddy got released, he would play pranks the way they would play pranks in the jail. He would come in and throw a glass of water round him and he'd be laughing. And he says he would jump up and go, 'What are you doing?' and fighting with him. There was that side of it, but we never experienced that.

If you look back at your life and growing up, it was hard. There were times when it was really hard. But knowing him, he couldn't have sat back and let it happen. He never made any decisions without talking to my mummy; whatever he did, he didn't make the decision alone.

I wouldn't say it was worth it. I would say it happened and we dealt with it. What is it they say? Ordinary people living extraordinary lives. It's not that it was worth it for us because we missed out on a lot, but the end result is what's going on now.

---

114 Tar Anall, a Belfast-based support group for republican ex-prisoners and their families. In the late 1990s, they had specific programmes to enable the children of serving republican prisoners to talk about their beliefs and feelings.

115 Coiste na nIarchimí, an umbrella organisation for the network of republican ex-prisoner support groups.

Mary Kennedy

Daughter of Mary Kennedy

Mary and Billy Kennedy, from Divis Flats in West Belfast, were the first and one of the few married couples to be interned at the same time. They had four children who were not taken into care but, as a result of the combined efforts of the extended family, neighbours and youth workers, were looked after until Mary was released. Their younger daughter, also called Mary, was at the centre of an international letter-writing campaign, led by the Northern Ireland Civil Rights Association, which brought a lot of media attention to the children's plight. Mary Kennedy senior died in 2011. Mary Kennedy junior was born in 1963.

I was eight or nine when my parents were interned. Before the arrests, our flat was raided 24/7. They didn't even rap the door. They'd just boot the door in, come in and the usual – get you up out of bed, pull the blankets off to make sure you're the only ones in the bed, under the bed and in cupboards. It got to the stage it was just a normal way of life. I mean, you were an outcast if the Brits didn't rap your door and search your house! There were sad times and funny times. But I think sometimes the funny times are easier to remember, because you try to bury the bad times. The one that always sticks in my head is when one of the fellows was hiding from the Brits and he jumped into bed between me and our Carol, and the Brit opened the door and said, 'Oh, sorry, ladies,' and closed the door again. Because he had long hair, they thought it was three girls sharing a bed.

This is what Mammy told me; when they rapped the door that morning, what my mammy assumed was that it was to arrest my daddy and she says, 'Billy, it's for you.'

And my daddy just turned round and said, 'No, it's not, Mary; it's for you.' She just assumed the Brits were coming to arrest a daddy. God forbid that they're here to arrest a mammy out of a house. But at the end of the day, there's a first time for everything.

I can't remember specifically the Brits knocking the door and taking them away. One night you want to bed and the next morning you got up, there was no mammy there, and then there was no daddy. It was just the four of us – Carol, Damien, Fergal and me – plus two foster brothers. Mammy was fostering them because their father was in jail. Carol was fourteen, Damien was twelve and Fergal was seven. One minute they were there and the next minute they weren't there and everyone else was there rallying round and trying to give us as much stability as possible. There was Brian McDermott, Tish Gunn, Tony O'Loughlin and Dee Kelly[116] – to give us stability, to get us out to school in the mornings, to make sure there was food on the table. From what I can remember, Social Services came in then and there was a house-mother came in to mind us. The house-mother ended up drinking and hitting us, so my granny came. She hit my granny, so she took me and Carol back to her house. Damien and Fergal went to my uncle Hugh's. If it hadn't have been for the neighbours, it would have been worse than what it was. My granny and all tried to keep us together as much as possible, but at that time my aunt also was in jail, so my granny had her two as well as us four plus two.

I remember getting on the bus with my granny from the CCDC[117] rooms where the job centre is now on the Falls, to go and visit my mammy in Armagh Jail. It was an all-day thing. You were up on the bus from about ten o'clock in the morning and getting home about tea-time. Once we were going up on the bus and they decided to try and smuggle alcohol in, so I had to wear two balloons, and as I was going in to get searched, the balloons burst. So Mary, at eight or nine years of age and smelling of alcohol, going in to visit her mother wasn't a happy sight! I got shouted at: 'How stupid were you to bust them balloons?'

Going up on the visits, there were the searches. It wasn't strip-searching us; it was the internees, what they had to go through to come out to visit us. But going up to visit your mammy and her not coming home with you, that was the hardest. You're eight or nine years of age; your mammy is supposed to be there with you. I just tried to make sense of it myself but it made none. 'Mammy wasn't here and I want my mammy back.' I don't think she ever got over it. You

116 Youth workers employed by the Northern Ireland Adventure Playground Association. Mary Kennedy senior worked as caretaker at the Divis Flats Adventure Playground.

117 The Central Citizens Defence Committee, set up in 1969 to monitor British Army and RUC actions against nationalists. They had a number of centres, one of which was on the Falls Road, close to Divis Flats. Minibuses left from this centre to bring relatives to visit internees in Long Kesh and Armagh Jail.

can hug and kiss your daughter, but you're not going home with her.

Then all of a sudden, these boxes of letters started coming in. Russia, you name it, they were from everywhere. I couldn't tell you where it started from. They were all to me. That was like from the frying pan into the fire. One minute your mammy and daddy weren't there and the next minute cameras were everywhere. Why pick on me? Why not pick on my big sister or my big brother or my wee brother? At the end of the day, it got my daddy and mammy out, but I don't think they asked my mammy's permission; you know, 'Is it okay if we use your Mary in this?' My mammy still has the letters in the attic.

I do remember at one point there was a march, 'Release the Prisoners', and I can remember being at the front of this march, carrying a banner. This was after Mammy got out. I remember her being angry because it was a march organised by the Sticks,[118] as in: 'How dare they use my child for a publicity stunt!'

I think my daddy was in and out and then in again. I can remember going to visit him in the Kesh with my mammy. And I remember being in the house more with my mammy than my daddy. I was used to him not being there; I was used to just us. Where any wee girl is concerned, as much as they love their daddy, it's harder to lose your mammy than your daddy. I don't think my mammy wanted us to visit him that often. I think she tried to give us as much stability as possible.

One day I was on the bus with my granny, going up to visit my mammy and Aunt Evelyn, and them coming out of the CCDC rooms, on the bus, and they told my granny: 'Your Mary's getting out now,' and my granny practically kicked me off the bus to go down and tell my granda. Then the icing on the cake was when the two of them walked in the door. But what a sorry sight she came home to! She was in shock as to the state the house-mother had left the flat in. One of the neighbours had to bring us bedclothes.

I think it made her, I wouldn't say depressed, but more wary, and it hardened her more against the Brits. She hated the ground they walked on – well, everybody did – hated to see them coming and did what she could to aggravate them.

But there was a Brit injured outside the door of the flat. He wasn't shot. A kid threw a brick and hit him on the side of the head. Mammy was in bed, not well, and it was Carol went down and got her. Mammy trailed him off the balcony. The Sticks were coming up the balcony to shoot him and she said,

118 A nickname given to members of the Official Republican movement.

'Not in front of my children. You're not doing it,' and she took him into the hall. She got shouted at. We got up the next morning and there were things written on the walls outside: Touts;[119] Brit Lovers; Touts Out.

The whole thing affected me in that I hated my mammy going out because I imagined she wasn't coming back. The only place she was allowed to go on her own was the bathroom. Even when she was going to the shop, it was, 'I'm going with you.' You were afraid of going to school and coming home and her not being there. As for my brothers and sister, Carol was still doing her thing, and Damien and Fergal were still doing their football and I was trying to answer letters to Russia!

Years ago, there was none of this 'oh, my God, I'm going to throw the rope up because of the Troubles', it was just put your head down, knuckle on, buckle down and get on with it. I know there are a lot of people who say 'oh, the Troubles did this to me'; you just led as normal a life as possible. You remember going to school in the mornings and people pulling you into shop doors and there's bullets flying. Try to say that to people and they look at you. Yeah, but it was life and it was the way you lived. You're walking to school one morning and a bus in the middle of the road is burning, but sure, you're on your way to school, the buses are burning and that's it; there's nothing you can do about it.

The experience hasn't softened me or it hasn't hardened me. I'm still just the same old me, only older. No wiser, like! Now, looking back on it, I wouldn't have lived it any other way.

119 A tout is an informer.

Cathy Nelis

Daughter of Mary Nelis

Mary Nelis has been politically active in Derry all of her life. She spearheaded a number of important community-development innovations in the city and was active in the civil rights campaign of the late 1960s. In 1974, she joined the Social Democratic and Labour Party but resigned a year later. By 1976, she was prominent in the Relatives' Action Committee, campaigning for the return of political status for politically motivated prisoners. Two of her sons were political prisoners in the late 1970s. She eventually joined Sinn Féin, was elected to Derry City Council and in 1998 to the Northern Ireland Assembly. Cathy Nelis was born in 1969.

My mammy grew up the eldest of four girls. It was the time when the norm was that girls, especially the eldest in the family, would work in the shirt factory. That was the only industry at the time in Derry. And even though my mammy was quite bright academically, when she turned fourteen, she was destined to work in the shirt factory. After a few years in the shirt factory, she met my daddy. My daddy came from a big family in the Brandywell area of Derry. His mammy died when he was two and so his family – there were ten of them – were reared by the daddy and the daddy's mother. Again, there weren't many educational opportunities for the family and my daddy didn't gain any academic qualifications. They got married, and very quickly, I think within a year of marriage, my mammy was pregnant with her first child. They lived for the first five years with my mammy's parents; they shared a bedroom with the three younger sisters. They left when my mammy was pregnant with her fourth child. Creggan Estate was being built at the time; that would have been the early 1960s. My mammy got a house then in Creggan. There was no tarmac on the roads: there was just houses built on top of one another; no social amenities, no schools. The fourth child came along then soon.

By 1969, I was born; my mammy had already had seven boys at that stage. She told me that the priest told her after the sixth child, because she was very ill as a result of the birth, that she shouldn't have any more children. But how do you go about doing that in those days? She went on to have nine children in total; she had another boy after me, born in 1971. Daddy at that time was over and back to England for work. So he would have been away for periods of time while my mammy reared us. Like most families, there wasn't a lot of income. You got by because the local shop would let you pay up for things, and you borrowed off neighbours and neighbours helped each other out. There was little luxury. We didn't have a TV; I don't remember a radio being on in the house. But I have very happy childhood memories. I don't have memories of growing up with poverty. I don't remember being hungry. I don't remember not having clothes. I don't remember not being happy. I think in those days because families were generally large, all the weans[120] were thrown into the street, so you made your fun on the streets, and that's the way it was. It was a very close-knit community.

My early memories include also aspects of the conflict, and the earliest ones would be British Army jeeps coming into the street. That would have been around '73 or '74; I would have been about four or five. And I remember Brits coming into the house, doing raids. They're not horrific memories; I don't think that they have traumatised me in any way. I don't remember being scared. To be honest with you, I remember being really excited. It was an event to fill an hour in the day, sort of thing. I remember on one occasion the British Army coming into the house and we had a cat – I got my first cat, it was a black cat – and I remember the cat making a leap for one of the British soldiers. It jumped on his head and this wee soldier nearly went berserk. And then it leapt from his head onto the curtains and my ma nearly went berserk! 'Never mind the Brit, watch my curtains!' you know.

Because there was a lack of amenities in Creggan and a lot of the fathers were away working, my mammy and a few other residents – I think it was probably mainly women – got together and formed a tenants' association. They started demanding that these basic amenities be put in place. That was the beginning of my mammy's introduction to community activism and politics – demanding that roads be tarmacked, provision of parks and local schools, for example. My mammy, around 1974, also joined the SDLP.[121] I suppose that's the beginning of my memories as well, of adults coming into the house, meetings being convened. And the reason I remember them was because it was the only occasion there were biscuits or cake brought into

120 Wee ones, children.

121 Social Democratic and Labour Party.

the house, and there were china cups borrowed from one of the neighbours.

Around 1976, my brother Donncha was arrested in the town and then they came and raided the house. Then a year later, they came and arrested John. I remember John's arrest; he was in the house. There was uproar in the street. So by 1977, my mammy ended up with two boys in jail. I remember on Saturdays she used to be away. She used to go to Belfast to visit the jail. I used to think she got on an aeroplane, for some reason! And she always brought back Chester bread and wee baps. I wouldn't look at them now, but we loved them; it was a treat. They were on remand in the Crum[122] at first. Then I remember a lot more activity around the house, a lot of meetings taking place. I remember Father Faul[123] coming to the house, for example. That brought us onto the street protests around the no-wash, blanket campaign. My ma just dragged us to protests, although I don't think, to be honest, she had to drag us; it was just something to do and it was exciting. There was at least one day a week when we used to go to a protest in the town, down in the centre of the town. Those few years for me were filled with riots on the streets, protests, a lot of activity around the house.

My mammy left the SDLP because the SDLP had basically refused to come out and support the prisoners, as did the Catholic Church. I specifically remember going to Mass in Creggan and you're sitting waiting for the priest to do the homily because you couldn't wait to get up and walk out. Probably a lot of teenagers who would have got away with not going to Mass in those days came to Mass deliberately to get up because the priest used to criticise what the prisoners were doing. So we used to walk out, and my mammy let us walk out. She walked out as well. Another reason my ma left the SDLP was that during Donncha's interrogation when he was arrested, a senior member of the SDLP asked my ma to go to his house and there was an RUC constable sitting there, and basically they were looking for my ma to force Donncha to do some kind of a deal.

She then became active in the Relatives' Action Committees.[124] They were mainly made up of relatives; there was a lot of prisoners at that time. My ma

---

122 Crumlin Road Jail in Belfast.

123 Father Denis Faul was highly active in civil-rights and human-rights issues during the conflict in Northern Ireland. Along with Father Brian Brady and Father Raymond Murray, he was one of a small number of Catholic priests who documented first-hand accounts of state human-rights abuses as part of a range of campaigns for justice.

124 Groups, mainly consisting of women relatives of prisoners, who campaigned on behalf of republican prisoners during the blanket protest of the late 1970s which led to the 1980 and 1981 hunger strikes for political status.

was away a lot in those years and my daddy was around. My daddy more or less looked after us and my mammy was the activist. My mammy also lost her oldest child in 1974; he was killed by a drunk driver. Also in 1977, another brother who was doing his O-Levels at the time at the College[125] – he would have been just going on sixteen – the cops came looking for him. The cops and the Brits had the College surrounded, but a local priest smuggled him out in the boot of the car and he was taken to Dublin. And he didn't come back from Dublin until the mid-'80s. She had lost one son, two in jail, one was forced into exile in Dublin and the rest of us were at home being looked after mainly by my father.

That rolls us on to 1980–81, the first hunger strike. My abiding memories of that are a lot of street activity, a lot of riots. And that time for me was the first time I had a sense of death; I had a sense of the seriousness of war. Up to then, it was exciting and you didn't really sense any danger, no fear around it, but the hunger strike was the turning point for me. And I know it was for a lot of other people that age, because people were dying and you got your first sense of 'hold on a minute, this is actually very serious'. We had moved round the corner to a four-bedroom house because I had got to the age where I needed my own room. I remember a lot of evenings sitting outside the house, maybe to twelve o'clock at night, on the steps because there was nobody else there except me and my wee brother; everybody else was out. I was afraid to stay in the house. I felt safer sitting outside. A lot of riots, a lot of protests, a lot of marches around that time. I don't think it affected our primary-school education. I did my 11-plus and ended up going to grammar school.

My mum was away a lot. She was at meetings. She went to Europe in '77–78 on a tour with the Relatives' Action Committee to try and draw attention to what was happening here in the jails. During the time she was away on tour, her father died, so she had to come back early. She went to America as well. They got speaking rights at the European Parliament and they did a protest at Strasbourg.

My mum tells the story that when she was away in Europe or America, there was a neighbour on our street who had a phone, Kathleen Mahon. And she phoned Kathleen Mahon and, of course, we were all over. She says I came on the phone and got on to her because there was no self-raising flour in the house. If that's any barometer of normality, obviously I wasn't too upset; I was getting on with my baking. I just feel I had a normal childhood; I wouldn't

125 St Columb's College, Catholic grammar school for boys in Derry.

feel hard done by. We weren't any different from any other family. People got very little. So in that sense, I don't feel that we were put out, and maybe it was because so many families were going through the same thing. I would say there was at least half a dozen families in that one street that had people in jail.

Raids became a part of life; that's just the way it was. We were all used to taking things from house to house so that when the Brits were raiding they were away ahead of them and back round by the time they were leaving. That was done by families in the street that weren't republican. The full street rallied. At the end of the day, you were going to support each other against the Brits, no matter what it was. There would have been families in our street who would have said to themselves, 'Well, I certainly wouldn't support what the IRA's doing.' Nevertheless, they would have supported the family in that situation.

That changed in the aftermath of the hunger strike and because the Church forced people to take a position. I think my mammy had words with Bishop Daly[126] because the Church had instructed all the clergy at that time to take a position in opposition to the prisoners. The Relatives' Action Committee then – it was actually my mammy and two younger women – did a protest in the grounds of the Cathedral. The three of them stood with blankets outside the chapel in the grounds of the Cathedral. That had a big effect. Your middle-class Catholics were disgusted. You can imagine it. I remember collecting the PDF[127] outside Creggan chapel at that time as well. I remember thinking: 'These people are going to Mass, and they're supposed to be good, but they're walking past me and they're not putting any money into the box.' They actually made comments; they would make criticisms, and snub you, give you dirty looks. Every Sunday, we would have been outside the chapel collecting the PDF. We all had our different Masses to do. Whatever weans were left in the house had to chip in.

I spent five years of secondary education at Thornhill.[128] I just felt very out of place from the day I went to Thornhill. There was a snobbery there; there

126 Father (later Bishop) Edward Daly was based at St Eugene's Cathedral in Derry. He was at the centre of one of the most iconic images to come out of the conflict, waving a white, blood-stained handkerchief as a group of men carried the body of Jackie Duddy, shot dead by British paratroopers on Bloody Sunday, 30 January 1972.

127 Prisoners' Dependants Fund, which collected money for the support of republican prisoners and their families.

128 Thornhill College, Catholic grammar school for girls in Derry.

definitely was a middle-class culture there, and you could definitely distinguish between those who had and those who hadn't. I went in with a second-hand uniform, and they had introduced a new gabardine at that time, so anyone wearing a gabardine, you knew that their family had money. Most of the girls going from the likes of Creggan or the Bog[129] were wearing the old ones. A lot of the teachers were quite middle class. There was one teacher who did speech and drama, and it was compulsory, you had to do it; her idol was Margaret Thatcher. To me, even at that age, she was the enemy; she was the cause of everything that was going on, and this woman was making us stand up and practise speaking like Margaret Thatcher! It was just anathema to me.

I hated being there. I didn't work. The only subject I worked at was Irish, and part of that was my rebelliousness. I remember references being made to me and another girl in my class whose brother was in jail; a couple of girls made comments one day. It was your classic situation; it was a Catholic grammar school and we don't want politics coming into the school. So they were taking you out of your 'normal' environment and bringing you here and you had to then transform yourself and fit into that environment, which is probably what I hated about it so much.

I did all the teenage things. My ma will tell you I was a nightmare; I was probably more work than any of the boys. I did all the teenage drinking and running to discos, not coming home until two in the morning, piercing my ears. So I had a typical teenage life, despite being in the middle of a really intensive conflict. But because it was a really intensive conflict in the '80s still, a lot of my peer group – they were a couple of years older than us, but we did socialise together – a lot of the fellows we were hanging around with at the time were killed as volunteers.[130] The conflict on the street was still very live for me, even as a teenager. And because you were losing friends at that age and you were losing other friends going to jail, you made that choice, whether you were going to become part of it; if you didn't become part of it, you were effectively stepping outside of a complete culture you were familiar with, including family and friends and the entire community.

When I was seventeen, I went to America to live. There were a few women out there who were activists, and one of them was a lecturer in New York and

---

129 The Bogside, a nationalist working-class area in Derry, the site of the Battle of the Bogside in 1969, the Free Derry No Go area of the early 1970s, and the killing of fourteen civil rights marchers on Bloody Sunday in 1972.

130 Members of the IRA, and other combatant groups, referred to themselves as volunteers.

she asked me to come along and speak to a group of her students about what it was like as a young woman growing up. I was just talking the way I'm talking now. And I had just been through Castlereagh[131] earlier that year and I was talking about that as normal as talking about what sort of coffee you like. It was the questions that the students were asking and the horror on their faces, like, 'How could they do that to you?'

That was the first time that I had that exposure, of being able to look outside in. And I was able to say: 'Hold on a minute. We have normalised that: we have accepted it; we have put up with the abuses.'

For someone else, that was: 'That's an abuse of your human rights.'

And I'm going: 'Welcome to the North!' I didn't say that at the time; I wasn't that cynical. But it was the first time I had that exposure.

After the hunger strike, my mother got a job in a book shop and she also did tutoring for an adult literacy class. So my mammy worked full time. She couldn't have not worked then; she'd got used to leading a really active life. We were all at secondary school, the younger ones, so she didn't need to be at home. She saved up the money and she was able to buy a house. She obviously was thinking ahead at that time, because the boys were getting out of jail. We had a four-bedroom house in Creggan, and she knew the boys would want their own space. So she bought a five-bedroom house down in the Bog. And, of course, the boys got out of jail and didn't want to live in the house!

She also set up a women's co-operative: Templemore Co-operative. She was trying to create work for local women because the shirt factories were all starting to close. My ma saw a wee niche for making Irish dancing costumes. So she set up the co-op in '85 or '86. I was involved in the beginnings of it; I used to do sewing myself. It was down in Dove House. She had also set up Dove House. That was an old people's home that was lying vacant. She and a few other residents fought a campaign to get that re-opened as a community resource centre. Then out of Dove House she set up the Templemore Craft Co-op. They didn't get any funding from the IFI[132] or anywhere. They lasted three or four years.

My mammy joined Sinn Féin in the '80s. She was elected to the city council in 1989 and she loved that because she was dealing with day-to-day issues on the ground. I think she did one and a half terms in the council and then she was elected to the Assembly. I don't think she liked that as much. It was

131 Castlereagh Holding Centre, Belfast, where police interrogated people they had arrested.

132 International Fund for Ireland, set up in 1986 to fund reconciliation initiatives.

taking somebody who loves working on the ground, developing local projects and asking them to go to Stormont. And, of course, she was coming up to retirement age anyway, so she retired a few years ago. She still does a bit of writing for the local newspaper and is still an active member of Sinn Féin.

We slag my ma. We say, 'If you were doing that now, you'd be up on child neglect.' But you have to put it into the context of the time. She was forced into circumstances that weren't her doing. She had little choice in her own life. Did she do her best? There were times I would say to her, 'Why didn't you let my da go out and do the activism? Because you loved it. You were getting out of the house.' And she probably did. She'd just given birth to nine weans. You can understand that. I would probably crack after three.

Most women in my ma's situation didn't have those opportunities. Most women wouldn't have got to Europe; most women wouldn't have got that trip to America. I remember looking at a photo of her and she was six stone. The anguish that she must have felt about what the two boys were being put through in jail. That would have been enough to drive a lot of mothers to drink or other unhealthy coping strategies. Her way of dealing with that was to get out and be active, and that's what kept her going. So I would say, alongside all that anguish, she enjoyed the activism as well.

If I'd been living through the times my mammy was, would I have done what she did? Probably.

Following in the Footsteps

The area that I came from, the family that I came from and the activity that was going on in that area, I don't think I really had any choice.

Billy McQuiston

Billy McQuiston

Son of William McQuiston

William McQuiston was a UDA commander in the Highfield area of West Belfast. His son Billy followed him into the organisation and into jail. As the peace process developed, Billy, known as 'Twister', became involved in community development and cross-community work. Billy McQuiston was born in 1958.

When the Troubles started, I was living in Highfield Estate. We moved to Highfield Estate in 1966, I think it was, when I was about eight years of age. Because it is an interface area surrounded on three sides by Catholic nationalist areas, there was like a siege mentality. We had the barricades up in the area, where men were defending the area at night. I was only a nipper at the time. To me, it was such an exciting thing. It was like a game of Cowboys and Indians. I used to run around with the men who were on the barricades. I would have brought them tea, gone to the shop and got cigarettes. To me, it was a big adventure that was going on in the area at the time.

In 1972, I was heading into the town centre on a Saturday afternoon. I was fifteen. Me and my friends used to go into the city centre to buy records, get a meal and basically hang around on a Saturday afternoon. On my way down to the town that Saturday, there was a bomb on the Shankill Road. The Balmoral Showrooms were blown up.[133] We were on the scene at the time. We were there when they were digging for the bodies. We didn't go into the town that day. We went back home and discussed what we'd seen. We knew there was an organisation just starting off in the area called the Ulster Defence Association. We knew that their meetings were the next day, Sunday, in a local hall. So we went and offered our services. I have to say that the reason we knew that was because my father was heavily involved with the vigilantes, manning the barricades. My father was the UDA commander in the area at that time.

133 On 11 December 1971, a bomb exploded in the Balmoral Furniture Showrooms on the Shankill Road, injuring nineteen people and killing two men and two young children aged two years and seventeen months respectively. Although no organisation ever claimed it, it was believed to have been carried out by the IRA.

We were accepted into the junior wing of the Ulster Defence Association. But because of our age, we weren't allowed to do operations. We were involved in things like training; we were sent on assault courses. During the UWC strike[134] we were involved in bringing food to people. There were times I would have been keeping a lookout when stuff was being moved, but very much on the periphery.

Around about September 1974, my father was arrested for a murder on the Springfield Road and he received a life sentence. There were mixed feelings. Number one, it was the loss of my father. I have to say that me and my father were always very close. I was the oldest son, the oldest of six children. I felt lost that my father had been arrested and that he was going to prison. I knew that he was going to prison for a long time. But I also felt a pride. 'My father has proven that he's doing his bit.' To me, he was a hero.

To be honest, when I look back on it, I felt that I had to live up to his name. 'My father's a life-sentence prisoner now and I have to live up to that name.' So I got heavily involved then in the military side of the Ulster Defence Association. Pretty quickly, I started rising up the ranks within the organisation. My father wasn't too overjoyed at my activities outside and he tried his best to curtail the activities that I did. He realised early on that he couldn't, that I was steeped in it, that that was the course that I was on. But he made me promise as the oldest son that I wouldn't let any of the other children join paramilitary organisations. So we didn't. As far as my father was concerned at that time, he was going to be in prison for a long time, and the way I was behaving I was going to prison and he didn't want any of the other brothers to be in prison.

My girlfriend was pregnant. She didn't really want to marry because of the life that I was leading then; she thought she was going to be left on her own at some stage. Eventually, I persuaded her to get married. We were only married about ten days when I was arrested robbing a bank in Crumlin village. I was actually informed on. We went into the bank and the police and army knew we were coming. They surrounded the bank and arrested us. I remember the morning that I went out to rob the bank I told her that I was going a message,

134 The Ulster Workers' Council was an amalgam of loyalist political and paramilitary groups which opposed the power-sharing executive that had been elected to run the devolved government in Northern Ireland. In May 1974, the UWC organised a general strike with the purpose of bringing down the government. With the help of widespread paramilitary involvement and the reticence of the British Army to intervene, the strike was successful; two weeks after it began, the government resigned.

and that I would be back about lunchtime. Bearing in mind that she was eight months pregnant at this time, I said that when I came back, we would go and buy the pram for the child. Eventually, when I did come back, the child was in school! I received eight years in prison.

That was the first time I was in prison. Prison held no fear for me. At that time, four members of my family were in prison. I had lots of friends that were in prison. As a matter of fact, I would have been at the prison at least once a week on visits. I was involved in transporting things into the prison. I was steeped in prison activities even before I went to prison.

My father was in the compounds; I was in the H Blocks.[135] I was on the blanket protest at that time. I went on the blanket protest because I didn't believe that I was a criminal. I thought I was a political prisoner. I wanted to be with my father and my comrades over in the compounds. All the time in my head, specifically in my younger days, was that I had to live up to my father. If my father was in the compounds, then I was entitled to be in the compounds. I used to get a visit with my father on a Sunday morning, once about every six weeks, and my father would have brought me down stuff from the compounds. He would have brought me down tobacco, because you were only allowed a certain amount of tobacco in the H Blocks. He would also have brought down two Coke tins with poitín in them and the two of us would have had two hours together on a Sunday morning and had a wee drink of poitín and a bit of craic and filled each other in on family stuff. To say that I enjoyed my Sunday mornings would have been a bit of an understatement. It was the highlight of the month.

I was released from prison at Christmas 1980 and I was straight back into UDA activity. I was arrested again in 1982 for pistol-whipping a guy. I'd called to ask him questions about something and he tried to assault me and I assaulted him back and he told the police that I had a weapon. I got five years in prison again for that. During that five years in prison, I was on the segregation protest.[136] When I was sentenced, I was moved from Crumlin Road to the Maze Prison. At that time,

135 Prisoners sentenced before 1976 received political status and were housed in the Nissen-hut compounds of Long Kesh Prison. Those sentenced after March 1976 were classified as criminals and were housed in the newly built H Blocks adjoining the compounds and officially referred to as HMP The Maze. Most republican prisoners and some loyalists went on protest, objecting to being labelled criminals. They refused to wear prison clothes and were dressed solely in blankets and towels. This was known as the blanket protest.

136 Republican and loyalist prisoners objected to being integrated in the prison system and fought for segregation through various means, including a republican bomb that killed two loyalist prisoners in Crumlin Road Prison.

at the Maze Prison, you had *de facto* segregation. You were losing ten days remission for every month that you were there, but there was *de facto* segregation.[137] So what we did was that people who were 'near the gate', who had less time to serve, they were made orderlies, which meant that they were working, so they didn't lose remission. So, towards the end of my time I was made an orderly, which meant I was eligible for parole in the last six months of my sentence.

I came back from parole and was sent to Magilligan Prison. At that time, prisoners at Magilligan were still fighting for segregation. I was one of the people writing comms[138] up to Magilligan Prison, telling them, 'Do this, do that. Try this method, try that method.' So they moved me to Magilligan Prison and because I had been so involved with trying to direct operations down there, as soon as I got there, I was made UDA commander. I carried on the fight for segregation. I was sent to Magilligan Prison with about five months to serve and I ended up serving about fourteen months. Because of the whole fight for segregation, I lost remission. That culminated that we felt we had to hunger strike. I was on hunger strike thirty-one days for segregation. The government did a deal with us and the protest ended, which the government reneged on a couple of weeks later, which culminated in another protest taking part. But by that stage, I had been released from prison.

I was released from prison in 1986 and straight back into UDA activities again. Within about six months, I was back in prison on a charge of demanding money with menaces. I served seven months on remand in Crumlin Road Prison for that and was found not guilty. Released from there, and within the space of three or four months, I was back in prison again. I was caught in Portadown with weapons shortly after an armed robbery. I received eight years in prison for that. I came out of prison in 1991 and again, straight back into UDA activities.

There were several attempts made on my life. I was only out of prison about two weeks when the Provisional IRA sledgehammered my door and tried to kill me in the house. I ran up to the loft and they shot the house up trying to get me.

At that time, one of my roles was to collect the welfare money and give it out through the welfare officers. I was Brigade Welfare Officer, so I paid the company welfare officers the money for the people in prison and they paid the prisoners' families a small amount of money for buses and cigarettes for

137 One consequence of failing to comply with prison regulations for integrating prisoners was that prisoners lost remission privileges.

138 Communications, letters written on cigarette or toilet paper and smuggled out of prison.

the prisoners. I used to do that on a Saturday morning in the offices of the UDA on the Shankill Road. On that particular Saturday morning, one of the welfare officers came in and told me that he wanted to speak to me. I said to him, 'Come on down into the back room.' And he said to me, 'No, come on and we'll get a quick pint. It's just a wee yarn I want with you.'

So me and him left the place and we had just got to the corner when the building was blown up. I was left the building less than twenty seconds when it was blown up.[139] The Provisional IRA put out a statement saying that they were trying to kill the West Belfast Brigade of the UDA. The West Belfast Brigade of the UDA didn't meet in there on a Saturday morning. Saturday morning was specifically about welfare officers paying prisoners. That's all it was used for on Saturday mornings.

Shortly after that, there was talk that the Provisional IRA were making overtures to people that they wanted a ceasefire. This information was filtering back to loyalist paramilitaries. So there was a debate going on within the loyalist paramilitaries about ceasefires. My own view on it was, if the Provisional IRA call a ceasefire, we had won; we had beat them. So it was down to us to call a ceasefire as well. One of my friends said to me, 'Well, it's like two football teams; we can't go out onto the pitch if the other team isn't going to arrive.'

For me, if the UDA was calling a ceasefire, there wasn't any role for me any more in that part of it. So I became heavily involved in community development within the area that I come from. We formed an organisation called Prisoners in Partnership. Our motto is *From Defending to Mending*. We believed that the community had given us support in defending them through thirty-odd years, so we now needed to pay something back, we needed to mend the community, bearing in mind that the community was a front-line community, that two thirds of the housing stock was unoccupied because people didn't want to live there because it was on an interface.

One of the things that cropped up early in my career as a community development worker was that, because of the area that I come from, surrounded on three sides by nationalist republican areas, I kept coming up against the peace wall.[140] Interface violence was going on between young people. So I joined a

139 In October 1993, the IRA targeted Frizzell's fish shop on the Shankill Road, claiming that there was a meeting of UDA leaders taking place on the first floor. The bomb exploded prematurely, killing the owner, his daughter and eight other people, including one of the two IRA bombers.

140 There are dozens of so-called peace walls in Belfast, physical barriers separating nationalist and unionist working-class areas.

group which was called Springfield Inter-Community Development Projects. We discussed it among ourselves in Prisoners in Partnership and we knew that this cross-community group was going. It was about twenty community groups right along the interface. We thought that we needed to be in there to try and solve the problems that were happening along the interface. The first few meetings were very tense. I found myself sitting across the table from people whom I would have given my right arm to be that close to a couple of years previously! But we tried to form relationships and worked together on problems. So I've been involved in community development and cross-community development since about '94, '95. And that's what I'm at today.

I think other people expected things of me because of my background, because of my father. As well as my father, I also had two uncles in prison. So I felt I had to live up to the family name. I think people just expected that I would do it because of my family name and because of who I was. At times, people felt that they didn't have to ask me where I stood on things or would I be interested in getting involved in something. They took it for granted because of my name that I would. For me, it was a duty and an honour.

When I first got involved in community development, I thought that I needed to learn about community development. In order for me to do the job right, I needed an education. So I did a course through the Ulster People's College, which gave me a bit of a hunger for education. The type of person I am, when I get involved in something I want to do it to the best of my ability. When I got involved in cross-community work, I got involved in conflict-resolution studies. I ended up doing a two-year Diploma in Queen's: Community Development in a Divided Society. It was a course that suited me completely. I am also the chairperson of Prisoners in Partnership and I thought that in order that I would give the best that I could to ex-prisoners that I had to learn something about that. So I did a trauma-counselling course.

When I started getting an education, some of my old beliefs were slowly changing, certainly when I got involved in cross-community stuff. Before I got involved in inter-community stuff, as far as I was concerned there was a great big monolith on the other side of the road there that wanted to exterminate my people. And as far as I was concerned, I wanted to exterminate them because they wanted to exterminate me. When I started getting an education and I started meeting people from the other side of the wall, I started seeing that this wasn't the case. A lot of my views were changing drastically. I found myself sitting in offices, pubs, etc, talking about things and people were looking and me and saying, 'With your family history and your family background, how are you coming out with that? Your da wouldn't think like that.' That was said to me on numerous occasions: 'What would your da say if he heard you saying that?'

My father knew I was involved in this stuff. My father served sixteen and a half years and he was released from prison just before I was released in '92. So my father knew I was involved in this stuff. I think my father was proud of me. My father was saying, 'Look, he's doing stuff there and he's getting himself an education.' So my father was proud of me in that respect. But it was held against me at times. It came up in conversation with my father sometimes. He would have raked me: 'Away down there and talk to your fenian[141] mates! Away and get that sorted out!'

I remember coming up to the vote on the Good Friday Agreement,[142] I did an interview with the *Guardian*; it was on the front page, standing beside a UDA mural in Highfield. And the mural in Highfield said:

Present Peace Now Stills Our Hand,
Death No Longer Stalks Our Land.
Our Weapons Are Silent And Shall Remain,
But If Needed We Will Rise Again.

They took a photograph of me. Basically, the headline was that if I can sign up to this, anyone can. I was asked to do this because of my background, because of my family. A French film crew got the hold of this and they wanted to do an interview with me. I did the interview. They asked me about my background and I said about my father being in prison. So they asked could they interview my father. I said, 'You have to understand, my father left school when he was twelve; he doesn't have a great education. My father will speak, but he'll speak from his heart. You have to understand that. He's a simple man. He knows what he wants and he'll speak his mind.'

So I asked him to talk to them and he said, yes, he certainly would. During the interview he said, 'If the war's over, then the war's over. And it's incumbent on people like us to right the wrongs we did in the past.'

141 'Fenian' is a derogatory term for a Catholic; another such term is 'taig'.

142 On 22 May 1998, referenda were held separately in Northern Ireland and the Republic of Ireland to measure support for the Good Friday Agreement. Some 71% of people in the North and 94% in the Republic approved of the Agreement.

And I thought that was a great thing; I thought, 'He's got it together, here. He knows exactly.'

I've always kept that in my mind. For someone who wasn't politically aware or doesn't really have deep thoughts about things, it was very astute of him. He was fantastic during the whole interview. Some of the things he said were very deep and I wasn't expecting some of the things from him. At the end of the interview, the reporter said, 'What would happen if somebody shot Billy, there?'

And he said, 'I'd go out and kill two of them tomorrow night.'

You know, great up to that, but where did you go there, Dad? He was going fantastic up to there; where did that come in? But I can understand it, because he's a family man. My father was very family orientated. He wanted peace, but if someone was to harm one of his children, he would go back to war tomorrow.

He was out of my life from I was fifteen, but you have to bear in mind that when I wasn't in prison, I was visiting him every Friday. And when I was in prison, I was with him every couple of weeks. My father was heavily involved in UDA activity. My father would have been away for weeks on end. It caused problems with my mother. Him and my mother, towards the end, they just weren't speaking. When my father was arrested, my mother still went to visit my father, but they weren't really man and wife. After about ten years that my father was in prison, my mother got a separation from him. But she still went up to visit him every week.

After a while, she took up with another partner and that caused a lot of problems at home. For myself, personally, it didn't. When we were talking to my father about it, he said, 'Well, I'm not there. We weren't getting on, even.' The way my father looked at it, he was grateful that they stayed friends and that she used to go up to visit him. He didn't really have a big problem with it. Well, he told me that, but I suspected that might just have been him trying to put a brave face on it. I think it did hurt him a bit. He harboured in his head that they might get back together because she was coming up to visit him. And I think that's why my mother did get the separation, because I think she saw that because she was coming up, he thought there was going to be a reconciliation, and for her, it was never going to happen. When they separated and she met another partner after a while, that caused a big rift in the family. Myself personally, I was taking my father at his word and I knew that he was putting a brave face on it. But if that's the way he was going to look at it, then that's the way I wanted to look at it. I have one sister and four brothers and the family split on it. Some took my mother's side and some my father's side, although my father told them, 'That's your mother's new life.' My sister wouldn't even go to my mother's house if her partner was there.

I remember one time I went down to my mother's house and my mother said to me, 'I was up seeing your da today, and look what he gave me. It's a wee budgie, but there's something wrong with it. They were going to kill the wee budgie because there's something wrong with it, but your da gave it to me.'

And I looked in the cage, and there was this thing and it looked nothing at all like a budgie. It had a big long neck; it had a big giant head. Its feet were like eagle's feet; they were like talons. And in total it had about twenty feathers. It was almost completely bald. And I said, 'He's taking the hand out of her.' I was down in my mother's house about four days later and I said to her, 'What about the wee budgie?'

And she said, 'Don't be starting about the wee budgie.'

I said, 'Why? What's up?'

She said her partner had come in from work and it started shouting his name: 'He's a baldy bastard! He's a baldy bastard!' My father had taught the 'budgie' to say it! But my mother took it in good spirit.

She got remarried and my father would have been friends with them. He would have gone for a drink with the two of them. But he didn't go to the wedding because my sister made such a fuss that my father didn't go. As far as my sister is concerned, that person doesn't exist. My mother and father should be still together.

My mother never wanted me involved in any of that activity. She wanted nothing at all to do with paramilitaries and didn't want us to be involved with paramilitaries. But I have to say that my mother, like most mothers, is like a mother tiger when it comes to her children. My mother has actually two criminal offences against her through the prison protests. Once during the protest for segregation in the Maze, she was in a protest at Shaftesbury Square, and when the police came to lift her off the street, she started beating them with her shopping bag. She was done for assault. While she didn't at any time agree with anything that we did, she certainly would have fought for anything she could to get us better conditions.

Would I do it all again? I would think that I would have to do it. I felt that I had to defend my area. My father was in prison for defending his area; it was my duty to carry on that activity. I felt that totally and I think I would do exactly the same again. Would I carry out the same actions knowing what I know now, with the different views I have now because of my education? Probably not. Probably, we'd have tried to go about it a different way, politically or whatever. The area that I came from, the family that I came from and the activity that was going on in that area, I don't think I really had any other choice.

My child was born when I was on remand in Crumlin Road Prison. It was a great joy for me. From day one, I made it a point to try and have a relationship with that child. Her mother brought her up to visit as much as possible. Before she went to nursery, she was up every week. When she went to nursery, I changed my visits to a day she could come up. I remember the first time that I got out of prison on parole, I said to the wife, 'Don't be telling her that I'm getting out. I want to surprise her.'

She was at the school. The school was at the swimming lessons that day. The wife said to me, 'She's at the swimming baths, but the bus comes up about ten past two.'

So I went up outside the school and I was standing outside the school, waiting on the bus coming. And the bus came up the road. And I could see her looking at me; she was straining her neck. She got off the bus and she came running over the road. I took her down home. 'This is my daddy. My daddy's here for me.'

She was showing everybody. We were sitting in the house and it seemed every five minutes there were one or two children looking in through the window. I don't know where all these kids were coming from. And I said, 'What's going on here?'

And I heard her saying, 'I told you I had a daddy.'

We found out later on her peers in school were saying to her, 'You haven't got a daddy. If you have got a daddy, where is he? Why do we never see him?'

So she had made it a point to go round and get all her friends and say, 'Look, that's my daddy; I told you I had a daddy.' When I heard that, it almost broke my heart, because then I realised the hurt that I was causing my family. But it didn't stop me.

When I was in prison, my wife lived with her mother. Her mother lived across the street from the house that I had at that time. I had to move because of the attacks on it. My house was fortified. I had CCTV. I had steel shutters behind the doors. I had steel gates on the stairs. My daughter was playing in the street and she grazed her knee. She ran to her grandmother's house. Sometimes that would have affected me; she's my daughter, she should be coming to my house. But when I thought about it, if she'd run to my house, by the time the security was off the house, she would have bled to death. And she was used to going to her grandmother. From she was able to write at all, I wrote to her one letter a week and she wrote to me at least one letter a week. So we did have a relationship. But I am conscious that I missed a big lot of her life. I am conscious that I caused her hurt. And I'm quite conscious that I wasn't a normal father, so to speak. The crux of that is that I have a grandson. He's two and a half years of age now, and every single second that I can spend with him, I'll spend with him. I missed my daughter growing up, but I will not miss my grandson.

She has never ever said to me 'you weren't here' or anything like that. She has never said to me that she resented that I'd done that. She was born when I was in prison, so she was brought up with me always being in prison. She has said lately that even when I was out, I was still involved in the UDA activity, so she could never depend on me being in the house. School plays and things like that, I always did my best to be there, but because of the work I was involved in, sometimes I couldn't. It hurt me, but at that time, to be honest with you, I just was so immersed in the whole thing. I met people recently who were gang members from Haiti, and we were discussing changes in ex-combatants here and one of the Haitians said to me, 'Explain the difference for you now with your family.'

I said to him, 'My mindset has changed over the years.'

He said, 'Explain how your mindset has changed.'

I said, 'Well, ten years ago, I would have died for my daughter. Today I want to live for my grandson.'

At that time, that was my thought; I would have been glad to die for my daughter. That was nothing to her. That was actually going to cause her more grief. My mind has changed now; now I want to live for my grandson. That's the difference.

Martin Meehan

Son of Martin Meehan

Martin Meehan senior was a lifelong republican, having joined the IRA in 1966 at the age of twenty-one. During the peace process of the late 1990s, he was a member of the Ard Chomhairle (national executive committee) of Sinn Féin and an elected member of the Northern Ireland Assembly. He died in November 2007. Martin Meehan junior was born in 1968.

My father to me was, like everyone's father, a hero as a child. He was very distant at times because of the length of certain prison sentences he was going through. However, when he was on the outside, he was very kind, very much a hands-on kind of father. He would have ensured you got to school and did your homework. However, he didn't have much time to devote to us because of his activity in the IRA and his role which, throughout the '70s, was fairly prominent in North Belfast. In that regard, we didn't see so much of him.

I really got to know my father when I was arrested myself in late 1989. I was arrested seconds after a gun attack on the RUC in the Oldpark area. I received twelve years for possession of a rifle. I went to the H Blocks where my father was already serving fifteen years. It was strange because, when I walked down the courtyard of the H Block, walking up to the entrance, someone shouted out the window, 'Are you all right?'

And I shouted back, 'Yes.' And I said, 'Who's that?' I didn't know who it was. And he said, 'It's your da.'

I was pretty chuffed that he was going to be on the same wing; it was H4. I went onto the wing and he was pretty emotional because, number one, I had just received twelve years, and he was looking back on his own life. At this stage, it was 1990 and he had another four years left to serve, whereas I was facing another eight years. He couldn't rationalise this in his brain for a considerable period of time.

We became very firm friends inside. We discussed everything from A to Z regarding the family, regarding my brother and sisters, my mother dying – she died when she was thirty-five in 1977 of cancer. We discussed politics, the military strategy of the IRA, drugs, social problems, everything. We spent the guts of three years together on the same wing, so we got to know each other extremely well. At times it was difficult because there's twenty-five men on a wing together in an H Block and me and my da were two of them. But I gave him his space and he gave me my space whenever each one of us wanted it. We walked round and round the yard like two goldfish in a bowl. We sat outside in the evenings and discussed things with other people. He was a great mixer, great craic, loved talking to younger prisoners, loved telling stories, not just about himself, about everything. He just loved life and got on pretty well with the screws; they all respected him, apart from the bigoted ones. Most prisoners respected him, whether it be loyalists or republicans. He was just a character, a real character.

He got out in January '94, and from when he got out, there wasn't much contact. But he was up once a month to see me, sent parcels up, letters every week, cards, postcards wherever he was going to – never failed to look after me. When I got out of jail, I moved back into his house in '96. I stayed there about three months. I just had to go and get my own place; I was too old to be living under my father's roof. He was never a drinker, never smoked; he'd have had a social drink, same as myself; I'm not a drinker, although I smoke a terrible lot. He was a very sociable guy, but there was a sadness in his eyes all the time. When I sat and looked at him, whether it be in jail or outside, there was always this sadness. And I could never figure out what it was. It must have been because of all the things that he had experienced.

I was very proud of him. He could have been a better father, obviously. He was in jail altogether twenty-two years. He was first arrested during the civil rights marches in '68 in Derry and he received six months for assaulting an RUC man. Then he was interned, escaped, on the run for about nine months, got recaptured in Ardoyne, back in again; he was the first person convicted of membership[143] and got three years for that. As soon as his three-year sentence was up, they released him and two weeks later he was re-arrested and re-interned, and he was the last internee to be released, around about Christmas 1975.

As I said earlier, my mother died in '77. She wasn't a republican, not at all. But she supported my da one hundred per cent. She was very much Catholic, very loyal to him, very loyal to us. But unfortunately, she got cancer. Never

143 Under Section 19 of the Northern Ireland Emergency Provisions Act 1973, membership of a proscribed organisation carried a mandatory minimum jail sentence of six months.

smoked, never drank – stomach cancer. Thirty-five when she died. My kids know about their grandmother dying; that's part of life. I remember a lot of things about my mother. My brother and my sister and I would discuss wee things. On her anniversary, we would put the notice in the paper so that people would remember her, to say a couple of prayers for her. I'm not a Mass goer because of my politics, ie the socialism part of it.

My da went back in again in '79. Prison that time was very difficult, because the family knew he was totally innocent of the charge that he was convicted of: kidnapping an informer. He didn't do it. We knew he didn't do it. We were with him that day in Newcastle, County Down, all that day. He wasn't even in Ardoyne. He lost his mother while he was inside and he wasn't permitted to attend the funeral and that devastated him. He also went on hunger strike for sixty-six days to prove his innocence, and the last six days he refused water also. And if it hadn't been for the intervention of Cardinal Ó Fiaich,[144] he would have been dead, because, as you know, Bobby Sands did sixty-six days. He was a very, very determined person, very headstrong, very loyal to the movement, to the army and to the Ardoyne community as well. He would have done anything to defend it. So in that regard, I would be very proud of him.

He got released in 1985, was out for approximately nine months. There was a British soldier abducted by vigilantes on 11 July 1986; he and another guy were acting suspiciously near the church in Ardoyne. No-one knew who they were; they thought they were loyalists. They tried to abduct the two of them, got one, and it turned out he happened to be a British soldier. The fellow was handed over to the IRA and the following day, my father and two other republicans were arrested in a street nearby, directly parallel to the house. He got fifteen years for kidnapping again. He had a career in kidnapping, as the judge said!

I had an older brother and two sisters. My grandmother raised us, his mother. She moved into the family home and took the mother's role. Shortly before his arrest in '79 for kidnapping the informer, he took up with another woman, Briege, and they got married in '85 when he got released. We stayed at home for a couple of years and the family disintegrated because my da was in serving twelve years, we'd this other woman; she had a baby with my da. Things just didn't work out in terms of us and her. I ended up in St Pat's Training School

144 Cardinal Tomás Ó Fiaich was the Primate of the Catholic Church in Ireland from 1978 until his death in 1990.

on the Glen Road in care.[145] My younger sister, she ended up in care as well, in Middletown, County Armagh.[146] The older brother, he ended up packing his bags and going to England; he stayed in London about seventeen years.

I was born in '68, so I grew up with the war situation. However, I was a Catholic, and I was a strong Catholic; my mother embedded that in me. To come to an arrangement in your mind that you may have to go out and kill people or you may have to hurt people, that was a hard thing to do. Also, my da's reputation was pretty high and I didn't want to undermine that in any capacity, and I also wasn't sure of what way I would be perceived as being an IRA volunteer. But, when I read the Green Book,[147] and I was given lectures and I was speaking to people, I just decided that people could take me as they find me. I'm not my da, even though I'm named after him.

Ardoyne was a hard place to grow up, very little money around, a lot of poverty, particularly if your father was in jail. You only got a couple of pounds a week for the family. It was very hard times. But the community were very strong, very tight. People still to this day would be very friendly. Families have been here for a hundred years. Everyone knows everyone. When I started doing Sinn Féin work when I was sixteen, seventeen, people weren't surprised seeing me painting graffiti on a wall – 'Vote Sinn Féin' – or putting a poster up or rapping a door. They weren't surprised to see me standing outside the Sinn Féin centre taking complaints. I would have been recognised from an early age as a republican, even though I might not have understood the full context of republicanism at sixteen.

The hunger-strike period catapulted a lot of people from my generation into the IRA. There was a young lad, Danny Barrett, a couple of streets away that was shot dead by the British Army from an observation post; the guy was sitting on his own garden wall, doing nothing.[148] He was fifteen, shot dead. The British soldier wasn't arrested, wasn't questioned, literally got away with murder. His friends, people I went to school with, were catapulted into the IRA. An

145 St Patrick's Training School on the Glen Road in Belfast was for orphaned, neglected or abandoned Catholic boys. Although children and young people with criminal records were not sent there, those in danger of being involved in criminality were.

146 St Joseph's Training School in Middletown, County Armagh, was the girls' equivalent of St Patrick's mentioned above.

147 A training and induction manual for new IRA volunteers.

148 The incident occurred on 9 July 1981. The British Army claimed that the teenager was armed, a claim denied by the police during the inquest.

awful lot of people joined the IRA in response to Thatcher. It politicised an entire working-class generation. An unbelievable amount of people that were determined that Irish people were treated as dirt and we weren't prepared to accept that. And the only way we could fight was through the IRA. The INLA in Ardoyne was non-existent then. The IRA was the only way forward.

I volunteered my services to the IRA when I was eighteen. I joined Sinn Féin when I was sixteen, so I was in the movement two years prior to joining the IRA. My family, even my extended family, would all be very socialistic. They all would be community orientated, strongly working class, dedicated to helping others. To me, joining the republican movement was an extension of that. To me, they were my family, my extended family. Close friends of mine also joined the IRA. So in that regard, it was a natural progression for me growing up.

Also, when I got stopped in the street by the Brits or by the cops, 'What's your name?'

'Martin Meehan.'

'Oh …'

Baton across the head! I was beaten, harassed, assaulted. When I fought back, I ended up in court. It was just a nightmare situation. The way I felt was 'fight fire with fire'. If they want to act the big guy, I can act the big guy, too.

I preferred to be seen as a Sinn Féin member. I was not one of these ones who had IRA tattooed on their forehead. I would have been one of these guys who sneaked in a back door in the dead of night rather than in broad daylight. I was more recognisable as a Sinn Féin person, which I enjoyed because, number one, it gave me security, number two, it gave me an added aspect of my life because being in children's homes, I was able to speak to people better. I was able to help people more because I had been through that phase of my life – particularly anti-social elements. I was able to speak to them on a one-to-one rather than looking down my nose at them. Not that I was anti-social; I was in the home because of a care order. But I was able to understand a lot of things: crime, poverty, social aspects to things.

I don't think anybody in the IRA expected me to be like my father. It was a different war in the '80s than it was in the early '70s. Plus, I was a highly politicised volunteer. There was really no politics in the early '70s; it was all military. So it was a different context; it was a different kind of a war. And also, coming into the ceasefire period, operations were scaled back; they were more targeted. In my da's day, there were rifles sitting close by. When Brits or cops entered the area, they were quick to access and volunteers were quick to act. In my day, there was a lot of bureaucracy. There were fewer loyalist attacks. There were no mass gun attacks the way it was in the early '70s. So in that regard, the IRA and IRA operations were more secretive and there weren't as many. So people didn't expect me to be another Martin Meehan. And I didn't want to be a leader; I just wanted to be an ordinary person, which I still am – very private. I'm not one of those who would stick my neck out or be on the television. It's not me. My daddy loved the limelight; I don't. I'm not one of these media babes. I don't like the lifestyle. I like to do my republican stuff in private rather than publicly.

My grandfather Jimmy, my da's da, was in the IRA in the 1930s. He was a close friend of Seán McCaughey, who died on hunger strike in 1946 in Portlaoise. He was interned in 1939 and he was held in Crumlin Road Jail until 1945. I have spoken to people from that period, old veterans, and my granda was a very dedicated volunteer, very well respected. It was even more secretive back then. He was a docker; he was a member of the dockers' union, same as my father. My great uncle was Irish Trade Union Secretary in the '60s, Joe Meehan. My great grandfather was involved with the unions as well, back with Larkin and Connolly, and in the dockers' strike in 1907,[149] he was secretary in Belfast. So you have those links; republicanism and socialism are to me intertwined. My grandfather died in 1967, before I was born. I never met him, unfortunately. I don't know very much about him; my grandmother never really spoke about him because he was a very private person. My great-uncle, Martin Clarke, was captured in the same house Brendan Behan[150] was captured in in Coventry. He received twelve years and he did the entire twelve years in solitary confinement, refused to wear a prison uniform. All his sons became IRA volunteers also. They lived in Ballymurphy in the '60s and '70s. Ironically, his sons stayed with the Officials.[151] In later years, after the ceasefire, we had a few Christmas drinks with them, my da and me. We had a lot of banter about Sinn Féin U-turns!

149 In 1907, led by union organiser Jim Larkin, 3,000 dockers in Belfast went on strike against their pay and conditions, and in particular the casual nature of their work. They were joined by other workers, including the carters, and hundreds of police in effect mutinied in support of a colleague who refused to accompany and protect a strike-breaking carter.

150 Brendan Behan, an Irish poet, novelist and playwright. As a teenager, he joined the IRA and was arrested in Britain in possession of explosives. He served three years in Borstal, as a result of which he wrote his famous book *Borstal Boy*.

151 In 1969, the IRA split. The smaller breakaway faction became known as the Provisionals, while the section that remained loyal to the leadership became known as the Officials.

That's the type of family I came from; so it's definitely in my blood. So is militarism, because my great-grandfather died in the Battle of the Somme. This is on my grandmother's side, her father. He was in the Inniskilling Fusiliers. He was a National Volunteer.[152] Ironically, when Roy Garland[153] was speaking to my father about this issue, he happened to mention the incident and his name to Gusty Spence in a later interview. So Gusty went, without being prompted, and got all the details – where his grave was etc – and sent it through Roy Garland to my da. My da was chuffed that he had found out where he was buried. He and the cousins who had been Officials went together and laid wreaths. And he took some soil from the grave and put it on his mother's grave back in Milltown.[154] He wanted me to go along with him and we should have been going this year sometime, but he died last year, so we'll never make that journey.

You have that militarism, socialism, republicanism throughout the history of the family. So I wasn't at all surprised that I had those kinds of feelings. In a normal society, I probably would have gone and joined the army. But unfortunately, if you join the army in this country, you go to jail or you get shot dead. To me, the IRA *was* the army, and it was a real army. People may look at history differently, but if it hadn't been for the IRA, there'd be no Ardoyne. Ardoyne would have been demolished in 1969; that's the reality. If it hadn't, it would have been demolished in internment week in '71.

It's hard to go to jail. It's hard to be interrogated in Castlereagh. It's hard to be harassed. It's hard to be beaten up. There's no romanticism involved. The romanticism about joining the IRA leaves you shortly after joining the IRA. It's a very hard life. It's a selfless life. A lot of people in the media talk about making money and godfathers of the IRA – where is it? I've never seen any money. I can't get a job. No-one would want to employ me.

My kids know I've been in prison. A couple of friends of mine had called and were talking and mentioned us being in jail. 'When we were in jail' was just a flippant remark. Later that night, my son asked me why was I in jail. This

152 The Irish Volunteers were formed in support of Home Rule for Ireland in the early twentieth century. With the outbreak of WWI, some followed the leadership of the Irish Republican Brotherhood and staged a rebellion against British rule in Ireland in 1916. Others, retitled the National Volunteers, joined British Army regiments and participated in the war.

153 Roy Garland, a unionist writer and political commentator who has written a biography of the leader of the Ulster Volunteer Force in the mid-1960s in Northern Ireland, Gusty Spence.

154 Milltown, Belfast's main Catholic cemetery.

was a few years back and I explained it to him. But where kids are concerned, if someone is in jail, it's for something bad. I tried my best to explain it to him. When his grandfather died and he went up to the house and he saw his granda lying with the flag over him and a guard of honour, he started asking more questions. At the minute, he's eleven; he's fully aware of the situation. I call the police the police; I don't call them peelers. They have been at the door numerous times handing me death threats;[155] I treat them with as much respect as I possibly can. I don't rant and rave. Me and my wife don't discuss politics in the house. I don't agree with discussing politics in the house. As far as I'm concerned, if I want to discuss politics, I'll go on the internet or go out and speak to people. I think a home should be for the family. I'm different to my father in that regard also. I go on holidays every year, we have a decent life, you don't have to worry about going back to jail. It's a different life nowadays. It's great. You don't see soldiers walking up and down the street.

I want my kids to be happy. And I've instilled that in them. The 11-plus was last week. My son is in P7.[156] He didn't do the 11-plus because me and his mother don't agree with it. I want them to be happy. That's the most important thing. I couldn't care less what politics they grow into if I can instil in them the happiness factor and just how to treat people. All the time, I would say to my kids, 'You are lucky.'

They say: 'Why do you always say that?'

And I say, 'Look at the kids in Africa. Look at the kids in India. You are lucky.' I bore them saying it, but I feel that you have to say things like that because kids have to realise that it is a hard world out there when they grow up. It's not about academic education. Education starts at home.

I voted 'Yes' for the Good Friday Agreement. I was in Sinn Féin up until last year; I had a heart attack shortly after my da died and I'm not really physically able to run about as I used to, so I'm no longer in Sinn Féin. I agreed with going into Stormont,[157] I agreed with everything up until a point – police. I find it extremely difficult, even though my da stood up in the Ard

155 Notifying him that they had information that loyalists were planning to harm him.

156 Primary 7, the final year of primary education at the end of which children move on to secondary education. Those who pass an examination called the 11-plus (because P7 children are around the age of eleven) acquire a place in the more prestigious grammar schools while everyone else goes on to attend secondary schools.

157 As a result of the Good Friday Agreement of 1998, a devolved Assembly and government were formed in which Sinn Féin participated. The Assembly sits at Stormont Castle in Belfast.

Fheis[158] and spoke in favour of it, because coming from the socialist end, police forces worldwide are not really geared towards the working class. Their reason for existence is not really to help the working class. That in itself is a difficulty, supporting people who murder people in this area. If the people within the RUC who murdered people were made accountable, that would be a step forward. I also find it very hard with the Special Branch, a force within a force, death threats. In 2001, my home was fired into by loyalists. My details have been handed over hundreds of times. I live in a kind of security cocoon still; I can't move out of Ardoyne. The trust factor isn't there. But that's just my personal opinion. I don't disagree with Sinn Féin's opinion.

I think times are a lot better than they were. I would like to see the police being more community orientated. Then and only then will people like me be able to trust. I come from the hunger-strike generation. That's the only difficulty I have with the whole peace process. Decommissioning?[159] I couldn't care less about the weapons. I'm glad in a way, because I never wanted it to end up like South Africa, that people can grab hold of weapons and do whatever they want with them. I'm glad they're gone and nobody can get hold of them. Who wants another Omagh,[160] for instance?

---

158 Ard Fheis, the annual conference of a political party.

159 The subject of IRA decommissioning of weapons and explosives was a protracted issue during the peace process. The IRA finally decommissioned in 2005. In 2009 and 2010 respectively the UVF and UDA followed suit.

160 On 15 August 1998, the Real IRA exploded a car bomb in Omagh, County Tyrone, which killed twenty-nine people, including a woman pregnant with twins.

Flair Campbell

Son of Lily Campbell

Lily Campbell, who died in 2008 at the age of seventy-seven, was a lifelong republican. According to her obituary in the Andersonstown News *(17 March 2008), in the early 1970s she was in charge of communications for the Belfast Brigade of the IRA and for liaison between the Brigade and GHQ. Flair Campbell was born in 1959.*

My mother was Lily Martin. She was born in 1931. Her family was put out of Toome for being Catholic. They moved to Ballymacarrett in East Belfast and were put out of there as well and then they finally settled in the Short Strand. She grew up there and she loved it; she was very proud of where she came from. She met her husband, Phil Campbell, from the Markets; I think she met him at one of them céilís.[161] They used to go on walks up the Cavehill, things that people don't do now. It's a bit of a walk, when you think, from the Strand up the Cavehill and back. Then she married and moved to Andersonstown in the late '50s. She had eight kids.

Her father, Seán Martin, was killed in an explosion in the Short Strand in 1940 when she was nine. He was a volunteer in the IRA and there was a faulty grenade in the house; they tried to throw it out the window but there were kids playing in the street. So, from what I hear, he told everybody to go out and then he was the only one that was killed. She was young; she said that she didn't really remember too much about it. The only thing she remembered was the sense of occasion, probably getting new clothes, and the horses, the horse-drawn carriage.

My da, Phil, was interned in the 1950s, just going into the '60s. And when he got out, like most republicans at the time, he found it kinda hard to get work. Even in the Strand, before they moved to Andersonstown, they'd hear most of the locals talking about the discrimination against Catholics in the

161 Irish dancing. During the mid-twentieth century, dance sessions were highly popular with young nationalists in the North.

shipyard or Sirocco Works.[162] The Short Strand had massive unemployment, yet was surrounded by industry and the hundreds marching past your door every morning going to work. You can imagine the friction, where people don't understand the politics of the situation and are just going, 'Get you out and get a job.'

'Where am I going to get a job? I'd have to change my name. I'd have to change my school.'[163] Which is one of the great things today: you see kids with Irish names, not scared of where they came from, educated through the Irish language, confident, and it's probably only due to people who fought for legislation and change.

There were eight in our family. Eamonn died in '63. He drowned. He was seven. I was about four or five when he died. At Andersonstown Leisure Centre, there used to be a river there, the Chalky River we called it, running from the Black Mountain through Andersonstown and on to the sea. And we used to cross over the river and play about. It used to lead down to a lovely wee oasis, a wee island, down at the back of the leisure centre. You got all sorts of brilliant nests and birds down there, summer and winter. We had birds that came to Andersonstown, yellow hammers, corncrakes, sand martins and curlews – birds you never see now. We used to play in it, me and my friend Jim and our Eamonn. And one day I couldn't get across to the river because of the traffic on the road. And I remember just sitting down beside Barney's shop and a woman gave me 2d[164] and I bought an everlasting lolly and I walked back up to the house. I just remember all this hullabaloo in the house and then, next thing, a wee white coffin. The only time I ever saw my mother crying was at the cupboard at the electric box underneath the stairs when she was looking at Eamonn's school books one day.

Coming into the mid- to late '60s, there was a lot of activity all around us, people out protesting and that. On the morning of internment, I remember being in the same street as my da, rioting with the Brits, and him looking at me and saying, 'Get home!' I suppose he was scared for me.

---

162 The Harland and Wolff shipyard and the Sirocco engineering works were among the largest employers in Northern Ireland; both were based in East Belfast. For most of their existence, they employed a very small minority of Catholic workers.

163 Names and school attended can provide strong clues to the religious background of a person in Northern Ireland.

164 Two pence, before the decimalisation of currency.

The next-door neighbours were out protesting. Everyone was out. Women were gathering stones in bin lids and throwing them down beside you. The British soldiers were in the grounds of St Agnes' church. They took over our school, De La Salle Christian Brothers in Edenmore Drive.

From the time the British Army took over in that summer term, I didn't go back till the next March and got abuse for it from the teachers. I ended up getting two black eyes and a busted face from one of the teachers. He was punching me; he knocked me unconscious, put me in hospital. My da went up to the school and the teacher hid from him. That was the Christian Brothers School for you! A friend of mine from school days, Danny, was the only wee lad in our class who came out then to help me; he got beat up, too. They expelled me. I went to the army[165] and they said, 'You're better off taking it through the system because he'll get a record and he'll not be able to teach again.' So I did go through the system, and every teacher in the school, bar one, signed a statement saying that I was a bad lad in the school. One teacher, our form teacher, refused to sign it. When Danny went back to school, they made him sit in the assembly hall for three days on his own for trying to stop the teacher beating me.

A year later, on the very morning my da died, me and Jonty spotted the same teacher on the Andersonstown Road, and we ended up putting him in hospital. We got charged and were going to be sent to jail only the teacher got up and said he understood the circumstances. We got heavily fined, and two years' probation. The teacher got off scot-free. This was 1975; I was just sixteen.

In the early '70s, Lily started to disappear out of the house. The older ones in the house looked after the younger ones. And more and more people started to come into the house, and meetings, and then weapons started coming into the house. And then the younger ones started getting involved. It was a bit awkward at times, because somebody was in the Sticks and somebody was in the Provos.[166] But then after the Sticks went on ceasefire, everybody gravitated towards the army.[167] That kind of resolved a lot of issues. It was very hard for my ma because she was always into education. She was always trying to get

165 IRA.

166 The republican movement split in 1970 over a number of issues, including the failure of the Dublin leadership to protect Northern nationalist areas in the attacks of the previous summer. Those who stayed with the Dublin leadership were called Sticks, Stickies or Officials, while the mainly Northern militants were known as the Provos, short for Provisionals.

167 Irish Republican Army, the 'Provos'.

us to stay at school. But you couldn't really devote the time that was necessary and be a volunteer; she was an active volunteer.[168] I knew that because of who she was running about with. And also I kind of ran about with her at times. She would let me help in certain things, like delivering messages; by that stage I could drive. So, it was handy, because she was a terrible driver.

I joined the Fianna[169] in 1971 at the age of thirteen. We were in the Boy Scouts in the '60s and everyone in that slua[170] of the scouts, bar one, joined the Fianna. It was an amazing jump from an organisation formed by Baden Powell over to one formed by Constance Markievicz. You'd internment, you had Motorman,[171] my da's brother Teddy was in jail and only released from Long Kesh to die – you had things happening every day. And the older ones were running about so it was kind of just, everybody, all hands on deck. I remember arguing with my mother; she was actually trying to stop me joining the IRA when one of my school mates was killed. He was only sixteen and a volunteer. And I was saying, 'Is it all right for other people's kids to go in the army but not your own?'

It was a big dilemma. She kind of just from that went, 'Do your own thing.'

In terms of us working together, it might have been easier for her that we weren't. She had to go on the run for a while. She had her own stuff to do; you were out of sight, out of mind. And when she heard the news and there was somebody arrested, somebody killed, she was wondering was that us.

Our paths hardly ever crossed when we were both active – only when she would say, 'Come on and give me a hand with this.'

Or I would say, 'Ma, would you drive me here?' Several different people, the likes of Brendan Hughes,[172] would later tell me things about her when he

---

168 Members of the IRA are known as volunteers. In Irish, the IRA is called Óglaigh na hÉireann, Volunteers of Ireland.

169 Na Fianna Éireann (warriors of Ireland), the youth wing of the IRA. It was formed in Dublin in 1909 by, among others, Countess Constance Markievicz, who later went on to be one of the military commanders in the 1916 Rising.

170 'Slua' is the Irish word for 'crowd'. It is also the name used for a group within the Fianna, in the same way as 'troop' is used for a group within the Boy Scouts.

171 Operation Motorman, in July 1972, was the move by the British Army to take over No Go areas: parts of Belfast and Derry controlled by the IRA.

172 Brendan Hughes, also known as 'The Dark', was reputedly Officer Commanding the IRA in Belfast in the mid-1970s. In 1980, he led the first hunger strike of republican prisoners in Long Kesh for the return of political status. He died in 2008.

was working with her. We were all just local, wherever local was. My ma was on a different level.

And it was only in later stages when I went into jail and came back out again, people were going, 'I used to work with your ma.' It was all respect, or slagging about her driving!

When my da died, my ma had to go to work for money; she was cleaning people's houses in the '60s, but then she went to work in the brewery canteen and in the canteen in the Christian Brothers School on the Glen Road. She was running back and forward. And then she went to night classes and started studying. I remember coming in and my ma would be sitting sleeping over books. 'Come on, Ma.'

'No, I've got to get this essay done.' After all those kids, after my da dying, after all she went through, she went back to school and got her degree. It was brilliant. Then she taught for a while in St Joseph's and then she went into Connolly House.[173] She was involved in setting up Twinbrook Tenants' Association.

It was about 1977 when I told her, 'Ma, I gotta go; I gotta leave.'

And she just said, 'Okay.' She was just that knackered, that exhausted. The next time I got in touch, they'd moved from Andersonstown to Twinbrook. I asked her why she moved and she said it was the constant raiding, harassment in the streets. My two sisters were in Armagh Jail, I was on the run. The house was getting raided sometimes two or three times a week. So she moved to Twinbrook, but it only took a while before she started being raided again. Then the SAS[174] hit the house, shot John, a neighbour, in the hand. They tied our Maura up in a chair and they threw her wee child across the room. The child was in a terrible state for a while, lost her hair as a result.

I was away for a while and got arrested and held in Portlaoise Prison from 1980 to 1986. My two sisters were in Armagh Prison in the late '70s. The three of us would have been out of the house at that stage. Lily had a hard ould time, because she would have been active as well. And she'd be travelling up to Armagh Jail and then having to take the journey down to Portlaoise. And at that time, you hadn't got the roads that you have now. Petrol was cheaper up here so they used to put this big drum full of petrol in the back of the minibus along with all the visiting relatives of the prisoners! Fair play

173 The offices of Sinn Féin in Andersonstown, West Belfast. It is named after the Irish socialist and signatory of the Declaration of Independence in 1916, James Connolly.

174 Special Air Service, special forces regiment of the British Army.

to the men who drove the buses, because they were an obvious and easy target for the forces against you. They were stopped, harassed, tortured, by the forces of 'law and order', even when they weren't working. The targeting was routine. You can imagine having to drive families to jail and you're getting up in the morning and you're checking under your car and minibus for bombs and you're thinking of your own family and you're thinking of all the people on the bus. You were watching what cars were coming up alongside you. They were very brave men.

Politics was never discussed as a subject, yet our parents were sure of their standing and gave us a good sense of justice. My ma seemed to know who was right and who was wrong. She would say, 'Who's helping who and why do they want to help?'

I remember a begging box coming into the house; the priests used to send you boxes for church collections to keep their houses lovely regardless of what poor conditions the people lived in. Every so often, there would be a new box delivered to your house and the boxes were numbered, so the clergy knew which house it went into and what returns were coming out. And it must have been the change of the new priest coming in who'd gone through the books. I remember this priest coming to the door one day to chastise the household. My ma wasn't ignorant; she let him in. The next thing, there was a whole big row and she scolded him and the wealth of the Catholic Church and she chased him. Both of us felt great that day. She resented the Catholic Church.

She resented the position of women in society. She would talk about some of the roles for volunteers as a woman. Lucky enough, she was an older woman, even though she was only in her late thirties, early forties, but that would have been twenty years older than most working with her. Once, she told me that she was passing on a comm[175] to this guy and he said, 'I don't take orders from a woman.'

She wouldn't tell me who it was. I said, 'What did you say to him?' And she said, 'I just left him. Stupid!'

She resented all the power structures that oppressed. I think she resented the fact that she had to get married and have kids. That was your lot. She used to say, 'We didn't know what poverty was because we didn't know what riches were. Our riches were in our imagination and our education.' She

175 Communication. During the no-wash protest in the late 1970s, prisoners in the H Blocks wrote letters on toilet paper or cigarette papers, wrapped them in cellophane, hid them in body orifices and passed them to visitors for delivery on the outside.

loved reading. And that was one of the things in the later stages, any time she was forced to be in hospital, you would see her stopping reading. You'd see the depression coming on. We needed to get her out of there. We needed to get her back home, get her reading again.

Even in her latter years, she was learning the Irish language. She wasn't great on her feet and her memory was kind of going. We went up to Oideas Gael[176] in Donegal for a week. When you go into an Irish class, they split you off, whatever level of Gaelic you have. We met this woman at lunchtime and she was saying, when you go into the class, they ask you what's your name, where are you from, what's your hobbies, who do you like, who you admire and who you don't like and so on. And she says, 'There's this wee woman in our class, and this guy says he admired Maggie Thatcher. And this wee woman went, "*Gabh mo leithscéal. Caithfidh mé ará seo i mBéarla*[177] just in case you don't understand. Were you dropped on your head, son, when you were a child? How could you admire someone like that?"'

Another day we were heading into Killybegs. There was a woman thumbing on the side of the road. We stopped to give her a lift and she got into the car. I said, 'Where are you from?'

She said, 'I'm from New Mexico. Do you know it?'

My ma says, 'New Mexico?'

'Yeah, do you know it?'

'No I don't, but I know it's hot and that it belongs to Mexico.' That was her on holiday; she was great at speaking her mind, but she could be tactless and hard at times.

It must have been very hard for our parents and our grandparents to live under the apartheid state that was there, that was created in the 1920s. The unionist monolith: it must have been so oppressive. Like people not being able to give their kids the names they wanted to give them, not being able to let them walk down this street or that street, not being able to see them have a job, not being able to argue back with the forces of law and order. Like in any oppressive system, you had to keep your head down. Everything had to be done under cover. Talking about freedom or independence had to be under cover. It's not all that long ago.

I'd like to say the love she gave us was at a different level than you'd see of people who are expressive today, people who hold their kids, praise and hug

176 An Irish language and cultural centre in Glencolumbcille, County Donegal.

177 'Excuse me. I'll put this in English.'

them. There was never that in the family. And she even said herself, even for her father as a child, maybe it's a good thing that you haven't got it in you to grieve. But I don't know about that. For her, from the '30s, being put out, going through the pogroms, then her da dying, then her son dying, then losing her husband through internment, then losing her husband, then losing her kids into jail, then she lost Ciaran, another son, in 2005. We couldn't tell her about Ciara, her grandchild, who was stabbed to death in 2007. It just would have wrecked her; she was going downhill. All through all that, she still found her way through education – always reading; some kind of solace, some kind of escape, some kind of connection to the world. And that's probably replicated in many a family right across the globe.

She died in March 2008. She was seventy-seven. She had had a heart attack, a stroke, diabetes, osteoporosis and rarely complained of her ailments even though in the last couple of years she needed constant care. I don't know how she hung on as long as she did.

We were lucky to have brave parents and an exceptional mother. She taught us the ability to critique, to ask questions. If you don't know, just ask. That's probably why we got hit all the time in school! Her ability to cut through crap I think was passed to her through her granny. My ma used to say you just have to look at how the British used 'divide and conquer' – you know, how such a small force could go in and take over a country like India and half the world. And people blame the Indians for being placid. That was their beauty. You should condemn Westminster for being a warmongering government. She was very sure of right and wrong in politics.

Robert

UVF Son of UVF Father

Both Robert and his father have served life sentences for conflict-related offences. Robert was born in 1956.

We grew up on the lower Shankill, very close to what would be the peace line now, Percy Street and Dover Street.[178] So obviously the Troubles had a big impact in that area. In 1968, with civil rights etc, I was only twelve. The only thing I remember about civil rights is trouble. I just know that after that, there were vigilante groups set up which my da was involved in. Being young and impressionable, I felt a bit of pride seeing my father out there defending the community. At that time I was involved in rioting and stuff that was going on, and probably my father was, too. It was actually years later I found out he was involved in the Ulster Volunteer Force. Not only my father, but wider members of my family would have been affiliated or would have supported that organisation. For me, it was like a natural progression. I don't think it had a bad impact on me. Looking back on my childhood, I wasn't going to bed at night worrying; it just became natural in those days.

When I became sixteen, I enrolled in the YCV.[179] I don't think my father was too happy, because by that time, it was 1972, and he probably saw what was happening in the country more than I would have at that young age – you know, the impact of what was going on. I know that he wasn't very happy that I had followed in his footsteps. I can remember the words he said to me: 'You do realise the road you've chosen; you will either die or go to prison.' But I wasn't the only one, I wasn't the only young lad out there.

I did have a great suspicion at that point that he was involved in the UVF because I had seen weapons about the house and I had seen my father being

178 In August 1969, mobs from the unionist Shankill Road attacked and burned down homes in the adjoining nationalist lower Falls Road. British troops were called in to restore order and erected barbed-wire barricades between the two areas. In time, this division was enhanced and now consists of a concrete, steel and wire 'peace wall', in places nine metres high.

179 Young Citizen Volunteers, the youth wing of the Ulster Volunteer Force.

stopped by the army and the police. And the men that used to come to the house, I knew about their involvement, too, so it was easy to put one and one together. At that time it wasn't something that was spoken about in public; it was quite secretive. It wasn't as free and easy as it would be today to talk about stuff like that. It was only because he knew that I had joined the YCV that I probably realised that he was probably involved deeper than what I knew. And then, after that, my involvement began as well. I always had great respect for my da. You always felt you didn't want to let him down. I'd say I definitely admired him, but I don't think that it ever came into my head that I sort of one day said, 'My da's in the UVF and because of that I want to be in the UVF.' I had my own mind; it was my own decision to join the YCV and it was my decision to follow through into the Ulster Volunteer Force when I was eighteen. He never influenced me, I will say that, in terms of pushing me towards anything. I just felt comfortable with it. I didn't think I had to do it because of my da.

In the early days, we belonged to the same platoon and he had some rank. I've never even asked him what it was. But when I was eighteen, I moved from that part to another part of the organisation. I felt I did a wee bit more than some other people, just to be seen as okay. I believed totally in what I was involved or I would never have joined.

The first time the house was raided was when I was about sixteen. Not probably as regular as a lot of other people's for some reason, but it was raided a few times over the years. It was part of life in those days. We weren't the only family; it was happening throughout Northern Ireland. At that time, you thought that you were part of that wider British fold, and it was the *British* army or the *British* police force; you were probably a bit schizophrenic. You thought that you were fighting for the same reason.

My mum was probably like the wife of any other paramilitary at that time; she just accepted it, too. It had to be done. She was quite loyalist herself, anyway, still is today. I don't think she has ever spoken to me about my joining up in all that time. I know she was very upset when I went to prison; that was very evident. But I cannot remember her any one time asking me anything; she just took it as read.

My dad ended up in prison in June 1977. He served about seventeen years. He got released about '93. There were a lot of arrests being made in 1977. Obviously, the police were looking for me at the time, so we had moved home. I remember I took a decision not to go and visit him when he was on remand for fear of myself being arrested. But eventually I went up; I went to see him one time on remand. I went up with my grandfather. The next time

I saw him, I was in prison myself. In November 1977 I was arrested. There were quite a lot arrested from the area I came from at that time. You were just waiting until they worked down the list. When I finally came through Castlereagh and went to Crumlin Road Prison, I was put in the base[180] and my father managed to come down and see me while I was in the base. I was put into a cell and then later on that night, I was moved up into a cell with my father, which was a very surreal experience. I didn't think it was just right that you were in prison with your father. You probably couldn't get up to the same things that other young men were getting up to in there. I know people say you're celibate when you go to prison, but I was *really* celibate. You couldn't get up to lots of skulduggery that maybe other young lads would have got up to. It didn't give me extra privileges; I felt it put extra pressure on me just simply because he was there.

Going to prison was hard, for him and the rest of my family, no doubt. I'd say they probably had a harder time than I did. If I look back to '77 in hindsight – I did this when I was in prison quite a few years anyway – you had a situation in my home where you had a very stable home life, which was very strange, given the things my father and I were up to. You had a full family at home, everybody working. Then all of a sudden, my mother lost her husband, she lost her eldest son, and home life then became very difficult for her. She then had two people to visit in prison, so financially it was very tight. I think she found it very hard to cope after a while and she ended up leaving my father, although she still visited me for a while, but it was very strained because I was my father's son. So I didn't see my mother for quite a few years. It was actually my first parole that I eventually sort of reconciled. On the whole, family members were supportive to different degrees. Some of them disagreed with the acts I carried out, but I was still a family member, whereas some of my family members totally agreed with what I did.

After your remand, you get your arraignment, so you don't have to appear in court as regularly. You're moved from Crumlin Road then to the H Blocks. So we were moved out to H Block 6. I went before my father because my arraignment was before his. I remember when he came down he was put into a different wing and again, for some reason, they came and moved me and put me back into a cell with him. But we were only there for a while and they decided to separate us, so they moved him to another wing. Eventually, the two of us got

180 After sentencing, a prisoner arriving in Crumlin Road Jail was held for the first night in a holding cell on the ground floor before allocation to a wing. This was known as the base.

sentenced. He received political status and I didn't, so he went to Long Kesh, the compound system, and I was put into the H Blocks, Maze Cellular.[181] After that, you were treated as if you were in two totally separate prisons. You may as well have been in prison in England, because the visiting arrangements were identical. The visits were brilliant; we really looked forward to them. We were allowed to write letters to each other, which we did when possible. During those times in the H Blocks, there was quite a lot of protesting going on, so there were times you lost your privileges and you had maybe only one letter per month and you had to decide: does that go to my father, my mother, my brother or a friend? To me, it was just a hazard of the life that I chose. It happened; you had to make the best of it. And I'm sure he did the same.

I know for a fact that when I went on a visit with my da, I didn't tell him everything that was happening to me, because you always had this thing in your head, you didn't want to worry somebody. And I've no doubt that he did the same with me. So we always tried to keep the visits on an up. I'm quite sure there were nights that, like myself, he was feeling down, but on those initial visits, because you only saw each other for a short period across a wide span, you didn't really talk about serious stuff. I think my father probably looked at my life more than his own. He had all this life beforehand – experience, marriage, children, etc – and I think he ended up with a great regret that I didn't. From I was just turned twenty-one until I was thirty-six, I spent those years, those formative years for home, marriage, children, whatever, that had all gone. But I was probably more pragmatic; I just accepted that that was that. I did what I did and I had to do the time for it.

There was a two-hospital system in the prison when we arrived. The compound men had their own hospital and we had ours in the H Blocks. Then they closed the one in the compounds, so that meant that anyone who was ill from the compound system went over to the H Block hospital. That was a way that we circumvented the visits. I could take sick and my father could take sick around the same time and you'd get a day or two in the prison hospital together. But I did take seriously ill. I spent ten months in hospital. I developed ulcerative

181 Internment without trial began in August 1971, with internees housed in Nissen huts at a former military establishment called Long Kesh, near Lisburn, about ten miles from Belfast. Later, when sentenced prisoners were conceded political status, they were imprisoned in Long Kesh. In the mid-1980s, H Blocks – prison units in the shape of the letter H – were built nearby for sentenced prisoners and the complex was known as Her Majesty's Prison The Maze, Cellular. Many prisoners, especially republicans, and their supporters continued to refer to the entire complex, including the H Blocks, as Long Kesh.

colitis, which required me to get an ileostomy, so I was quite ill. I think that was the saddest visit we ever had. It just so happened that before I was getting taken out to the hospital on the outside, to Musgrave Park,[182] I had a visit with my da and he was shocked because he hadn't seen me for, I think, six months. I'd lost so much weight; I think I had dropped down to nine stone. At the end of thirty minutes, there was no transport to bring us back to our relevant prisons and they still separated us – put him in a room and put me in a room, even though I was ill. Once the thirty minutes were up, the thirty minutes were up. I know it was very annoying to him because he went back and wrote a letter to me that night about how he was feeling. It was quite a long letter.

At the start I was so young, I was in the H Blocks, there were protests going on, you were probably a wee bit wilder, for want of a better word, whereas my father had been quite settled. Definitely, by the time I came back out of hospital, that was 1987, I think, I had ten years under my belt and my father had ten as well. By that time, you had mellowed; the regimes had changed; it was a lot easier being a prisoner in the H Blocks then.

There came a point about 1989 where I just wanted a change because it was starting to feel a bit stale for me. By that time, I had become involved in education, so my priorities were changing slightly. I did an honours degree when I was in and then I did an MSc when I came out. I decided to move to Maghaberry Prison.[183] Then there was a deal done with the remaining compound men, because they had obviously dwindled down to tens of people, that if they gave up their political status and moved to Maghaberry and into the same régime as myself, then they would be favourably looked at for release on their next case review.

In Maghaberry, we were on the same wing; he was just round the corner, but there was free association, so we could see each other every day, walk the exercise yard. We used to have a cup of tea and go and sit together in the cell and catch up on what really happened. We did become extremely close. There was the fact that we both went to prison and we still have it today, a great affinity for each other. To be able to sit down and talk to your father properly is fantastic, about things that really matter, about what's going on in his life, what's going on in mine.

---

182 Musgrave Park Hospital, a regular hospital with a separate section for the treatment of military personnel and prisoners.

183 Initially, in Maghaberry Prison, unlike in the H Blocks, there was no official segregation of loyalist and republican prisoners, and all prisoners there were seen as conforming.

He was very supportive of me all the time. In the compounds, they were able to do leatherwork, so they were able to have an income. There were fractures within the family, so in terms of my needs, in terms of clothing etc, my brother would have helped me out sometimes, but it mostly came from my father: a pair of training shoes, jeans, a pair of shorts. If I needed some educational books, some friends on the outside would have bought them for me, but also my father. The mathematical books were quite expensive, so my father would have paid for that, as well as other people. There was always that support. Even now. I'm greatly supportive of what has happened in Northern Ireland; so is my father. He is supportive of me within my work.[184] I can't remember a time lately when we would have had a difference. We definitely would have had differences before I went into prison. We weren't as close then because I was the Young Turk coming up. Probably the lifestyle I would have led then was totally different from my father's. It was only through being in prison with him for so long that that relationship deepened.

It turned out when my father went up for review, they didn't let him out; they kept him for another year. We were both actually going together on the same day for review, and because of this cosy deal that had been done with the compound men, it looked as if my father would get released and it was always expected that I would do another year. But when it came about, they released me and kept my father for another year. It was quite difficult to leave him. I was crying my eyes out. I don't know whether it was just leaving my dad or because I knew people that I'd spent all that time with in prison. It was a pull to leave that camaraderie and all those people behind.

It seemed to me my father came out and kicked his life off from the day he left it behind. He went back to the same type of work, back to the same type of hobbies. The only difference was he didn't bother with paramilitaries afterwards; I mean, he wasn't active militarily anymore. It's probably more lately, where my father is getting quite old, that we would sit down and talk quite a bit. I would say we look back with nostalgia. Although we were in different places and the regimes were totally different, on the real level we probably suffered the same stuff. We both got locked up at night, me in a cell and him in a compound, but the front door was still locked.

The experience definitely changed me. I hate this bit where people say you went to jail and you got educated. That presupposes you were stupid before

184 Robert is involved in community development in projects that have grown directly out of the peace process.

you went in or you didn't bother. I did go to a grammar school before I went in and I know from looking back that academically I was okay. I mightn't have been the smartest cookie, but I was okay. Even when I started to take up my education again when I was in prison, I found that I was quite ahead on some of the courses that were on offer. The lads that studied politics and sociology were probably further ahead than me, because I studied mathematics; politically there's not a lot of impact there. It was from reading other books that I got thinking what was it all about and why we were in – which I'm still struggling with today, to be honest. A big impact for me was moving away from here just as much as going to prison. I only spent six or seven days in Northern Ireland when I got released. I went to university in England and I eventually ended up staying there. I only went to do a year's course. I enjoyed the freedom of being out of jail, but I also enjoyed the freedom of being out of the Northern Ireland environment.

If I had a son, I wouldn't agree with him doing what I did. We have moved forward so much. I would disagree now with using violence as a means to an end. I think the conditions are here in Northern Ireland where young kids don't have to do that. At the time, at my age then, there wasn't a political thought in my head. I just saw my community under attack. But even those words I'm using now, I wouldn't have used then. It was totally different then: communities fighting every night, bombings, killings, doorstep shootings; the whole situation has vastly changed. I hear people saying that there is an element of youth running about out there who feel they have missed out on something, being involved in paramilitaries or going to prison. People like myself and others have a bit of responsibility there. Maybe over the years we have been too romantic about what it was like in prison. I've heard that from other people. Personally, I have never heard a young person say that to me. Maybe it's different characters I meet, but I personally have never heard a young person say that. In fact, most of the young kids haven't a clue. Now the kids mix freely, which didn't happen when I was growing up. That whole social change has had a big impact.

I have to be honest and say it wasn't all bad. What I found was that prison was split into three chunks. You had that rebellious period when you first went in, then this calm-down period with the realisation you're going to be there for a while; there was no such thing as an amnesty going to happen all of a sudden. Then you get a middle period where you see you're not going anywhere for a while; there was no light at the end of the tunnel – sentenced to life in prison with a twenty-five-year recommendation, so you sort of have in your head at that time you're going to do twenty-five years; you can't do anything about it. And then there's the last part when all of a sudden you start seeing people in before you getting out on parole. And then, wallop! You do get out on parole, you meet a girl.

Possibly my last two years were, for different reasons, as difficult as the first two years. You couldn't wait. You found it harder to concentrate because you were getting out a week at Christmas and maybe a week at the summer; you were living your life in six-month chunks. I've had a great life ever since. I don't want that to come across as flippant. It's just I've tried to move on as fast as I can because of how old I'm getting and try to help out wherever best I can. I've packed so much into the last few years that those years in jail are starting to recede in my memory.

I didn't create the situation; the situation created me. But the acts are mine personally. I can't complain then that I got caught, I got punished. You just have to accept it. I hear some people saying that we were all victims. But there is no way that I would see myself the same as the victim of one of my actions.

David Stitt

Son of David Stitt

David Stitt, the son of a UDA man of the same name, was born in 1971.

I'm the son of David Stitt, David Green Stitt; he gets 'Peaser' Stitt because 'peas are green'. My da's one of five brothers and one sister and they're from Comber Street in the Short Strand. They lived there up until 1969 when obviously things were getting a bit sticky. The Provisional IRA moved them out of their house. My dad came back home from work and the Provisional IRA had Comber Street cordoned off, with gunmen and a heavy machine gun at the top of the street. They were burning out Protestant homes in Comber Street and various other parts of Short Strand. When he came home, they had the furniture out in the middle of the street. He had a fight with a fellow who was supposedly his best friend, a fellow he grew up with, a Catholic guy. He was on the barricades on behalf of the IRA and he helped to move my da out of his house. To cut a long story short, they were given ten minutes to get whatever belongings they had out of the house and it was burned out.

That spurred my dad on to be more proactive against the Provisional IRA. He had an axe to grind; he got a wee bit bitter from then on. He joined his local defence association; there was no Ulster Defence Association then. In the early '70s, there were gun battles here, there and everywhere and he was active in that, him and his friends. They did as much as they could with as little as they had. My dad used to tell me they had nothing. They had maybe a long shotgun and a Martini Henry rifle and an old .45 First World War British Army officer's pistol. He and his brother Tommy were involved in starting the LPA[185] up. My dad's brothers were all active: Ronnie, Billy, Freddie, Tommy – they were all active members of the UDA, fighters, activists on the front line.

I came along in 1971 and in 1973 was the first UDA show of strength. I was out on that. I don't remember, but I was there with full combat gear on and my wee boots, walking with my da with his combat gear on and he held my hand.

185 Loyalist Prisoners' Association, a support group for UDA prisoners and ex-prisoners.

So the UDA and loyalist paramilitarism were just part of my life from an early age. My dad brought me everywhere with him. Me and my da would be like two brothers. I'd a really good relationship with him when I was growing up. I remember him telling me stories about the police hitting the house when I was two or three years old. We've had rifles in the house and machine guns in the attic, but the police just didn't find them. And running around in the car with me, moving gear when I was in the car in the baby seat. This is just the way it had to be then. My da would go down to UDA headquarters in East Belfast. I would go down with him. I remember it as well. I'd go down there every Saturday, sitting with all the big lads, Andy Tyrie, the Supreme Commander as they called him then, of the UDA.[186] I've seen it all first-hand. I've seen all the big lads, and that was just part of my life from then on.

My mother had a brother, Sidney Leeman, 'Soup' Leeman, from East Belfast. He's dead now. This guy was a freedom fighter extraordinaire. This guy was on the front line. He was the man in East Belfast. I was impressed by that guy. I was going up to the jail every week with my dad, who ran the prisoners' buses. I was up seeing relatives of mine. My uncles were in. My dad's friends were in. Little did I know when I was coming up to visit people when I was two or three years old that I was smuggling stuff in. I was going up every Saturday to see people I didn't know, but then I built up relations with them. I looked up to those men, defenders of our community. It was impregnated in me from an early age. Teachers used to be asking: 'What do you want to be when you grow up?' I wanted to be a UDA man when I grew up. It's as simple as that. I couldn't wait until I was the right age to join a loyalist paramilitary organisation.

I was originally from the Newtownards Road. We lived in Sanders Street opposite the Short Strand until about 1974. In 1974, I moved to Tullycarnet.[187] In our housing estate, we all knew somebody who was involved. When I was sixteen, I watched what Michael Stone did in Milltown Cemetery[188] and that

---

186 Andy Tyrie was the leader of the UDA from 1973 until forced out in 1988 by hardliners for being too political.

187 A working-class housing estate in East Belfast.

188 In March 1988, three IRA members, who had been shot dead by undercover British agents while on active service in Gibraltar, were buried in Milltown Cemetery in West Belfast. As their bodies were being lowered into the graves, loyalist Michael Stone attacked the mourners with guns and grenades, killing three people. He was chased, caught and beaten by the crowd before being rescued by the police.

impressed me big time. I said, 'If this man can do this, I can do something to contribute to the loyalist cause.'

So I joined my local active service unit of the UDA in 1988. I put my hand up for anything and everything that they had to offer. I held a job down; I was a welder in the shipyard. I worked during the day and as soon as I came home, I washed and changed. I always touched base with my local commander that night to see what we had on offer. From an early age we were firearms training – machine guns, pistols, incendiary devices, blast bombs, basic military training and targeting. My dad taught me how to shoot a rifle, about composure, about your breathing, about squeezing the trigger. You were an apprentice paramilitary. You were getting your training from older, more experienced men. The Protestant community was getting it bad at that stage of the game because the IRA was hitting Enniskillen,[189] Teebane.[190] The UFF[191] hit back with various retaliations and took the war to the IRA and the Catholic community.

The first time my dad knew I was in the UDA was when I was sixteen; he found a .357 pistol in my hot press. I was coming back later on that night to get it to be dug in out of the road again. I came back in that night about eleven o'clock. I was looking in the hot press at the back of the towels; it wasn't there! Then my da was at my shoulder. 'What are you looking for?'

I said, 'Nothing.'

He said, 'I know what you're looking for. Come on down the stairs.' So we went down the stairs into the kitchen and he said, 'Don't be bringing any guns into this house ever again. That can put you into jail just like that. Don't be so stupid.'

I said, 'Where is it? I need it.' We had a garden, then a garden fence and a bit of waste land at the back of our house.

He said, 'Hold on. It's out in the waste land.' He had dug it in 'cause he knew the craic. He had his pyjamas on – out, over the garden fence, with a coal shovel in his hand, dug it up and handed it back to me. So he knew from then on that I was involved. And that's when the house started getting hit regularly.

---

189 On Remembrance Sunday, 8 November 1987, the IRA bombed the war memorial in Enniskillen, County Fermanagh, killing eleven people.

190 In 1992, the IRA bombed a bus carrying construction workers at Teebane crossroads, between Omagh and Cookstown, County Tyrone. Eight people were killed.

191 Ulster Freedom Fighters, a *nom-de-guerre* used by the UDA when claiming military operations. It was an illegal organisation, unlike the UDA which was not banned until 1992.

During those years, from sixteen to twenty-one, if there was stuff going on, if there was somebody got murdered or an attempted murder, if your name got caught in the loop, you were in Castlereagh. The police were coming up to your house, five o'clock rap, into the Land Rover and you were away to Castlereagh. If Castlereagh was full up, they took you to Gough Barracks[192] for the statutory two-day interviews, extended sometimes to seven days by the Secretary of State. The first time the house was hit was when I was fifteen during the 'Ulster Says No' period,[193] when police officers were being intimidated out of their houses and there were riots everywhere. I was arrested under the Prevention of Terrorism Act. I was taken to Strandtown[194] because I was a juvenile.

When my dad found the pistol in the hot press, he knew I was fully fledged. He had a yarn with me a couple of weeks later, asked me what team I was in, because obviously his friends were still there and he wanted me to be looked after. I told him what battalion I was in and who was my commander and he went and had a wee word with my commander. He always said to me, 'Don't be getting involved, because there are only two places you're going to go: jail or Roselawn'[195] He wasn't too happy about it, but then he learned to warm to it as I got to eighteen, nineteen, twenty; I was becoming a young man myself then and he didn't treat me like a wee boy anymore. He knew what I was doing. He was sort of proud of me in a way, what I was doing. It wasn't the way it was in the early '70s where they all went out and had a bit of a gun battle at the top of the street. There was more thought involved. There was a load of serious stuff going on. He sort of warmed to it.

To buy weapons, the UDA and UFF needed money. We had to have a lot of money to keep a military campaign going. The war didn't just run on its own. So in 1993, my military commander had organised an armed robbery of a Cash and Carry. Seven of us went out to do it. The police had been tipped off beforehand by an informer within our ranks. They were lying in wait. They let us go into the place, let us do our stuff with an articulated lorry which we

192 Castlereagh and Gough Barracks were two RUC holding, or interrogation, centres in Belfast and Armagh respectively.

193 In 1985 the Anglo-Irish Agreement for the first time gave the government of the Republic of Ireland some official say in the affairs of Northern Ireland. Unionists united to protest loudly under the slogan 'Ulster Says No', organising mass demonstrations, disruptions of the meetings of public bodies, and attacks on members of the police force, the RUC.

194 An RUC station in East Belfast.

195 A cemetery in East Belfast.

had hired out, filled it up – we were in there for about an hour. Got the cash and the cigarettes and went to go outside the place and the police were waiting outside. They popped up, undercover police and army, and opened fire on us. They fired thirty-five shots at us. Me and my cousin got away on foot. They chased us, firing at us down the Ravenhill Road. I was arrested about two miles away from the scene at the gates of the Ormeau Park. I was walking through the gates when an undercover car came down, two of them bounced out, got the pistols out, put the pistols to my head and got me to the ground. I was in Castlereagh Holding Centre for three days.

Before you go to the court to be formally charged, you have an informal visit in the police station. My mum was a Sunday School teacher and a Christian for twenty-five years, right throughout my life. They came up to visit me. My mum turned round to me and she said, 'Did you sink any of your mates?'

'No.'

'Did you make a statement?'

'No.'

She told me there and then she was proud of me. And my dad was proud of me. It was a great thing for us; if you did get caught with anything, you didn't sink your own people. You held your own self-respect when you went in. And you didn't make a statement. Yes, you were caught bang to rights, but you didn't take anyone else down with you. I was charged with armed robbery.

When I went into prison in 1993, I hadn't been in prison before. Okay, I was suspected of things, but I'd no criminal record at all. I had a job. My best friends, wee Terry Mercer – he's dead now, committed suicide – and Jimmy Birch, would come up and visit me once a month. My mum and dad were up every week, bringing me food parcels. My da was smuggling stuff in for me; that's what he did in the early '70s when he went up to visit people. I was only in jail about three weeks when I got my arm broken by the police going through the tunnel from the jail to the court.[196] My cousin was slabbering to the police. A fight broke out. They put me in a restraint lock and I got my arm broken. Mum and Dad came up and saw me with my arm in a cast; they were none too happy. They thought it was the prison officers. My mum went up to the prison officers in the visiting area and gave them a bit of what for. I said, 'Mum, it wasn't them; it was the police.' They were raging and they wanted to help me. They were scared for me because they knew republicans had planted a bomb in

196 A tunnel ran from the Crumlin Road Prison under the main road to the Crumlin Road Courthouse. Prisoners went through the tunnel to emerge in the dock of the court.

the canteen. I was in jail and I still wasn't safe. So they were worried sick.

When we were in the Crumlin Road Jail, the Provisional IRA planted bombs in the canteen.[197] We were trying to be active back against them; we were trying to smuggle in explosives also. It was 23-hour lock-up. 'Self-segregation', it was called, for twenty-three hours and you had an hour's exercise every day. There were 103 loyalists when I was on remand in Crumlin Road Jail in 1993 and thirty-five republicans. That shows you how much a threat loyalists were at that stage. Loyalists outnumbered republicans three to one. When they were out in the yard for an hour, we were in the canteen having our dinner, and when we were out in the yard, they were in the canteen. It was controlled movement. On the landings, you had loyalist and republican cells alternating. You were next door to these guys, but we never associated with each other. You fought; you were trying to kill each other. When we were going to visits, when we saw republicans, we were running for them, and likewise they were running for us. It was survival of the fittest. They were blowing us up and we were trying to get explosives in. Obviously, republicans had more capabilities with Semtex, so we went to attack them, because we outnumbered them three to one. We used to do them with galvanised steel mop buckets, improvised weapons like razor blades in the toothbrush. We went to town on these guys when we got them. And likewise when they'd have got one loyalist out on the landing when he was going to a visit and there were four of them together, they'd have rushed that one loyalist and given him the tanking of his life. That's the way it was; we had a deep hatred of each other.

We were in the Crumlin Road Jail when the Shankill Road bomb[198] went off. We were walking around the yard; next thing, we heard the bomb go off and that was not nice. There were IRA men living next door; we wanted to get at them, it was as simple as that. We were trying to kill them.

The IRA got segregation for sentenced prisoners through their hunger strikes and dirty protest. We decided to go for segregation for remand prisoners. When you're on remand, you're innocent until proven guilty – well, that's what they say. You're guilty until proven innocent as far as I'm concerned. We

197 There was a protracted campaign in Crumlin Road Prison for segregation between loyalist and republican prisoners.

198 On 23 October 1993, the IRA sent two members with a bomb into Frizzell's fish shop on the Shankill Road, intending to blow up UDA members thought to be meeting above the shop. The bomb exploded prematurely, killing one of the bombers and nine other people in the shop, including the owner and his daughter.

said we're all UDA men here: we're innocent until proven guilty; we don't want to be living next door to these republicans; we're political prisoners, we want political status, remand or not.

In June 1994, there were 103 of us there at the time; seventy in A wing and thirty in B wing. A wing's exercise yard was massive, probably one football pitch long. B wing's yard was a small triangular affair, very small; about a third of a football pitch. There was a massive, big steel gate which kept A wing and B wing separate. The loyalist prisoners, both UVF and UDA, decided that we would go for segregation. So the OCs[199] of the different wings decided we would have a riot; we would take the yard. We were lobbying our politicians, we were lobbying the number one governor for segregation. They were literally pishing up our legs; they didn't care. It got to the stage we were fighting every day: the tensions were high; it was just after the Shankill bombing; we decided to go for it.

When we were out in the yard that night, we had agreed not to come in. We'd already collected weapons from up in the cells; people had small iron bars, improvised knives, petrol bombs. We had access to petrol; we would steal petrol – the lighter-fuel petrol. We weren't coming in: we were tooled up; we were going to fight with the riot team; this was our protest for segregation. They called us to lock and we didn't respond. They said they were going to send the riot team in. They had a shelter with a corrugated-iron roof, a flat roof, probably about fifty-foot long by fifteen feet wide, on steel poles. When it rained and we were out in the yard, we stood underneath this to keep dry. No sides on it because obviously, they needed to see you, the security cameras; this thing was on stilts. So we decided to break this down and use the corrugated-iron roof for a ramp to get up on that big roof. If we got up on the roof, the riot teams couldn't get us.

Meanwhile, while we were pushing this down, rocking it forward and back, me and Torrens Knight, who did the Greysteel massacre as they call it[200] – Ice Man is his nickname – and another wee man called Glen from the Shankill, climbed up onto the first roof and up the drainpipes and got onto the big A-wing roof. Meanwhile, the boys down in the yard got the corrugated iron, they got it broke down and the poles that were holding it up, they used them to bust the locks of this big gate that was segregating A wing from B wing. So the prisoners were all together then. Then they used the big corrugated-steel ramp to get up on the first roof; it was like a boiler house. Everybody got up

199 OC, Officer Commanding the prisoners.

200 In revenge for the Shankill bombing, the UDA attacked a bar in Greysteel, County Derry, in October 1993, killing eight people. Torrens Knight got eight life sentences for the attack.

on the boiler-house roof, pulled the ramp up to the boiler-house roof and then put it from there onto the main roof and a hundred-odd people walked up on it. We stripped the roof, Bangor Blue slates. The British Army was drafted in. We slated the British Army. The prison officers' riot team came over to an adjacent wing opposite; we slated them, too. Then they despatched the British Army up and they started firing rubber bullets at us from the other wing. They weren't getting us down; there was no way.

We stayed up there for a night. It was on the news and I'm standing up on the apex of the roof, smoking away. My ma didn't know I smoked. And here she was, 'Look, there's our David and he's smoking!' I'm standing on top of the roof with a big stick and all she was worried about was that I was smoking a cigarette! They jumped in the car and came up to see me.

You could see people over there, you could see figures, but you couldn't make out who they really were. There was a crowd of loyalist supporters and a loyalist flute band. It was a great ould time, to tell you the truth. Negotiations went on. There was an Ulster Unionist councillor on the Shankill called Joe Coggle. We had A wing stripped of its slates; you could see right through into the attic. He came up into the attic and the OCs of the wings went down and negotiated with him. We were there for conditions: we wanted segregated; we had the piss pots in the cells then for slopping out. Crumlin Road was infested with cockroaches. The number one governor promised us the moon and the stars to get us down. We got down. He got us locked up and next week, 'No, you're not getting anything; tough.' That didn't stop us, though.

The OCs decided to wreck the jail from the inside. We'll never get up on that roof again. The cells – make them uninhabitable. We'd steel beds. Break the bed ends off your bed like an iron bar; make a hole in the wall. If you can make a hole in the wall, get into the next cell, make a hole in that wall. It was loyalist, republican, loyalist, loyalist, loyalist, because there were only thirty-five of them. Everybody do it; A and B wing. It was all organised; we're going to do it at eight o'clock at night when the screws had gone home. There were only the night guards there. Somebody shouted out the door, 'Right, go for it,' and we were away. We busted our bed ends; everybody had, like, a long iron bar for a digging tool. I was doubled up in the cell with a fellow called Mark from Tullycarnet. Off we went, through the walls. There was a republican next door called Paddy. We were blasting away at the walls; they were two feet, two and a half feet thick. It was an old Victorian jail. Behind the plaster were big rocks. We took the rocks out and away we went again. We had our picture boards up on the wall, wooden picture boards where you had your family photos.

Next minute, we saw light. Paddy's picture board had come off. And he came up, put his eye up to hole in the wall and he said, 'You boys come in here, I'm going to cut the head off you. I've got a knife'.

And my mate says to him, 'Is that right? We've got a 9mm pistol.'

Paddy ran up to the door, screaming, 'They've got a gun. They've got a gun.'

Obviously, we didn't have a gun; it was just an ould bit of bluff. The prison officers came and let him out. We made the hole bigger, got into his cell. Took his letters for intelligence to help our boys outside and motored on into the next one. Norman and another guy from the Shankill, we met them. They were digging away at their cell. We started giving them a hand. We did fifteen cells in a row by the time we were finished and we couldn't go any further. There were seven of us sitting at the end cell. Everybody had done that, A and B wing, and we did all three landings.

They had nowhere to put us. There were 103 of us. That was our plan: we wreck this place, they'll have to move us to the Maze. We knew there was a spare block down there: H1. The Ninjas came in, put the shields up to the hole in the wall and took us through that hole one at a time, marched us down to D wing and put us in any spare cell they had. They handcuffed Mark and me to a bed and left us there for two days. They just treated us like scum. Then they came and said, 'Right. You're going.'

'Where are we going?'

'The Maze.'

That's it; we got segregation for remand prisoners! They put us in the horse-boxes and took us straight to the Maze and put us in H1. It was an amazing feeling.

The prison officers in the Crum were bastards, to put it mildly. You'd get the odd nice screw, but nine times out of ten, they were scumbags, you know, psychological torture, stealing your mail, wee jibes about your family. Maybe you've a girl coming to see you; wee jibes about her when you get back to the wing. 'Oh, she was nice. Wonder who's nailing her tonight?' We'd a great hatred for these guys. Most of them were alcoholics; they'd come up with drink on them. Letting the wrong people out at the wrong time. Creating fights for a laugh.

The Maze screws were a different kettle of fish. We got in and they had cups of tea and cake on a tray; the screws were serving it. And here's me, 'What the fuck's this?'

They put us all in the big canteen and everybody went in individually to see the number one governor in the circle. And he says, 'Davey, you were up in the Crum. That's a different régime. Forget about that. We've a different way of dealing with things down here. This is like a hotel and the customer's always right. You're the customer; you're always right.' The Maze was a wonderful place. We were all together, euphoric atmosphere. We had a sense of achievement that we went through that campaign to get where we were.

I was in the Crumlin Road for a year. We did the protest in 1994. July '94 we were moved to the Maze. I was in the Maze six months on remand; H1 was the remand block. I got sentenced in December 1994. I then got moved over to H2, which was the UDA-sentenced block; that's where all the lifers were. When I got sentenced, I remember writing on the back of a soap box: 'Three years, nine months left to do', and we'd already done a year and a half. My cousin Billy Stitt was in with me. And I said, 'That's our release date.'

It was meant to be 1999 and it was only 1994. And I remember us looking at ourselves and going, 'How are we going to do this?'

'We're just going to have to get into a routine and go for it.'

'Big chin' – that was the saying in there. 'You've a big chin. Take it on the chin.' I was a year and a half on remand, a year in the Crum and six months in H1. I did two and a half years in H2. I got out in January 1997.

While we were in prison, leading up to the IRA ceasefire, Ray Smallwoods[201] was assassinated. In my eyes, the republicans were given carte-blanche. They knew they were going to call a ceasefire. They said, 'We've a few scores to settle here,' and the British Government said, 'All right, go ahead. We'll give you a few weeks to settle your scores.' Before they called their ceasefire, they hit Joe Bratty and Raymie Elder,[202] two people who were connected to the Ormeau Road bookies.[203] They did Bratty and Elder and Ray Smallwoods, who was a leading light for us; they wanted to shut us up. Ray Smallwoods was a forward-looking, leading-light man out of the John McMichael[204] camp. They knocked us right back. They kept us behind for a good five or six years until we got on our feet politically. If we had had Ray Smallwoods, we would have been further along than we are now. The

201 A former prisoner who became a leading light in the UDA-affiliated Ulster Democratic Party in the lead-up to the ceasefires of 1994. He was killed by the IRA in July 1994.

202 Two leading members of the UDA in South Belfast, killed by the IRA in July 1994.

203 On 5 February 1992, loyalist gunmen burst into the Sean Graham bookmaker's shop on the lower Ormeau Road and shot dead five people. Bratty and Elder were UDA leaders in the area where the shooting occurred.

204 John McMichael was the military commander of the UDA in South Belfast. In the 1980s, he attempted to turn the organisation towards electoral and community politics. He was killed by an IRA bomb in 1987.

ballot box and the gun was going well for the republicans and we were going to get a wee touch. We were trying to get astute in that way. I had a bitterness there. They called their ceasefire and we couldn't get back at them.

My mum's from Dee Street. She was brought up with loyalist paramilitaries, too. Her brother, Soup Leeman, he was involved. Her other brother, Michael Leeman, he was involved. She was married to a guy that was in the UDA. She would never have let anyone say anything bad about me. She went to her pastor to get him to write me a reference to get me compassionate bail because my uncle was dying. He wouldn't do it. So from then on, she left that Church; straight away. She left that Church and she wasn't a Christian no more. She went, 'What? Hypocrites! For twenty-five years I'm a Sunday School teacher here and you'll not write him a reference? You can stick your Church!' She told them that. And she walked away from the Church in 1994. She was proud of me; I know she was.

I have a younger brother, five years my junior. He wasn't a combatant. I went into jail when he was fifteen. That spurred my da to put a complete security blanket around him. He was kept out of everything. And I also contacted from jail the fellows that were running the active service unit in the area. I said to them, 'He hasn't to get involved in anything. It would kill my ma and da if the two of us were in here.' My wee brother went along with that. My da bought him a wee car, gave him an interest that way.

I'm not ashamed of my past, but I wouldn't bum and blow about it in the house. If my daughter asked me, I would tell her because I'm proud of what I did. I'm proud of what loyalists did. In my eyes, we were doing a good job up till the ceasefire. The gangsters and drug dealers got a hold of us after the ceasefire and gave loyalists a bad name. That's a bad aspect of loyalism which I'm ashamed of, you know, Jim Gray,[205] the Shoukris[206] and the like. These people gave us a bad name, sucking the life out of the communities, the very communities we were defending. They were having the opposite effect on them and turning the communities against us. Now we've got rid of all these people I'm proud of what we're doing now.

I'm working for Charter for Northern Ireland, an East Belfast ex-prisoners' group. We're moving in the right direction as far as conflict transformation

205 A UDA commander in East Belfast. He was shot dead, probably by loyalists, in 2003.

206 Andre Shoukri was a UDA commander in North Belfast. Together with his brother Ihab, he was expelled from the organisation as moves were made to turn from criminality to more political pursuits. Ihab died of a drug overdose in 2008.

goes. We're going from strength to strength. We've got the community groups active. We're putting stuff back into the communities. We're running events in the communities. We're looking after the pensioners; we're looking after the youth; doing cross-community work in our areas to try and cross the bridge. I'm proud of my past and I'll tell my child that. I'm a very proud loyalist and I would never hide it from anybody, friend, family or whatever.

If the IRA was on ceasefire, the loyalists had to be on ceasefire; we were a reactionary force to them. Who were we going to fight? There was nobody to fight. It was hard to maintain the ceasefire and we had a few wee falls off the wagon on the way. But time's a great healer; we have to move on. It's all about our people and developing our own communities now. We have to get ourselves off our knees, back onto our feet.

The Past is Past

I know who my father is. I know he had this other life and he has done things that I wouldn't really want to ask about or want to know about. But now, it's just, he's here, and he's the kind of father everybody else is. The past is the past.

Ciarraí Harkin

Donna

Stepdaughter of Hugh

'Hugh' is a UVF ex-prisoner who currently works in restorative justice. His stepdaughter 'Donna' did not wish either of their real names to be used. Donna was born in 1972.

Hugh is my step-dad. My mum and Hugh got together around about 1986 and he was just gradually introduced to the family, to me and my sister. My younger sister is considerably younger than me. I would have been around the age of twelve, old enough to know that he was Mum's boyfriend but not old enough to know anything else. We all got on great and Mum and Hugh got married.

Hugh was a member of the UVF and shot somebody when he was about fifteen, and to be honest, that's about as much as I know. I wasn't aware of anything until I was directly told. It's not as if I had suspicions. There was never any talk around the family with regards to 'he served twelve years in prison'. There was never any slip-up, if you like. As far as I was aware, he went to school, left school, went to work in the shipyard and he was in the shipyard up until my mum met him. I didn't have any idea. But at the same time, once I was told about his background, once I was told about what he had done and that he'd spent time in jail, there wasn't a shame element that I'd ever picked up on from his family. It's not 'don't ever say, don't ever talk about it, don't ever mention it, it didn't happen'. The family are very, very proud of him as a person, and what he has achieved in his life since then has taken precedence over what happened when he was so young.

I remember I was told in the park. I was out with my mum and I was in a park, not far from where we lived. And I was told the reasons why I was being told. We came from West Belfast and we'd moved over to North Belfast where Hugh had a lot of family, and a lot of people knew him and knew of him, and his crime was committed there. So I was told just in case somebody else said something to me. They didn't want me being told by a stranger, basically, and wanted to make sure that I could ask questions and I could be informed and ask what I wanted about it. I was about sixteen, seventeen. It shocked me, very much, but I never told anyone initially, not because I was ashamed, but because I believed it was obviously something very personal to him and I wanted to respect him and his family.

It's very strange, because I went to a Protestant school. My best friend then (and now) was Colin, a Catholic guy from West Belfast. Hugh used to take me over to his house and drop me off; there were never any issues. Colin's like my brother; we're very close. I never once thought, 'What's Colin going to think?' because I was absolutely certain he liked Hugh for being the person he was then and still is today. When I told him, he was shocked, but it never affected the way Colin felt about him then or now. I've only ever told Colin and one other person. I've never said to anybody else because I don't feel it's my place to discuss Hugh's background; it's not my business to tell anyone, it's up to him. My sisters don't talk about it, but not because we feel like we shouldn't do, just because it doesn't come up. It's not mentioned.

I just thought, 'I don't really want to know. If that's something that happened, and that's part of his background, then it's in the past and I don't need to know.' I know that I asked him questions. I know that I asked him who he shot. I know that I asked him was he on his own, and why did he do it. But I couldn't tell you what the answers were. It was either the same day that my mum told me or it was very shortly afterwards; it might have been the next day. I wanted to know as little as possible and I haven't asked many questions since then. My attitude was: it's Hugh's business.

When I was young, I lived in England and then my family came back to Belfast. My first experience with loyalism would have been whenever we came from England to Belfast because it was all red, white and blue, and there were army vans everywhere. I remember screens being erected along the Stewartstown Road when there was rioting.[207] I also remember being in Wallace Park in Lisburn with friends on bikes and we got chased out of the park because I told another group of kids that I thought I was a Catholic. When I questioned my mum, she said to me, 'Well, we don't really practise any religion, darling, so you're not really anything.'

I had to go back and ask my mum again what a Protestant was when I started secondary school, because everyone said they were Protestant and I wanted to know was I a Protestant because I went to that particular school.

207 The British Army erected screens at interface areas, especially when an Orange Order parade was passing by a nationalist area. The screens were usually made of hessian on wooden frames and were four or five metres high.

She said, 'Yes.' My mum was born and grew up in West Belfast. My mum's family were burned out of their house because there were only a couple of Protestant families that lived on the street. My family are all Protestants. My uncle was in a band for years,[208] but I would never have associated my family with things I would have heard on the news about here. You know, loyalism – that just happened to mad people that didn't have anything else to do. What were they fighting over?

What I take from it is that I think there were these people on both sides that were really victims of circumstance. I've met friends of Hugh and people that he was in contact with and is still in contact with, men who were in exactly the same position as him. It intrigues me as to how one person in a family ... what sets them off to go and do what they did if there are other brothers in the family and they've got the same mum and dad, because it can't be down to bigotry. It can't be down to being told, 'Catholics are bad. Catholics are evil.' Hugh wasn't brought up in that type of environment. He was brought up in a Protestant environment but not in a bigoted environment. He has a brother who never committed a similar crime. It's not Catholic-orientated; it might be republican-orientated if it's a political issue, but it's not on a religious basis.

I have always been of the view that I haven't really wanted to know, haven't wanted to delve into it. Probably, maybe subconsciously, I haven't wanted to because I haven't wanted him to feel like he has to sit down and justify himself or explain himself. It might be because, subconsciously, I don't want to know in case I hear something I don't want to hear. I know the bare bones of it; maybe I don't want to hear because I don't want anything to blemish my relationship with him. Because he's a fantastic person, he's my dad and I love him, no matter what. He has been fantastic for me, fantastic for my sister, and the family as a whole.

If we were in the house and there was something on TV about political prisoners – for example the Good Friday Agreement – and people were getting early release[209] and I would openly show my disgust at that and say, 'I think that's completely appalling,' he wouldn't get into political debates with

208 Loyalist bands accompany Orange Order parades and participate in band competitions. At their simplest, they consist of young people, mostly men, playing fifes and drums, although there can also be relatively sophisticated pipe bands. The most demonstrative and sectarian of these bands are often referred to as 'Kick the Pope' bands.

209 As a result of the 1998 Good Friday (Belfast) Agreement, all remaining republican and loyalist prisoners were released by July 2000, even if they had not served their full sentences.

me. I studied Law at Queen's but I would not come from a 'lock everybody up' angle by any means. But I would look sometimes at things and just think, 'How can our government just release these people after a couple of years for what they've done?'

He wouldn't get into conversation or discussion with me about it. I never remember him talking from a political stance or saying, 'People did things at the time and they thought they were right.' There's never been any talk of justification for what he did or people like him have done.

I have a huge problem with people being out on early release. They were given a sentence and they didn't serve it, but I understand that it had to happen as part of the peace process. Hugh did his time. It's weird, because I wasn't living here during the '70s when the Troubles were at their height, so I don't know what it was like. When we lived in West Belfast, there were bombs, there were bomb scares; my school was affected. But full-on terrorism, if you like, that other people remember, I didn't grow up with it. But I do think that there's a huge climate change, and without speaking on Hugh's behalf, that would seem to be his attitude as well. He believes that what he did was right at the time. He didn't just go out gung-ho to get involved in anything. He went out with a purpose, to do what he did because what he was doing was right.

The person he shot was obviously a victim. The ramifications for his family and friends are huge, without a doubt. They're all victims. But Hugh is a victim as well, and people like him, living where they lived and being brought up in circumstances that maybe, if they were somewhere else geographically, they might not have been brought into. People from the Malone Road wouldn't have been involved in the Troubles as he was growing up, being a fifteen-year-old in North Belfast when York Road's being blown up. And the same for people on the other side, somebody from the New Lodge; they're coming from a working-class estate and being affected by a bomb or a shooting happening on the Falls Road, for example. I strongly believe that they were all victims. The situation at the time would have had a huge influence. These people haven't murdered since. These people aren't serial killers. Hugh hasn't gone out and murdered a Catholic since; that would just make him evil and a bigot. I'm not condoning what he did, but there's not the same kind of mindset behind it.

If you're fifteen and you go out and do something, you might not realise the extent of what you're doing or the ramifications of what you're doing. But there must come a point when you have to take responsibility for it. It might not be when you're fifteen. It might be when you're in your twenties. It might be when you have your own child that's fifteen and you're thinking, 'When I was this age, look what I did to my life. Look what I caused. I took someone's life.' But being fifteen, a child, is definitely a major factor.

My daughter is very, very close to Hugh. They have a great relationship and he completely dotes on her. Telling her about Hugh's past wouldn't be something I would be ashamed of saying, but I would direct her to Hugh. I think that it's his place. If she starts asking questions or if we feel that there's a need to let her know, then I'd pass that responsibility on to him. It won't be a 'sit down, let's bare all'. I've always been of the opinion that if a child's old enough to ask a question, then they deserve some sort of an answer, depending on their age and their ability. I can't think for the life of me what would ever prompt her to say anything, but considering the work that Hugh does at the minute, maybe there will come a time. If he continues to do restorative justice work, she might say to him, 'How did you get involved in this and why are you so passionate about it?' And he might feel the way to explain to her is to give his background. But that would be up to him. I would never say anything to her without consulting him first.

When he came out of the Maze, he went to work in the shipyard. He didn't go into restorative justice until a lot later. It's really only been over the last six or seven years when I would hear him talking more openly about the type of work he does and the importance of educating young people, steering them out of trouble and trying to get them to be more community-orientated.

From the day that I was told by my mum about Hugh, nobody else ever said anything to me. It's weird, because I could probably have continued up to the age I am now and might never have known a thing. I'm glad my mum and Hugh made the decision to tell me. I'd rather know, because it is a huge part of who he is, but it doesn't by any means define who he is. If I want to delve further, Hugh's here and I can just go and ask him, as he's very honest and open. Up until now, though, I've just chosen not to.

Ciarraí Harkin

Daughter of Richard Harkin

Richard Harkin is a Derry-based republican ex-prisoner and Sinn Féin activist. Ciarraí Harkin was born in 1983.

My father has been involved since he was very young. He has been a member of the Irish Republican Army since, I think, as far back as when he was about twelve. My father explained that in those days when he was growing up, everybody became a member. It was just normal life. I've heard stories about the actual Troubles, the shooting and rioting, but I don't remember any of that. My experience of it is that it's pulled my father out of home a lot. So he lost a lot of his time. We actually had to move out of Derry, because my father was on the run. So I lived in Donegal for the first five years of my life. My mother had to leave with him as well. She had three of us before we moved back to Derry. A lot of the time my father wouldn't have been there.

Once we moved back to Derry, we thought everything would settle, even though I really had no sense at that stage, because it was just this man who comes and goes. Through the years in Derry, we experienced house raids; they would have come in and raided the house and basically got you up for school in the morning! It wasn't as routine as that, but there were quite a few times when there would have been a heavy knock on the door and the police officers would have come into the house and searched their way through while Mammy was getting us up for school.

My father was arrested then, ten years ago this year, for planting a bomb under a car in Newbuildings.[210] The job had just been done and they were coming home and they arrested him and three others. He was sentenced to twenty years and he eventually served eight and a half. There were five children in our house and we were all under the age of eight. So my mother was left with five children under the age of eight; the youngest was a year. I was seven.

Going to Belfast, going to visit, I only got to see him once a month or once every six weeks. My mammy got to see him once a week, but pulling us out

210 Newbuildings, a village about three miles south of Derry City.

of school, we just couldn't do that. It was the Crumlin Road he was in first for two and a half years. It was really terrible going through searches. I really wouldn't want young children to go through that. You don't only have to go through one; you've to go through a waiting room, and then searching, and then a waiting room and then searching, and then a bus home – all that for about twenty minutes every six weeks. Then when we got older, he was moved to the Kesh, but it was the same process. You didn't look forward to going to see him, but you wanted to see him. It was just the botheration of it all.

For the first year or two or three, we were too young to question. I think it just became normality. Then, once I did get a bit older, you do start to ask questions and you do realise that you are a bit different, that things in your life are a bit different from other people's. I remember hating it. I remember saying to my mammy, 'I don't want to go up on a visit.'

You sat there being watched constantly – the screws, as they called them, just walking up and down. In the Crum, it was a big room with white plastic picnic tables and four chairs around it and it was open; you didn't have any privacy. It was rotten. It was always awkward. Sometimes, when you went up after four or six weeks, you didn't know where to start. You didn't want to sit telling him what you had done for the last six weeks. And looking back on it, I don't think we ever asked my daddy what he'd got up to in the last six weeks. Later, they were allowed phone calls and that was a lot better. My daddy would phone every night and we had to make sure everyone was in the house to speak to him. That brought us closer. Once the phone calls came, it was every day, you know, 'What did you do today?' and you would have chatted. You didn't get that much time on the phone, because there were five of us. And my mammy would want to speak to him.

In school, we had a lot of free time; we were allowed to do anything we wanted and I decided to sit down and write a poem about going to visit my daddy. It was called *Strangers*. I remember coming home and my mammy read it and she started crying. When I think back, obviously I was affected in some way, because this poem was written in school. It was put up on the wall during an exhibition. And then I had to read it out in the Guildhall Square.[211]

Then it was strange when he was coming out, because we were not used to a man, a male figure in the house. I remember saying to my mother, 'What if I come out of the shower?' I mean, I've got brothers, but we just weren't used to that older male figure. It was strange, probably because of my age. I

---

211 The main square in the centre of Derry, often used for political meetings and rallies.

was a fifteen-year-old girl. Even though I had two brothers, now there was a male figure, a man! And even though he's my father, I had never had that experience every day. Whenever he came out, it did feel like he was a stranger, even though we had seen him and we had spoken to him. For the last two or three years he was inside, we could speak to him every day.

I used to feel very guilty if I had to go somewhere and leave him. If everybody was leaving the house and my daddy was sitting there by himself, I felt I needed to entertain him as if he was a guest. It was strange. And I remember talking to my mammy about it. And she was saying, 'Ciarraí, it's your daddy's house, too, and you'll just have to adjust.'

Now, looking back, I wouldn't say it really affected my life as such. If anything, I've just kinda blocked out any politics. I wouldn't have an interest. People just assume because of my father that my beliefs and his are the same. When it comes to voting, people say, 'We know who you're going to vote for.'

But they shouldn't assume, because I might not. My daddy does a lot of work in the community now for Sinn Féin. A friend of his came to me and asked if I was interested in being a Sinn Féin councillor, doing work in the community for Sinn Féin. I hadn't a clue what exactly Sinn Féin do, or what my father does. I would have the option to know. That's one thing about my daddy: he'd always said, 'Anything at all you want to know, I'll tell you.' He wasn't going to come and speak to us, but if we ever wanted to know anything, he'd never hold anything back. But I just decided I don't want to know. I know what I know and that's all I want to know.

I don't need to know. I see my father as two different people. To me, he's just Daddy and he's really loving, really caring, and we know he'll always be there for us if we need him. But there's another life that he was involved in and I don't need to know what violent things he's been doing. I would say to him, 'You know the time you were arrested for planting the bomb, did you realise that you were setting out knowing obviously that you could get jailed and that that was somebody's father, somebody's son, somebody's brother?' Did he understand that? And I said, 'What if it had happened to you?' It could have been the other way about. He knows that we don't agree.

He was telling us a story of them being shot at by the SAS and there's actually a scar on his back where the bullet skinned him. I'd say my daddy's life would be really interesting if I wanted to find out about it. Maybe someday I will, but I don't really feel that I need to know now.

When I look back, I don't feel any anger or hatred for the British Army, because I don't know enough of what was going on in the inside to hate anybody. The way I feel is that they were just doing their jobs. My daddy has said to me that he's not happy about a lot of the things that he's done, but that when there's a war on, your feelings are so strong and there are certain things that you had to do. I wouldn't be seeking any justice or feeling any resentment.

People like my daddy who joined were obviously very young, so they were in a way brainwashed in the beginning. They were led on by people who passed their beliefs or hatred about the British Army, passed on at a very young age. I don't hate him for anything that he's done. I would prefer to blank out that part of his life and just know him as my father. In my head, I know it was not just that one incident he was arrested for. I've been told by other people, which I didn't even ask for, other things that he might have been involved in. The way he said it to me was that the IRA was an army; they were fighting a war, same as the British Army who are going to Afghanistan now. There was a war going on when he was growing up and he was in an army, fighting a war for his country, and that's what he says he was doing. And there were things that they did.

When you think of it, we don't like any kind of wars or any kind of violence. And when you think of the British soldiers going across now to Afghanistan, the same things are happening: there are bombs exploding and people dying and that's what went on here. And that's what I prefer to see him as, as a soldier, even though they don't have a uniform. There's a difference between British soldiers and people in the likes of the IRA where they're not being paid, so it has to be something they strongly believe in.

I think my daddy is really glad that none of us are actually involved. I've got two brothers who couldn't care less about the Irish Republican Army. My older brother is interested in what happened and would know a lot more about things than me; he would ask many more questions. We don't have the same views as my daddy. It's never been forced upon us. It's never been in any way talked about unless we want to go there. It's never been brought into the home in regards to my daddy in a forced way talking about it, trying to pass things on to us; that never happened.

My mammy did try to keep us safe from anything that was happening around us, trying to create a normal world for us. I think it's because it hasn't been brought into the home. I think if my daddy had come in every night and told us a story of what he had done … my father would rather leave it up to us. If we want to know, that's fine, but if we don't, he's not going to force it on us.

My mammy and daddy were lucky that none of us caused much hassle. But anything that she thought was wrong or she had to scold us for, we always would have got the threat: 'Now, I'm going to have to speak to your father about this.'

My mammy had to deal with a lot of stuff on her own, but she always would have shared what happened with him. Sometimes she didn't tell us she was going to say something and you'd go up on a visit and when he gave you that disappointed look it was terrible. I used to think, 'God, I'd rather have a slap.' When I was growing up, a lot of friends of mine would have been drinking or smoking and I used to think, 'I couldn't do that because of what my daddy would think.'

I suppose I could say that my life is a lot different from my friends'. Not now; I'm happy in my life now. My experiences growing up were a lot different. But to be honest, I wouldn't say that it has affected me to the point where it's going to affect the way I'm going to deal with pressure.

I used to be embarrassed saying my father was in jail, even though I didn't know, when I was younger, the difference between political prisoners and criminals. On another occasion, another child is going to think automatically, 'That's a bad man.' And I didn't want people to think that, because I knew he wasn't, not to me.

I remember having conversations with my close friends in the street or my close friends at school then when I was younger about daddy being in jail, but I don't think anybody judged me. Because I went to an Irish language school,[212] there are people involved in setting up these schools who have been involved.[213] So there'd be a lot of people who would look up to you more because of who your father was. I don't feel any reason to be proud of things.

There's young boys of eighteen, nineteen or twenty – it's as if it's happening like it was years ago. They're starting to be brainwashed now. They won't even look at me, you know, boys that I would know from the street, whom I've grown up with, because of who my father is. I'm not known as Ciarraí Harkin; I'm known as Richard Harkin's daughter. I'd prefer to be known as myself because I don't have the same beliefs. Years ago, I had been asked by Sinn Féin

212 During the 1980s and 1990s, a substantial number of schools – nursery, primary and secondary – were opened across Northern Ireland in which lessons were delivered through the Irish language. Initially, the running costs fell solely on parents and supporting communities, but eventually the sector was fully funded by the Department of Education.

213 Involved in republican politics or military activity.

to go on TV. It would have been when I turned eighteen; it would have been my first vote. I had to do it in Irish. 'My name's Ciarraí Harkin and this year I'll be voting for Sinn Féin.' I wasn't even asked was I a member of Sinn Féin! It was just taken for granted because of your background, whose daughter you were. I was young and naive. These things should be kept secret. You don't have to tell people who you're voting for. I do vote for Sinn Féin, but people assume that I'm going to do that.

My sister just had a baby six weeks ago; it's the first grandchild and my daddy just completely melted and my mammy's saying, 'This is his time. He has lost so much from you that he's spending a lot of time with the baby.'

He has lost a lot with us, so he's just going to do it now with this new baby. I did ask him, 'Now that you see Clodagh and us, would you do it again?'

And he said he would. He says that looking at the granddaughter and taking her away from him or him staying away for a long time from her, he would really miss her. And he said it was the same when we were younger, spending time away from us; we were always on his mind and that he missed us. But when we were younger, there was a lot more things happening.

Sometimes you think, 'That is really selfish. I've never felt number one to you. A father and his children should come first.' Things like that do come up. At times like that, you think, 'Maybe I was affected more than I think.' I remember saying to him, 'We've never been a priority for you.'

He didn't deny it, but he cried; probably because he accepts that it was true. Now that he doesn't have to be called away, that he's not actively involved and has plenty of time to think about things, and we're older … I've told my daddy how we feel and how we've been affected, because our life has been a bit different from the normal childhood because of the things he has done.

When my daddy got out, I was already fifteen; I was already kinda grown up. And the time before he went in, we were living in Donegal, on the run, and didn't see much of him. So I suppose he hasn't been much of a father, but now he tries so hard and he's really making up for it; he's really loving and really caring, so I can't look at him as an evil person who would do things that you would hear about.

I'm obviously so glad that my father is still here. In all the things that have been going on, he could have quite easily been blown up or shot. Our family is very close. And I think with my daddy being inside, it brought us even closer. Like, my father would never leave, even if he was going to the shop, without giving you a kiss. That's the way we are now, and I'm happy with the way family life is.

I just like to keep the two men separate, their two lives separate. I know who my father is. I know he had this other life and he has done things that I wouldn't really want to ask about or want to know about. But now, it's just, he's here, and he's the kind of father everybody else is. The past is the past.

CONCLUSION

The adults interviewed for this book acknowledged that they had suffered directly as children as a result of the parent's involvement. They spoke of police and army raids on their homes, the tension and sometimes ignominy of jail visits, the absence of the parent, usually, but not always, the father, and the tension of the parent's return after long absence. For the most part, they did not dwell on the material and financial difficulties of life with a parent in prison, but focused on their relationship, or lack of it, with the imprisoned – or in two cases, dead – parent.

One of the most obvious consequences of the parent's involvement was the constant attention of police and army who raided their homes. Áine Fryers states that one of her earliest memories is of an early morning raid. For Fiona Bunting, while her father was still alive, the raids occurred a couple of times a week. David McMaster remembers being 'tortured' by raids. However, Ciarraí Harkin jokingly says that one advantage of the raids was that they got the children up in time for school.

But these experiences were no laughing matter. For eight-year-old Mary Kennedy, there was a more devastating experience: the internment of her mother and father. A long-term consequence was that when her mother was released, Mary was scared of letting her out of her sight in case she would disappear again. John Lyttle had the devastating experience of stumbling on his father and his colleagues at work, interrogating a man in the family home, and it is clear that the memory of that night is still crystal clear to him all these years later. Fiona Bunting's reaction to having to step over her father's body outside her bedroom as she went to seek help for her mother, also shot by loyalists, was complex: both forgetting the details of the incident and carrying a deep rage for many years.

Either through death or imprisonment, one of the most persistent experiences for these people as children was the absence of the parent. Dan McCann was shot dead when his daughter was three years old; she says that she had 'a void where someone else has a person'. Jeanette Keenan's father Brian went on the run in 1971 when she was ten, and as a result of this political exile, followed by a long period in prison, he did not return home until 1994. Martin Meehan's father, also called Martin, spent over twenty years in prison on three separate occasions while Martin junior was growing up. And Steven McMaster's father David was jailed when he was six months old, so that the first time he saw his father outside of prison was fourteen years later when his father was on parole. Gearóid Adams saw little of his father until he was five years old. And for Ciarraí Harkin, her father Richard was 'just this man who comes and goes'. Billy McQuiston's father was 'out of my life' from the age of fifteen. One consequence of such absences, as Seán Ó hÁdhmaill found, was that he had to take on the role of the man of the house.

A theme which comes out strongly in many of the stories is the culture of silence which surrounds these experiences. Mark Ervine's mother told him his father David was painting the prison in which he was in fact incarcerated. Sometimes the silence was self-imposed. Ciarraí Harkin talks about her father as if he were two separate men: the one who had the 'other life' of activism, and the one she now knows and loves. Likewise, Donna separates out the previous military involvement of her stepfather Hugh and her current respect for the man she knows after he was released from prison.

That release proved a source of tension for a number of those who spoke. Mark Ervine contrasts the enjoyable times he had when visiting his father in prison with the disciplinarian he encountered after release. Áine Fryers resented her father treating her like a sixteen-year-old. Ciarraí Harkin found it strange to have an adult man around the house for the first time. And Seán Ó hÁdhmaill feels he only avoided possible tension because he moved to university in Dublin at the time of his father's release. Perhaps most startling of all is Steven McMaster's account of how he took the opportunity of his father's release to move in with him in an attempt to understand why his father had thought and acted as he had; Steven was disturbed by what he discovered.

The daughter of Dan McCann says she does not like what she already knows about her father and his involvement and fears there may be 'more of the same, or worse'. Others interviewed expressed some resentment of the parent's actions, albeit less total than that of Dan McCann's daughter. Áine Fryers resented the IRA for sending her father to England where he was caught and imprisoned. At the same time, Fryers concedes that she ended up supportive of her father's politics. Likewise, Jeanette Keenan acknowledges that war was a 'necessary evil' and her father had the conviction to play his part in that struggle. Mark Ervine concludes that his father's success in moving loyalism along a political path outweighs his own past differences with his father.

At the same time, the testimony of many of those interviewed is riddled with ambivalence. Jeanette Keenan can, at one and the same time, wonder where her community might be in terms of equal rights without the involvement of people like her father and fail to understand how he could ever leave his kids behind to pursue politics. Ciarraí Harkin judges her father's decision to choose politics over her and her family as 'selfish'. And for all that, her love of her father comes through in her testimony, Fiona Bunting is clear that, unlike him, she would always put her kids first.

The raids, the parental absence, the culture of silence, the stress of prison visits and of homecoming, as well as the suspicion that their parent had abandoned them in favour of political or military activity – all these took their toll, with some of those interviewed (like Liz Rea) reporting nervous breakdowns and others (like Fiona Bunting and John Lyttle) acknowledging that they struggled for years to come to terms with what had happened.

Despite that, many of those interviewed remark that what they went through felt normal at the time. There was no alternative against which to measure their traumatic experience, as Mark Ervine argues, adding that he didn't find growing up as he did particularly stressful. Dan McCann's daughter, used to seeing periodically the dramatic television footage of her father's funeral, says that for a long time she believed everyone who died got a funeral on television. Flair Campbell shows no indication that he thought it odd that he and his mother were IRA members simultaneously. Robert, a UVF ex-prisoner like his father before him, remembers the family home being raided, but adds stoically that theirs wasn't the only home being raided. And also talking of raids, Cathy Nelis says she doesn't remember being scared and doesn't feel traumatised as a result.

Is this merely a post-hoc defence? Or can it be that these children managed to survive horrible experiences, emerging eventually as mature and balanced adults? There is copious evidence of the latter in these pages. This may not be the case for all children of combatants in Northern Ireland, only a small fraction of whose stories appear here. But in the end, the resilience of the people interviewed here shines through.

What are the mechanisms of such resilience? There are undoubtedly individual characteristics which helped some people to survive better than others. But there are also social factors: the support of close friends and tight families, embeddedness in strong communities of resistance, sharing the political and ideological ideals of their parents and community.

In the end, the people interviewed for this book were not passive victims, but survivors who managed to ride the crest of the conflicts they experienced. Ultimately, despite the trauma, and despite their feelings of ambivalence, resilience won out. That in this sense, these children of combatants in Northern Ireland are not unique, that there is evidence, as we saw earlier, of similar resilience among South African and Palestinian children, is ultimately a positive conclusion.

Further Reading

Cairns, E (1987), *Caught in Crossfire: Children and the Northern Ireland Conflict.* Belfast: Appletree Press

Castillo, C (2007), *Calle Santa Fe.* Paris: Agnes B Films

Connolly, P, Smith, A and Kelly, B (2002), *Too Young to Notice? The Cultural and Political Awareness of 3–6-Year-Olds in Northern Ireland.* Belfast: Northern Ireland Community Relations Council.

Connolly, P and Healy, J (2004), *Children and the Conflict in Northern Ireland: The Experiences and Perspectives of 3–11-Year-Olds.* Belfast: Office of the First Minister and Deputy First Minister

Cúnamh (2000), *Déagóirí le Chéile: Research Report.* Derry: Cúnamh

Feldman, A (2002), 'X-children and the militarisation of everyday life: comparative comments on the politics of youth, victimage and violence in transitional societies', *International Journal of Social Welfare* 11: 286–299

Fields, R (1973), *A Society on The Run: a Psychology of Northern Ireland.* Penguin

Fraser, RM (1973), *Children in Conflict.* London: Martin Secker and Warburg

Garbarino, J (2008), *Children and the Dark Side of Human Experience: Confronting Global Realities and Rethinking Child Development.* Berlin: Springer

Guevara, A (2006), *Aleida Guevara Remembers her Father, Che.* Melbourne: Oceanbooks (DVD)

Gunn, S and Krwala, S (eds) (2008), *Knocking On: Mothers and Daughters in Struggle in South Africa.* Johannesburg: CSVR and Capetown: Human Rights Media Centre

Jamieson, R and Grounds, A (2002), *No Sense of an Ending: the effects of long-term imprisonment amongst Republican prisoners and their families.* Monaghan: Expac

Little, A (2009), *Give a Boy a Gun.* London: Darton, Longman and Todd

Maegusuku-Hewett, T, Dunkerley, D Scourfield, J and Smalley, N (2007), 'Refugee Children in Wales: Coping and Adaptation in the Face of Adversity', *Children and Society* 21: 309–321

McEvoy, K, O'Mahony, D, Horner, C and Lyner, O (1999), 'The Home Front: the families of politically motivated prisoners in Northern Ireland', *British Journal of Criminology* 39(2): 173–197

Punamäki, R (1996), 'Can Ideological Commitment Protect Children's Psychosocial Wellbeing in Situations of Political Violence?', *Child Development* 67: 55–69

Qouta, S, Punamäki, R and El Sarraj, E (1995), 'The Impact of the Peace Treaty on Psychological Wellbeing: a Follow-up Study of Palestinian Children', *Child Abuse and Neglect* 19(10): 1197–1208

Shirlow, P (2001), *The State They Are In.* University of Ulster, Coleraine, Social Exclusion Research Unit

Slovo, G (1997), *Every Secret Thing: My Family, My Country.* London: Abacus

Smyth, M (1998), *Half the Battle: Understanding the Effects of the 'Troubles' on Children and Young People in Northern Ireland.* Derry: Incore

Spence, L (2002), *Unheard Voices: The Experiences and Needs of the Children of Loyalist Political Ex-prisoners.* Belfast: EPIC

Sutton, M (1994), *Bear in Mind these Dead: An Index of Deaths from the Conflict in Ireland 1969–1993.* Belfast: Beyond the Pale Publications

Tar Anall (2000), *Left in Limbo: the Experience of Prisoners' Children.* Newtownabbey: Island Pamphlets

Tar Anall (2005), *Still in Limbo?* Newtownabbey: Island Pamphlets

Tomlinson, M (2007), 'Suicide and Young People: The Case of Northern Ireland', *Child Care in Practice*, 13 (4): 435–443

Wiwa, K (2001), *In the Shadow of a Saint: A Son's Journey to Understand his Father's Legacy.* London: Black Swan